Protocols by Invariants

Cambridge International Series on Parallel Computation: 7

PROTOCOLS BY INVARIANTS

Anneke A. Schoone
Utrecht University

CAMBRIDGE
UNIVERSITY PRESS

Published by the Press Syndicate of the University of Cambridge
The Pitt Building, Trumpington Street, Cambridge CB2 1RP
40 West 20th Street, New York, NY 10011, USA
10 Stamford Road, Oakleigh, Victoria 3166, Australia

© Cambridge University Press 1996

First published 1996

Printed in Great Britain at the University Press, Cambridge

Library of Congress cataloging in publication data available

British Library cataloguing in publication data available

ISBN 0 521 44175 7

Contents

Preface

Originally, the research reported in this book was motivated by the way the material used for an introductory course on Distributed Computing (taught in the spring of 1985) was presented in the literature. The teacher of the course, Jan van Leeuwen, and I felt that many results were presented in a way that needed clarifying, and that correctness proofs, if existent, were often far from convincing, if correct at all. Thus we started to develop correctness proofs for some distributed protocols. Gradually a methodology emerged for such proofs, based on the idea of "protocol skeletons" and "system-wide invariants". Similar ideas were developed by others in the context of formal proof systems for parallel and distributed programs.

I thank the ESPRIT Basic Research Action No. 7141 (project ALCOM II: *Algorithms and Complexity*), the Netherlands Organization for Scienctific Research (NWO) under contract NF 62-376 (NFI project ALADDIN: *Algorithmic Aspects of Parallel and Distributed Systems*), and the Department of Computer Science at Utrecht University for giving me the opportunity to do research on this topic, and for providing such a stimulating environment. I thank my coauthors Jan van Leeuwen, Hans Bodlaender, and Gerard Tel, and also Petra van Haaften, Hans Zantema, and Netty van Gasteren for all the discussions we had.

Later the idea came up to write a thesis about this subject, and I especially thank my thesis advisor Jan van Leeuwen for his stimulating support. The first four chapters of the thesis served as preliminary versions for the first four chapters of this book, while chapter 5 on commit protocols was added later.

For proofreading several versions of the manuscript I owe thanks to Petra van Haaften, Jan van Leeuwen, Friedemann Mattern, Doaitse Swierstra, Richard Tan, Gerard Tel, Marinus Veldhorst, and Hans Zantema.

1

Introduction

In the past two decades, distributed computing has evolved rapidly from a virtually non-existent to an important area in computer science research. As hardware costs declined, single mainframe computers with a few simple terminals were replaced by all kinds of general and special purpose computers and workstations, as the latter became more cost effective. At many sites it became necessary to interconnect all these computers to make communication and file exchanges possible, thus creating a computer network. Given a set of computers that can communicate, it is also desirable that they can cooperate in some sense, for example, to contribute to one and the same computation. Thus a network of computers is turned into a distributed system, capable of performing distributed computations. The field of distributed computing is concerned with the problems that arise in the cooperation and coordination between computers in performing distributed tasks.

Distributed algorithms (or: protocols) range from algorithms for communication to algorithms for distributed computations. These algorithms in a distributed system appear to be conceptually far more complex than in a single processing unit environment. With a single processing unit only one action can occur at a time, while in a distributed system the number of possibilities of what can happen when and where at a time tends to be enormous, and our human minds are just not able to keep track of all of them.

This leads to the problem of determining whether the executions of a distributed algorithm indeed have the desired effect in all possible circumstances and combinations of events. Testing algorithms has now become completely infeasible: some form of "verification" is the only way out. But verifying a distributed algorithm by verifying all possible executions still is infeasible. Hence the need for a more formal approach that aims at assessing properties of an algorithm which hold for *all* possible executions simultaneously. This is the course taken in *assertional verification by system-wide invariants*.

Although a lot of work has been done in devising proof systems for distributed algorithms with desirable properties such as modularity and compositionality, our approach is entirely pragmatic.

1.1 Distributed Computing

A distributed computation is not so much a computation in a distributed system, as a computation which is distributed in a system. We will first discuss what distributed systems look like in section 1.1.1, and then give the model and notation that we use to describe a distributed computation in such a system (section 1.1.2).

1.1.1 Distributed systems

To deal with the complexity of distributed systems, computer networks are designed and implemented as layered structures. (See for example the books by Tanenbaum [Tan88], Halsall [Hal85], and Sloman and Kramer [SK87] on this subject.) In the hierarchy of layers, each *layer* implements a set of functions in order to provide a service to the layer above, making use of the services provided by the lower layers, without any knowledge of how these services are implemented. The set of rules governing the interaction between two layers in one network node is called an *interface*, while the set of rules concerned with the interaction within one layer between network nodes is called a *protocol*. Thus most distributed algorithms can be called protocols.

The layered structure simplifies the implementation and maintenance of a distributed system, due to the separation of concerns between layers. The system is also more flexible, since one layer can be changed by itself, provided the interfaces remain the same. The layered structure has also led to standardization: since 1977 the International Standards Organization (ISO) has been developing a full reference model for the communication system, the main purpose being to make communication between computers from different manufacturers possible. This model consists of seven layers, and is briefly discussed in section 1.1.1.1.

In section 1.1.1.2 we discuss how we model a distributed system, and in section 1.1.1.3 we give an overview of the assumptions about the network that we encounter in the design of distributed algorithms.

1.1.1.1 The ISO reference model. The ISO reference model is also called the Reference Model for Open Systems Interconnection (OSI). The term "open" means

that systems which follow the standards in this model are open to other systems that adhere to the same standards. The reference model has been set up to provide standards for communication between mainframes of different manufacturers, and is currently extended for arbitrary distributed systems. The seven layers identified in the model are (starting below in the hierarchy): the physical layer, the data link layer, the network layer, the transport layer, the session layer, the presentation layer, and the application layer. In each layer, the entities sent can be different, both in size and in added control information, such as address information, error-detecting codes, and sequence numbers. If it is not necessary to make a distinction between these entities, we will just call them "messages".

The *physical layer* is concerned with the transmission of *bits* over a physical circuit. Issues in this layer are, for example, by what electrical signal a bit is represented, and what kind of plugs and sockets are used.

The *data link layer* turns the raw physical circuit into a link that appears as an error-free connection to the network layer. The entities transmitted in this layer are usually *frames*, as opposed to single bits. It performs error and flow control: frames can get lost or garbled and, as it may be necessary to retransmit frames to remedy this, one also has to deal with frames that arrive out of order or that are duplicates of frames that have arrived already.

The *network layer* deals with switching and routing issues. The units that are transmitted are usually *packets*. It is the responsibility of the network layer to deliver every packet sent at its destination, wherever that may be. Thus the question of how to determine a route for every destination from a given source is an important issue in this layer. In this layer it can be assumed that packets do not get lost, garbled, duplicated, or reordered on a single link, as the data link layer is supposed to filter those errors out.

The *transport layer* is concerned with setting up and closing *connections* between two nodes in the network, and doing this in the most efficient way. This is the first *end-to-end* layer: communication is between arbitrary network nodes, whereas in the lower layers there is only communication between neighbors. In this layer, it is again necessary to consider loss, duplication, and reordering of messages. This is due to the fact that, although the network layer is supposed to provide a new route in case a link on the way goes down, it cannot prevent message loss due to the link failure, or duplication if a supposedly lost message is retransmitted over the new route, or reordering of messages if the new route proves to be faster than the old route.

The *session layer* is to provide *sessions* between application entities, for example a transaction between a banking terminal and the bank's computer. Authentication might be required here. The session layer is often merged with the transport layer.

The *presentation layer* deals with the representation of information, and the necessary formatting and conversions. Examples are data compression, data conversion, e.g. between different character codes, and data encryption, to provide security. It also deals with the fact that terminals can differ widely in for example line and screen length used, and the use of special characters.

The *application layer* is the highest layer, and deals with the communication between software systems and user programs at different network nodes. Examples are distributed databases and electronic mail systems.

1.1.1.2 *Modeling a distributed system.* As yet there is no universally accepted definition of a distributed system. After the informal description above, we will now give a more abstract definition, related to our model of distributed computations.

> A *distributed system* is a set of processes which communicate by message passing.

It is also possible that processes communicate by shared memory, but we do not consider this here. However, we model the "communication by message passing" by shared variables, albeit in a limited and strictly prescribed way (see section 1.2.1). If two processes in the set have the possibility of communicating in both directions with each other (this need not be the case for all pairs of processes), we say that they share a *link*. Hence we only consider bidirectional links. We will talk about *sending* and *receiving* messages over the link, although this link need not be a physical channel or transmission line. The set of processes together with their communication links can be represented by a *graph*, with processes as nodes or vertices and links as edges. As we only consider bidirectional communication links, this graph is an *undirected* graph. If we are mainly concerned with the graph representation of the distributed system, we will often use the terms *network* and (network) *nodes*.

An *event* in a distributed system is one of the following: (1) the sending of a message, (2) the receipt of a message, or (3) an internal event. Internal events can either be located at a process, such as the local execution of some program segment in a distributed algorithm, or can be located at a link, for example, the loss of a message in transit. We will model the latter type of internal event by means of processes also, so-called *link processes*. To avoid confusion, we will often use the term *processor* for a process that is considered to be located at a node in the network, although of course the correspondence between processes and processors need not be one to one.

In this book we exploit a layered structure more or less as provided by the OSI model. For each layer, we use the services provided by lower layers by making the appropriate assumptions. For example, the communication protocol in the data link layer guards against the loss of messages. Thus in the network layer, we have the assumption that there is no loss of messages. Conversely, an assumption that is made in most chapters is that a link between two network nodes behaves like two FIFO queues of messages, one queue for each direction. This does not mean that we restrict ourselves to networks where this is actually the case, but we assume that this can be achieved by communication protocols present in the lower layers of the network, and that the question of how to achieve it is not our concern now. In the next section we give an overview of the typical network assumptions that are made throughout this book.

1.1.1.3 Network assumptions. There is a wide range of assumptions possible

in distributed computing. For example, a network can be static or dynamic, nodes can be anonymous or have a unique identity, and communication can be reliable or unreliable. These different assumptions provide a way to focus attention on some aspects of distributed computing, while abstracting away from others, as they relate to the layered structure of a distributed system.

We can divide the network assumptions into those that pertain to the topology of the network, and those that pertain to the communication in the network. We will first discuss the assumptions related to the topology of the network.

We assume that a network consists of *processors* (nodes) connected by *undirected communication links*. Although directed networks are possible, we do not consider them. We assume that the processors have *unique identities*. As for the communication links, we consider two possibilities: either the links that are present remain present during the period considered and no new links arise, giving rise to a *static network*, or the links can come up and go down, giving rise to a so-called *dynamic network*. If two processors are incident to the same link, we call those processors *neighbors*. Unless otherwise stated, we assume that processors know the identity of their neighbors. In the way we formulate distributed algorithms or protocols we assume that there is only one link between two neighbors, but this is not really necessary. We also assume that the network contains no self-loops, i.e., links from a processor to itself.

Next there is the possibility of *processor failures*. Possible assumptions include: fault-free processors; processors that may crash and recover again (transient failures); processors that can crash, but are not allowed any activity any more after that (fail-stop); and *Byzantine* processors, making malicious faults. We model the failure of a processor (except in the last chapter) by the simultaneous failure of all its incident links, and the coming up of a processor by the coming up of some but not necessarily all of its incident links. We will sometimes need the assumption that a processor failure does not include the loss of all memory of that processor, i.e., the processor can have access to stable memory, on some non-volatile storage medium.

Usually we assume that the network we consider is *connected*, but this is not always necessary. An assumption that is sometimes made is that every processor knows (an upper bound on) the number of processors in the network. A quantity like this can be used for example to limit the generation of messages or work (see section 3.2) in the system. Another parameter of the network that is useful in this respect is (an upper bound on) the *diameter* of the network. This can be used to kill messages after they have traveled over a sufficient number of links. It can be used even for dynamic networks, if there is an upper bound on the number of links that can go down, because there is a relation between the maximal diameter increase of a network and the number of links that go down [SBvL87].

In distributed computing, there are numerous algorithms designed for special network topologies, but we will only consider the general case. Sometimes we will discuss only the very simple topology of two processors connected by a link, if we study protocols for communication between two processors and assume that addressing is done correctly (in chapters 2 and 4). Then it is not necessary to consider the other parts of the network.

Processors can send messages to their neighbors over links, and processors can receive messages from their neighbors. However, messages cannot be received before they are sent. For this type of communication by *message passing*, there are two frequently used models. One is based on the idea of a handshake or *rendezvous*: if two processors want to communicate, the sender is blocked until the receiver is ready to receive. Thus the sending and the receiving action are *synchronous*: they take place at the same time. This model is used in programming languages like CSP [Hoa78], ADA, and OCCAM.

In the other, *asynchronous* model of message passing the sender is not blocked and it can take arbitrarily long to receive a message after it has been sent. In our terminology, it can take arbitrarily long for the message to arrive at its destination and be received after that (the receiver might be blocked until the message has arrived). In this model, processors need buffers to retain arrived messages until they can be processed. It is the model we will be using most in this book. A third model that is possible is to assume that messages arrive within bounded time.

Depending on the circumstances, we make different assumptions about the possible *communication errors*, i.e., the failures in message passing. These include *loss* of messages, for example due to a link failure, *garbled* messages, i.e., messages whose contents were changed during the transmission, and *duplication* of messages. We assume that a message cannot originate spontaneously on a link. As for garbled messages, we usually assume (except in section 2.3) that a garbled message can be recognized as such, and thus can be purged and considered "lost". Duplication of messages can occur if messages can be routed by different routes, due to link failures. Routing by different routes can also cause the *reordering* of messages, i.e., that messages arrive at their destination in a different order than the order in which they were sent. Finally, if an assumption about the network is that messages arrive within bounded time, one can distiguish so-called *timing failures* if in fact they do not arrive in time.

1.1.2 Modeling distributed computations

For an appraisal of the general features in distributed computing, we start by considering the essential building blocks and only use complete protocols as illustrations. The building blocks are basically the separate statements of the actions that must be carried out in a distributed system, without specifying when and where they should take place. We can assemble bigger blocks by adding restrictions, e.g. in the control flow or the communication. We call such an assembled block an *operation*, and a set of statements or operations a *protocol skeleton*. If we assemble the statements or operations of a protocol skeleton into larger operations, we call the resulting protocol skeleton a *refined* protocol skeleton. Successive refinements can yield a complete protocol, while different successive refinements may yield another protocol for the same problem. Thus a protocol skeleton stands for a class of protocols, all of which can be obtained from this same skeleton by some refinement.

In denoting protocols, we use a mixture of English and an imperative programming language. As it is not necessary for understanding, we will not discuss things like parameter passing or give the syntax of the programming language.

1.1.2.1 Protocol skeletons.

As said above, a protocol skeleton consists of a number of operations, each of which consists of a piece of (sequential) program. Operations can be carried out any number of times, by any processor, and at any time, and thus in any order. We assume that only one operation is carried out at a time. An operation is viewed as an atomic action, i.e., it cannot be interrupted. We do not specify anything about an assumed order in which the operations may take place, but an operation can contain a so-called *guard*: a boolean expression between braces { }. An operation may only be executed if it is *enabled*, i.e., if its guard is true, otherwise the operation is called *disabled* and nothing happens. For example, a processor can only execute the code for receiving a message if there is indeed a message present to receive.

The method we use for the correctness proofs of distributed algorithms is that of
assertional verification by system-wide invariants. The idea is that if an assertion (a
relation between process variables for example) holds initially, and is preserved by
all possible operations, then it will hold always in the distributed system, whatever
order of operations takes place in an actual execution of the distributed algorithm.
Such an assertion is called a system-wide invariant. The advantage of the use of
protocol skeletons in assertional verification is that refinements preserve invariants.
If one has a refined protocol skeleton which can be viewed as a special instance of
a protocol skeleton, then any system-wide invariant which holds for the protocol
skeleton will hold also for the refined protocol skeleton. This is the case simply
because the invariant was proven correct for any order of operations in the general
case, and hence also for the special order of operations which will take place in the
refined protocol skeleton.

The basic statements, and thus basic operations, in a distributed program for a
processor i are: send a message to j (S_i), receive a message from j (R_i), and do
an internal (local) computation (I_i), where j is any processor connected to i by
a link. Operations and variables are subscripted by the identity of the processor
that performs and maintains them, respectively. Usually, we only consider uniform
distributed computations, in which all processors cooperate and contribute in the
same way to the computation. Hence it is almost always the case that all processors
have the same operations to execute, on their own local variables. Thus, if we give
a protocol skeleton for processor i, we implicitly mean that the protocol skeleton
contains those operations for *all* processors i. Thus we can give the basic protocol
skeleton as follows.

Basic protocol skeleton:

S_i: **begin** send a message to some neighbor j **end**

R_i: {a message has arrived from j} **begin** receive the message from j **end**

I_i: **begin** compute **end**

As it is usually necessary to specify what the initial values of the processor
variables are, we will do so for the variables used directly before the code of the
operations, after the keyword **Initially**.

Apart from the operations that must be carried out at the processors, a protocol
skeleton may contain operations pertaining to *link processes*. Link processes were
described in section 1.1.1.2 and will be considered further in section 1.2.1. The
name of a "link operation" is subscripted by the names of the processors incident

to the link. We also assume that the protocol skeleton contains that operation for *every* link in the network.

We can use the operations as *building blocks* for larger operations that we also consider as atomic. One might ask under what circumstances we are allowed to view operations as atomic. Lamport discussed this in general [Lam82], and for the case of message passing [Lam90]. Surprisingly, under some conditions one can even view the sending of a message and its subsequent delivery at the receiver in an asynchronous environment as one atomic action. In chapter 5 another approach is taken. There we discuss a class of protocols (atomic commitment protocols) that ensure that a set of operations is always executed as if it were one atomic action.

If we combine operations into larger ones, we add extra structure to the order of communication and/or the order of computation. This can be done in different ways, and yields different protocol skeletons. Some ways are more or less standard, and the resulting protocol skeletons will be referred to as *modes of computation*. Given a mode of computation, an idea of what information a message should contain, and a way to compute the wanted information from the received information, we have a general framework for a protocol.

We distinguish the following four modes of computation: *phasing, message-driven* computation, *simulated synchronous* computation, and *synchronous* computation. We will now describe each mode for fault-free static networks. Extensions to cope with possible errors and failures would obscure the basic ideas at this point. If errors may occur, we have to add the appropriate error operations (see section 1.2.1.2), and extend the basic protocol skeletons for these modes of computation with some means for coping with the errors. We will refine some of these protocol skeletons further to arrive at protocols for specific purposes. In chapter 3, we investigate the interrelation between the distributed computation per se and the mode of computation used, for the case of computing minimum-hop distances.

1.1.2.2 Phasing. The idea of phasing is to divide all the work to be done in a computation over different phases, and to allow a processor to begin working on the next phase only if all the work of the current phase is completed. Thus phasing adds some structure to the order of events in a computation, which was totally arbitrary until now. We add a variable for the current phase at each processor i: $phase_i$, and a new operation is added for the transition to the next phase: P_i. The most general protocol skeleton P which makes use of phasing is as follows.

Protocol skeleton P:

Initially $\forall i$: $phase_i = 0$.

S_i^P: **begin** send a message belonging to phase $phase_i$ to some neighbor k **end**

R_i^P: {a message has arrived from j}
　　　 begin receive the message from j and record it; compute **end**

P_i^P: {all messages of phase $phase_i$ have been received from all neighbors}
　　　 begin $phase_i := phase_i + 1$; compute **end**

Note that the internal computation operation I_i is now divided over operation R_i^P where the computation pertaining to the received message is done, and the operation P_i^P, the internal computation which effectuates the phase transition. Comparison of the operations S_j^P and R_i^P reveals a problem introduced by phasing. As in operation S_j^P a message belonging to the current phase $phase_j$ is sent, we can define the phase number of a message as the value of $phase_j$ at the moment that S_j^P was performed. However, in the corresponding receive operation R_i^P, nothing is mentioned about a phase number of a message. Ideally, the messages processor i receives while $phase_i = p$ would be the messages that i's neighbors sent while their phase number had the same value p. Now the problem is, what does processor i do when a message belonging to a different phase arrives: may it be received? There are several possible ways to deal with this problem.

First, it might be the case that the assumptions about communication on the links combined with the properties of a more specific protocol skeleton suffice to prove that the arrival of messages of the wrong phase cannot happen. Secondly, we could just refuse to receive the message if it belongs to a different phase, and add a guard to that effect to the operation R_i^P. We should take care not to introduce the possibility of deadlock then. Thirdly, the message could be received but ignored, as if it had been lost. The fourth possibility is, in case the message belongs to a later phase, to buffer it until the processor reaches the right phase. The fifth possibility is to just let the processor receive the message and perform the appropriate computation. It will depend on the circumstances what choice we make.

Another problem is the guard of operation P_i^P: "all messages of phase $phase_i$ have been received". There must be some way for processor i to evaluate this guard. One possibility, if the number of messages per phase is not fixed, is to include the number of messages to expect in a phase in the first message belonging to a phase, or to somehow mark the last message belonging to a phase (in the case of FIFO links).

1.1.2.3 *Message-driven computation.* The added structure in the order of computation in this case is that messages may only be sent upon receipt of another message. Usually some relation is specified between the contents of a received message and that of the messages to be sent. We will use the term "appropriate" for this relation as long as we do not want to specify it. Thus we do not have a separate, autonomous sending operation any more. But now we need a way to start the sending of messages. Hence we introduce an operation A_i^M (awaken) in protocol skeleton M which can be executed either spontaneously (after initialization), or upon receipt of the first message. Thus we include a test of whether processor i is awake in operation R_i^M, and if it is not, we let i awaken first, i.e., execute operation A_i^M. In most applications a processor is supposed to awaken only once. The boolean $awake_i$ records whether i is awake or not.

Protocol skeleton M:

Initially $\forall\, i$: $awake_i = false$.

A_i^M: $\{\neg awake_i\}$
    begin $awake_i := true$;
        forall neighbors j **do** send the appropriate messages to j **od**
    end

R_i^M: $\{$a message has arrived from $j\}$
    begin if $\neg awake_i$ **then** do A_i^M **fi**;
        receive the message from j; compute;
        forall neighbors k **do** send the appropriate messages to k **od**
    end

In a static network, all processors eventually awaken if and only if in every connected component of the network there is at least one processor that awakens spontaneously, and messages are not lost, garbled, or delayed infinitely long. Thus we will assume in the sequel that there is at least one processor in each connected component of the network that awakens spontaneously. In a dynamic network, some action comparable to awakening will be taken upon a change in link status (i.e., the going down or coming up of a link). This will be discussed in section 1.2.1.3. For this formulation of the message-driven mode of computation we need the extra assumption that messages are not lost, garbled, or delayed infinitely long. This is because the sending of a message is now restricted (by the availability of a message to receive) and a processor might not have the possibility of sending a message so often that it gets through. Whether duplications of messages can be handled correctly in this mode of computation depends entirely on the specific algorithm. Summarizing, we have the following assumptions for the message-driven mode of computation.

Assumption 1.1.1

(1)   At least one processor in every connected component awakens spontaneously,

(2)   messages are not lost, garbled, duplicated, or delayed infinitely long.

This form of computation is called message driven, because events only occur once a message is received. Thus the situation that no more messages are around is of special interest in this mode, as all processors are then waiting for a message and nothing will happen any more when this is the case. This situation is called *termination* (TERM). To detect it, a termination detection algorithm is often superimposed upon the message-driven computation (see e.g. [Tel91]).

1.1.2.4   Simulated synchronous computation. In this mode, which is frequently used to simulate synchronous protocols on an asynchronous network, we combine the added structure of phasing and of the message-driven mode of computation. Hence assumption 1.1.1 applies here, too. Although we did not require in the case of phasing that the message received was of the same phase as the receiver, we will do so in this case, as it has the advantage that a message can contain less information. However, we then need a way to ensure that no messages belonging to the next phase are received if they happen to arrive early, as is possible in this mode. To this end we add a new variable in each processor i: rec_i, which is a boolean array that records for each neighbor j in $rec_i[j]$ whether all messages of the current phase from neighbor j have already been received or not. Hence it is necessary that the receiver of a message has some way to decide whether a message received is the last message of the current phase or not. As a consequence, we require that at least one (possibly empty) message per phase is sent to each neighbor.

There are several ways to implement this: for example, sending the number of messages to expect in each phase, or combining all messages of one phase over one link into one large message. Again we are not interested in an actual implementation, as long as a processor can decide the question. This leads to protocol skeleton SS.

Protocol skeleton SS:

Initially $\forall i$: $awake_i = false$, $phase_i = 0$, and $\forall$ neighbors j: $rec_i[j] = false$.

A_i^{SS}: $\{\neg awake_i\}$

> **begin** $awake_i := true$;
>
> > **forall** neighbors j
> >
> > **do** send the appropriate messages of phase $phase_i$ to j **od**
>
> **end**

R_i^{SS}: {a message (of phase $phase_i$) has arrived from $j \wedge \neg rec_i[j]$}

    begin if $\neg awake_i$ **then do** A_i^{SS} **fi** ;

        receive the message from j and record it; compute;

        if this was the last message of phase $phase_i$ from j

        then $rec_i[j] := true$

        fi ;

        if $\forall$ neighbors k : $rec_i[k]$

        then $phase_i := phase_i + 1$; compute;

            forall neighbors k

            do   send the appropriate messages of phase $phase_i$ to k;

                    $rec_i[k] := false$

            od

      fi

    end

Note that operation P_i^P is now included in operation R_i^{SS} to ensure that all operations except awakening are only done upon receipt of a message. A link can contain in one direction messages of two different phases. Assuming that messages have to be received in the order in which they arrive at a processor, we now need the assumption that they arrive in the same order as they were sent. Otherwise the guard of operation R_i^{SS} could cause deadlock. Thus we assume that links behave as FIFO queues. In section 3.1.1.3 we will prove for refinements of this protocol skeleton that the phrase "of phase $phase_i$" is not necessary in the guard of operation R_i^{SS}.

Assumption 1.1.2 *On any link, messages in any one direction are not reordered.*

1.1.2.5 Synchronous computation. In synchronous computation it is usually assumed that all processors awaken simultaneously, and that messages are transmitted with a fixed delay. In an environment where messages can be lost, the latter assumption can be used to conclude that a certain message must have been lost because it did not arrive in time. For our purposes, however, it is usually sufficient to weaken the assumption to the following, in addition to assumptions 1.1.1 and 1.1.2.

Assumption 1.1.3

   (1) *All processors awaken spontaneously, and*

   (2) *transmission delay is sufficiently bounded such that the non-arrival of a message can be inferred.*

In synchronous computation not only are all messages of one phase sent "at the same time", but also all messages of one phase are received "at the same time". It is usually not assumed that more than one message can be received over one link at the same time, hence the information of all messages is assumed to be merged together in one (larger) message. As in protocol skeleton SS, the operation P_i^P is included in the receive operation.

The variable rec_i is not used any more, as the registration in the protocol skeleton of which messages have been received is replaced by a registration of which messages have arrived, but this is provided by a lower layer, and thus not specified here. If this protocol skeleton is used in a really synchronous environment, i.e., an environment in which messages have a fixed delay and where there is a way to let all processors start (awaken) simultaneously, then the guard of R_i^S becomes true automatically each time the fixed delay has elapsed. The protocol skeleton S is as follows.

Protocol skeleton S:

Initially $\forall i$: $awake_i = false$ and $phase_i = 0$.

A_i^S: $\{\neg awake_i\}$
  begin $awake_i := true$;
      forall neighbors j
      do send the message belonging to phase $phase_i$ to j **od**
  end

R_i^S: $\{$from every neighbor the message belonging to phase $phase_i$ has arrived$\}$
  begin forall neighbors j **do** receive the message from j **od**;
      $phase_i := phase_i + 1$; compute;
      forall neighbors j
      do send the message belonging to phase $phase_i$ to j **od**
  end

1.2 Verification

Having discussed several models for distributed computation, we need to precisely model the different possible network assumptions before we can start to design and verify algorithms.

1.2.1 Modeling the assumptions

An elegant way to model some assumptions for the distributed system is to introduce *system operations*, i.e., operations that model the behavior of the distributed
system, in addition to the behavior of the algorithm under consideration. Joseph *et
al.* [JRT86] use a comparable approach in their model as they augment the finite-
state machine used for the basic protocol with transitions pertaining to system
operations such as the loss of messages on a communication link. For the case of
communication errors, we consider a communication link as a separate process, and
the occurrence of an error on that link as the execution of an operation acting on
the contents of that link, i.e., on the variables maintained in the link process. We
can thus precisely define in each protocol skeleton what errors we allow, by adding
the corresponding operations. Likewise, the going down and coming up of a link
can be represented by operations. In considering time-dependent algorithms, we
also need to introduce the concept of *time*. This also can be done by a system
operation (see section 1.2.1.5).

We discuss communication in a fault-free static network first (section 1.2.1.1).
The operations for the most common communication errors are given next (section
1.2.1.2), and dynamic networks are modeled in section 1.2.1.3. We define transient
failures in section 1.2.1.4 and "time" in section 1.2.1.5.

1.2.1.1 The fault-free static network.
In a fault-free static network, it is
assumed that messages sent are not lost, garbled, duplicated, or delayed infinitely
long. Thus a message sent always arrives unaltered in finite time at its destination.
We also assume that the messages on a link in any one direction are not reordered:
links have the FIFO property, i.e., a message sent first on a link arrives first. We
use the following formulations.

If two processors i and j share a link, then i and j are called neighbors. The link
between processors i and j, denoted as (i,j), is represented by two FIFO queues
of messages $Q[i,j]$ and $Q[j,i]$ containing the messages from i to j and from j to
i, respectively. Hence we consider only undirected networks. We denote the fact
that a message with contents m is on its way from processor i to processor j over
the link (i,j) as: $<m> \in Q[i,j]$.

In a static network, links are fixed and known to their neighbors. If j is a
neighbor of i, then sending a message from i to j means appending a message to
$Q[i,j]$, and receiving of a message from j at i means deleting the first message,
i.e., the head of $Q[j,i]$. Thus we can formulate the *send* and *receive* procedures
for i as follows.

proc send $<m>$ to j = { j neighbor of i } **begin** append $<m>$ to $Q[i,j]$ **end**

proc receive $<m>$ from j = $\{\, j$ neighbor of $i \wedge <m>$ head of $Q\,[j,i]\,\}$
begin delete $<m>$ from $Q\,[j,i]$ **end**

Note that the guard of the receive procedure will have to be subsumed under the guard of the operation where the procedure is called.

1.2.1.2 *Communication errors.* Communication errors frequently considered in the literature are: loss of messages, garbling of messages, duplication of messages, and the arrival of messages out of order, i.e., arrival at the receiver in a different order than sent by the sender. We will name error operations as E_{ij}^{l}, where the subscripts denote the link on which the operation acts, including the direction: thus E_{ij}^{l} acts on the contents of $Q\,[i,j]$. The superscript denotes the kind of error: l stands for loss of messages. We distinguish the following error operations.

E_{ij}^{l}: $\{\, Q\,[i,j] \neq \emptyset \,\}$ begin delete a message from $Q\,[i,j]$ **end**   (loss)

A garbled message remains in existence, but with a content that is no longer valid. It is usually assumed that such a message can be recognized, e.g. through a parity check. We do *not* consider Byzantine or malicious faults, hence we assume that a message cannot be changed into another valid message. We denote a message with invalid contents as an "empty" message: $<\lambda>$ (λ for empty string). The garble operation is as follows.

E_{ij}^{g}: $\{\, Q\,[i,j] \neq \emptyset \,\}$ (garble)
    begin forsome $<m> \in Q\,[i,j]$ do $<m> := <\lambda>$ od end

By the statement "**forsome** $<m> \in Q\,[i,j]$ do something **od**" we mean: for one arbitrary message in the queue $Q\,[i,j]$ do something. By the statement "$<m> :=$ $<\lambda>$" we mean: change the contents of the message into λ, but do not change the position of the message in the queue.

Duplication of messages arises when transmissions or copies can be generated by some mechanism in the network.

E_{ij}^{d}: $\{\, Q\,[i,j] \neq \emptyset \,\}$ (duplication)
    begin forsome $<m> \in Q\,[i,j]$ do append a copy of $<m>$ to $Q\,[i,j]$ **od**
    end

The use of different routes can also cause reordering of messages with a common destination.

E_{ij}^r: $\{ \mid Q\,[i,j] \mid\, \geq 2 \,\}$ (reorder)

    begin forsome $<m>,\ <m'>\ \in Q\,[i,j]$

        do interchange $<m>$ and $<m'>$ in $Q\,[i,j]$ **od**

    end

The counterpart of the assumption "messages are not delayed infinitely long" does not need a separate error operation, as it is described by E^l.

1.2.1.3 *Dynamic networks.*

In a dynamic network, links can go down and come up. It is usually assumed that a link that goes down can cause the loss of some or all of the messages that were in transit on that link. The assumptions stated above for links in a static network also apply to links in a dynamic network, whether they are up or down. To model the loss of messages when a link goes down or is down, we change the send procedure. If link (i,j) is up, then sending a message has the same meaning as in the static case. If the link is down, sending a message from i to j means: possibly appending the message to $Q\,[i,j]$. This corresponds on the one hand to the message getting lost and on the other hand to the situation that the message was still in i's output buffer when the link came up again. If the link is down and $Q\,[j,i]$ not empty, receiving a message just means getting the head of $Q\,[j,i]$, corresponding to getting the next message in i's input buffer. Note that this need not be empty when the link is down. Thus we get the following *send* and *receive* procedures.

proc send $<m>$ to j =   **begin if** $linkstate(i,j)$ = up

                              then append $<m>$ to $Q\,[i,j]$

                              else possibly append $<m>$ to $Q\,[i,j]$

                              fi

                    end

proc receive $<m>$ from j = $\{\ <m>$ head of $Q\,[j,i]\ \}$

                                    begin delete $<m>$ from $Q\,[j,i]$ **end**

To model the going down of a link, we add an operation for that link which provides for the corresponding possible loss of messages. As a counterpart to the operation for going down, we also add an operation for the coming up of a link. It is of course necessary that processors somehow become aware of the changed status (up or down, respectively) of an incident link. We model this by adding special messages $<up>$ and $<down>$, which we call *control messages*. We assume that when a link changes status, control messages are added to the message queues corresponding to that link, and that the processors incident to the link eventually become aware of the changed link status when they receive the control message.

Thus the status of the link cannot be observed directly by the incident processors, and therefore a processor may try to send a message over a link which is down.

When link (i, j) comes up, an $<up>$ message is appended to both $Q[i, j]$ and $Q[j, i]$. When link (i, j) goes down, a $<down>$ message is appended to both $Q[i, j]$ and $Q[j, i]$ and, moreover, we allow that arbitrary non-control messages are deleted from $Q[i, j]$ and $Q[j, i]$, corresponding to the situation that some or all messages are lost when the link goes down. It is probably more realistic to only delete messages after the last $<up>$ message, but it is not necessary to make this assumption. We do *not* allow that control messages are deleted.

Thus we get the following operations U (coming up) and D (going down) for links.

U_{ij}: $\{linkstate(i, j) = \text{down}\}$
    begin append $<up>$ to $Q[i, j]$; append $<up>$ to $Q[j, i]$;
        $linkstate(i, j) := \text{up}$
    end

D_{ij}: $\{linkstate(i, j) = \text{up}\}$
    begin delete all, some or no non-control messages from $Q[i, j]$;
        delete all, some or no non-control messages from $Q[j, i]$;
        append $<down>$ to $Q[i, j]$; append $<down>$ to $Q[j, i]$;
        $linkstate(i, j) := \text{down}$
    end

Here $linkstate(i, j)$ is a ghost variable which can have values *up* and *down*. It is not a variable which can be accessed by any processor, but it is introduced in order to formulate properties related to the status of the link more precisely.

One might ask why we chose to append the control messages at the end of the message queue upon a link status change. In the case of a U operation this is clear: the $<up>$ message marks the beginning of a sequence of messages sent while the link is up, and thus is transmitting reliably in some sense (depending on the communication errors allowed). But for the case of a D operation, the $<down>$ message is in a strange position. Messages that were in a position in the queue in front of (before) the $<down>$ message might have been lost, due to the D operation, as well as messages sent in the queue behind (after) the $<down>$ message, due to the send procedure. Apart from the fact that it is not quite clear where else to insert the $<down>$ message, one can think of the following situation as an adequate motivation for our choice. A transmission line that has been operating satisfactorily suddenly degrades so much that the physical layer decides to declare the line down. But reporting that the line is down to the layer

above (the $<down>$ message), may come *after* the first loss of a message due to
the failure of the transmission line.

In chapters 3 and 4 processors going down are modeled by the going down of
all incident links of a processor that are still up, and processors coming up by the
coming up of some but possibly not all links incident to a processor. There we do
not assume that a processor which goes down loses the contents of all its memory.
In chapter 5 we will see applications that explicitly maintain information in "safe
(stable) storage" to cope with processor crashes. We refer to chapter 5 for the
precise models used in that case.

Summarizing, the assumptions for a dynamic network are:

Assumption 1.2.1
  (1) Messages are not lost other than by a D operation, a send procedure, or an
       E^l *operation (if included),*
  (2) messages are not garbled, duplicated, or delayed infinitely long, other than
       by the appropriate error operation (if included),
  (3) links change status only by the appropriate U or D operations, and
  (4) initially, all links are down and the initial topology of the network is defined
       by the appropriate U operations by way of initialization.

To protocol skeletons intended for dynamic networks we must add new operations
RU and RD for all processors to model the special action to be taken upon a
change in link status: receive an $<up>$ message and receive a $<down>$ message,
respectively. Alternatively, we can extend the code for the R operation with a
test which determines whether the message received is a control message and the
appropriate consequent action. If the distributed computation at hand computes
something which depends on the actual topology of the network, such as for example
minimum-hop distances, part of the computation may become obsolete as a result
of a change in topology. There are two ways to deal with this: the protocol can
partially recompute (which leads to the problem of deciding what part must be
recomputed), or it can restart the computation from scratch (which leads to the
problem of reinitializing).

1.2.1.4 Transient failures. In the previous sections, we discussed communication failures and changes in the topology of the network. In the protocols in this
book it is always specified which specific failures a protocol can and cannot tolerate. Usually, a protocol is extended with some extra feature to tolerate that specific
failure. For example, a communication protocol that tolerates loss of messages has
the possibility to retransmit messages and has some way for the receiver to decide

whether a received message is original or a retransmission. There exists another approach to fault-tolerance altogether: the use of *self-stabilizing* algorithms.

In 1974, Dijkstra introduced the property of self-stabilization in distributed systems and applied it to algorithms for mutual exclusion [Dij74]. To define a self-stabilizing algorithm, we need the concept of the *global state* of a system. The *local state* of a processor consists of the values of all local variables of that processor. The global state of the system consists of the local states of all processors, together with the contents of the message queues. For the purpose of a self-stabilizing algorithm, the set G of all global states is partitioned into 2 sets, the set L of all *legal* states, and the set I of all *illegal* states. An algorithm is called self-stabilizing if the following two conditions hold. First, starting from an arbitrary global state, it reaches a legal state within a finite number of steps. Second, any step taken while it is in a legal state leaves it in a legal state. Consequently, self-stabilizing algorithms do not require any initialization. For a traditional algorithm, the initial state would be a legal state, and all reachable states would be legal states. The illegal states would not be reachable for a traditional algorithm, for by assumption the algorithm would not start in such a state.

Consider now the occurrence of a transient processor failure, e.g., corrupting the contents of some memory locations. Due to the definition of a self-stabilizing algorithm, the resulting global state can be viewed as a (probably) illegal state, and hence we know that the algorithm will take only a finite number of steps to reach a legal state. In this way, the algorithm tolerates all transient failures (given that the algorithm has time enough to reach a legal state). A disadvantage of the use of self-stabilizing algorithms is that it is not locally observable for a processor whether the system is in a legal or in an illegal state. Self-stabilizing algorithms are not used in practice yet, as far as we know. However, the research on this topic has greatly increased lately. In this book, we will not discuss self-stabilizing protocols further. More on self-stabilization in general can be found in [Tel94, chapter 15], while self-stabilization in communication protocols (discussed in chapter 2 of this book) can be found in [AB93].

1.2.1.5 Time. In distributed computing, there are many protocols that use time in some sense or other. In those protocols it is assumed that processors locally have access to timers and/or a local clock. Clocks are local variables which are advanced or increased by "time", and in all processors by (more or less) the same amount. They are also supposed to show (more or less) the same value (i.e. time). Timers on the other hand, are decreased by "time", and in all processors by (more or less) the same amount – the same amount by which the clocks are increased. Timers do not generally show the same value, however: a timer can be set to some value, and it is usually the understanding that if the timer has reached a certain value (e.g. < 0) then some action has to be taken by a processor. Such an action is called a *timeout action*. Examples can be found in chapters 2 and 5. If we think of analog clocks, the increase in clock values is by some positive real value. However, in computers clocks are digital, thus they increase by a number of *ticks*, hence a positive natural number. To model this, we assume that all processors i have a local variable $clock_i$, and that "time" affects all *clock* variables in the same way. We thus introduce a system operation TIME, which changes all local variables $clock_i$. For the ideal case that all clocks show exactly the same time, we have to augment the protocol skeleton for some protocol using time with the following.

Initially $\forall\, i, j : clock_i = clock_j.$

TIME: **begin** choose $\tau \in \mathbb{N}^+$;
  forall i **do** $clock_i := clock_i + \tau$; $timer_i := timer_i - \tau$ **od**
 end

This has to be interpreted as: some operations of the augmented protocol skeleton are executed before the clocks are advanced by τ. As the assumption that all clocks show exactly the same time is not usually realistic, it is often relaxed to the assumption that the drift of all clocks is ρ-bounded, that is, in real time τ a clock is increased by an amount τ' with $\tau/(1 + \rho) \leq \tau' \leq \tau.(1 + \rho)$ (see e.g. [Tel91]). In the model, one might now want real valued clocks to reflect how far on its way a clock is towards the next tick. Thus the operation TIME is changed to:

TIME: **begin** choose $\tau \in \mathbb{N}^+$;
  forall i
  do **forsome** τ' with $\tau/(1 + \rho) \leq \tau' \leq \tau.(1 + \rho)$
    do $clock_i := clock_i + \tau'$; $timer_i := timer_i - \tau'$ **od**
  od
 end

We will not discuss drifting clocks further, as the extension from exact clocks is straightforward. Of course, assuming the existence of an operation TIME creates the need for a protocol on a lower level of the distributed system to keep the clocks within the desired bounds, or "synchronized" as it is called in the literature (see e.g. [RSB90]).

Distributed algorithms often use so-called *timestamped* messages. These are messages to which an extra field is added, containing the value of the local clock of the sender at the time that the message was sent. Timestamped messages can be used to limit the lifetimes of messages in a network: at the receiver the timestamp in the message is compared with the local clock, and if the difference is too large the message is discarded (see section 2.2). Another use of timestamped messages occurs in cases where messages in transit in the network might be reordered. Then the timestamps are used to reconstruct the original ordering of the messages at the receiver. Time-stamping mechanisms do not need strictly synchronized clocks (cf. Lamport [Lam78]).

The problem of how to keep local clocks in a distributed system synchronized is not addressed in this book.

1.2.2 Assertional verification

In the preceding sections we have described how distributed algorithms can be viewed as sets of atomic actions. Once an algorithm and the distributed system in which it is executed are defined precisely, we are left with (1) determining which assertions reflect the correctness of the algorithm (the *specification* of the algorithm), and (2) proving that these assertions hold. This is the subject of assertional verification.

1.2.2.1   Correctness properties.   The properties that reflect the correctness of a distributed algorithm are usually divided into *safety properties* and *liveness properties*. The latter are also called *progress properties*. Safety properties are of the form: if something happens, it is not something bad.   Liveness properties are of the form: eventually something good will happen.

In the case of the distributed computation of some value, a safety property might be: "either a processor holds the correct value, or there is a message under way to that processor containing the correct value". A liveness property in this case might be: "a processor will hold the correct value in finite time".

In the case of a communication protocol where information has to be transferred from a sender to a receiver, a safety property would be: "the information received by the receiver is a subset of the information sent by the sender". A liveness property in this case would be: "eventually the amount of information received by the receiver is increased". Note that if the protocol is supposed to keep on transferring information forever, then termination cannot be considered correct behavior.

A distributed algorithm whose safety properties hold is called *partially correct*. In this book we are mainly concerned with the partial correctness of distributed algorithms. This stems from our wish to state algorithms in a form that is as general as possible. Thus we are usually not concerned with e.g. implementation, which often means that some flow control is absent. This can have the effect that it is no longer possible to prove *total correctness*, i.e., that all desired liveness properties hold also. In section 2.2 we illustrate some pitfalls which can occur in designing an implementation of a protocol skeleton, while trying to maintain the safety and liveness of the latter.

It is less clear what liveness properties are necessary for the total correctness of a distributed algorithm. It is evident that the property of "no *deadlock*" is necessary for liveness, but it is usually not sufficient. In terms of protocol skeletons, deadlock-freedom translates to: before valid termination, there is always an operation that is enabled and thus can be executed. Note that deadlock-freedom can be expressed as an assertion (see also [JRT86]).

Consider again a communication protocol where information has to be transferred from a sender to a receiver. Even though the receiver keeps receiving messages, it might very well be possible that the amount of information received is never increased, because the same message is received over and over again (because the sender is repeatedly transmitting the same message). A situation like this is sometimes called *livelock* or *no progress*.

In this case, we might formulate a progress property like: "in finite time, the information at the receiver increases". However, in practice, this is not a sufficient condition for a communication protocol, as Yemini and Kurose noted [YK82]. Think of the situation that every new piece of information takes twice as long as the previous one to arrive. Thus if a certain performance is desired, then this should also be part of the specification. However, for proving such performance properties other methods than assertional verification by system-wide invariants are necessary.

Although we are mainly concerned with safety properties, we will sometimes prove some "weak progress properties", that is, properties that show that progress is always possible. Chandy and Misra [CM88] assume a *fairness* rule in the execution of their programs that implies that every operation is selected infinitely often. With such a rule it is possible to prove that certain events will happen eventually. As we did not assume any sort of fairness in executing operations, we cannot prove statements of the form: "something will happen", as the case that nothing happens at all (i.e., no operation is executed) is valid, too, in our model.

The closest we can get to proving progress properties is that it is sometimes possible to prove that only a finite number of operations can be executed before a certain desired state, such as termination, is reached. This is done in the following way. One has to find a function F from the set of system states to some well-founded domain, such as the natural numbers, or tuples of natural numbers. A well-founded domain is a set of elements, together with a partial ordering on those elements, such that every decreasing sequence is finite (and thus ends in (some) smallest element). This function F should have the following property: if any operation of the protocol skeleton is executed, the value of F is strictly decreased. If we can find such a function, we know that only a finite number of operations can be executed.

1.2.2.2 The proof method. The method we use in the proofs of safety properties of distributed algorithms is that of *assertional verification by system-wide invariants*, first used by Krogdahl [Kro78] and Knuth [Knu81] for the case of protocols, and later advocated by Lamport [Lam82] for use in distributed computing. Chandy and Misra [CM88] based their design and proof system for parallel programs UNITY on this same method, albeit for a different programming model. As early as 1976, Keller [Kel76] presented an abstract conceptual model for the verification of parallel programs which contains all the basic ideas in this verification method. The tradition in assertional verification started by Owicki and Gries [OG76] is based on a different philosophy, namely the need for a proof system that satisfies the principle of compositionality (see section 1.2.2.3).

A (system-wide) *invariant* is an assertion which holds in the initial state(s) of the system, and which is preserved by all possible operations, i.e., if the assertion holds before execution of the operation, then it will also hold afterwards. An assertion is *always true* if it is preserved by every possible execution sequence of operations. Thus if an assertion is invariant, it is also always true. However, the converse does not hold [Kel76, vGT90]. In the literature, the distinction between "invariant" and "always true" is not always made carefully.

As the proof rules for the notions "always true" and "invariant" differ, we must take some care in using them. Consider the assertions a, b, and c for some protocol skeleton P. Let a and b be always true, and let $a \Rightarrow c$ hold. Then also the assertions $a \wedge b$, $a \vee b$, and c are always true. Hence the notion "always true" is closed under conjunction, disjunction, and implication. However, it is not closed under parallel composition: if a is always true in both P and Q, then a need not be always true in $P\|Q$, the parallel composition of P and Q, i.e., the union of the set of operations in P and Q, together with the respective initial conditions [vGT90].

For invariants a and b on the other hand, we have that $a \wedge b$ and $a \vee b$ are invariant for P, and if a is also an invariant for Q, then a is invariant for $P\|Q$ [CM88]. However, if $a \Rightarrow c$ holds, this does not necessarily mean that c is an invariant for P [vGT90]. We can only deduce that c is always true for P, as a invariant implies a is always true, and the notion "always true" is closed under implication.

The assertions used in our correctness proofs usually describe the relation between the contents of several variables of a protocol skeleton and are stated as logical formulas. To limit the number of parentheses in formulas we assume that the binary operator for conjunction ($\wedge$) has a higher priority than the binary operator for disjunction ($\vee$).

If a safety property for a distributed algorithm is expressed as an assertion, then for the verification of the algorithm it is sufficient to show that the assertion is always true. It is not necessary that the assertion is also invariant. Only, in our opinion, showing that an assertion is always true by checking the definition of "always true" is not acceptable, as this leads to an infinite proof obligation. Hence we begin by proving assertions invariant, as the notion "invariant" has a finite proof obligation, and then deduce that (consequences of) these assertions are always true. Keller called this way of proving assertions to be always true the *induction principle* [Kel76]. Note that every assertion which is always true can be proved by means of an invariant [San90, Mis90]; the problem is to find a suitable invariant. In an actual proof that an assertion is invariant, we will often refrain from mentioning the operations for which it is clear that they cannot influence the assertion because they do not alter the variables involved.

This is the basic proof method for safety properties for one protocol skeleton. Suppose we have a protocol skeleton together with a proof of its safety properties. Given a modification of the protocol skeleton, is it possible to arrive at a partial correctness proof of the modified protocol skeleton by *modifications* in the original proof, or do we have to redo the whole proof completely? The need for modification of a protocol skeleton arises in many situations. Apart from the change that is made if scheduling restrictions are imposed on a protocol skeleton, a protocol might have to be ported to a different system, or it might have to be combined into a larger protocol with other components. Sometimes we change a protocol skeleton just to facilitate the proof of its safety properties.

Below we list some of the changes to protocol skeletons that are considered and that occur throughout this book, together with the necessary changes in their partial correctness proofs.

- Strengthen the guard of an operation: the proof remains valid.
- Add an *auxiliary variable*. An auxiliary variable does not influence the execution of the operations in any way. Hence the variable may not appear in the right hand side of an assignment to a protocol variable, nor may it be referenced in the conditions of the control structures: the proof remains valid because the behavior of the protocol skeleton is not changed. However, it is possible that additional properties can now be derived.
- Delete an auxiliary variable, together with all references to this variable: properties which mention this variable thus become meaningless; however, derived

properties without this variable remain valid, because the behavior of the skeleton is not changed.

- Add an operation: one must augment the safety proof and check that the invariants remain valid under the new operation also.
- Delete an operation: the proof remains valid, as it holds also for the case that the deleted operation is never executed.
- Combine two or more operations into a larger one: to maintain the safety properties, verify that the use of the original operations in the larger one is consistent with their guards.
- Merge two protocol skeletons P and Q into $P\|Q$: verify that the initial conditions of P and Q do not conflict, and verify that the invariants of P are preserved in Q, and vice versa.

Note that if we weaken the guard of an operation or add an operation that does not preserve the invariants used in the safety proof, we might have to redo the whole proof. The last chapter of this book contains two examples of transformations of protocol skeletons for which this is necessary.

Up till now, we have only discussed assertions which are invariant or always true, and thus are assertions which are independent of time. However, this does not mean that assertional verification cannot be used for time-dependent algorithms, i.e., algorithms where explicit use is made of clocks, timers, and timestamps on messages. Usually the only feature of "time" that is used is the ordering of events that it implies. In section 1.2.1.5 we showed how we can incorporate the concept of time in our model of computation. Thus we can state assertions about "time" as assertions about values of the local variables $clock_i$. Chapter 4 contains an example of this.

1.2.2.3 Related proof methods.
As for total correctness, we already mentioned in the previous section that our model of computation does not allow complete total correctness proofs. Although freedom from deadlock for some protocol skeleton can be stated in an assertion, this does not mean that freedom from deadlock for this protocol skeleton automatically carries over to freedom from deadlock for a refinement of it. As the order of operations in the latter might be more restricted because extra guards were introduced, freedom from deadlock for the refined protocol skeleton will have to be described by a *different* assertion, which will have to be proved separately.

As for the problem of livelock, if we weaken the condition that "execution of the algorithm cannot go on infinitely long before some desired state is reached" (either termination or some other desired state in case of continuous algorithms), to the condition that "operations do not become enabled infinitely often before some desired state is reached", it is sometimes possible to prove this weaker form of "no livelock". This is done in the following way. Define a function F from the set of system-states to some well-founded set W, where F has the property that execution of every operation changes the system-state such that the value of F strictly decreases. (A well-founded set is a partially ordered set in which no infinite decreasing chains exist.) If such a function F exists, then it implies that only a finite number of operations can be executed before the desired state is reached.

The well-founded set W in our case is always a set of (N)-tuples of non-negative integers, for some value of N. We then define the following total ordering $<_W$ on W:

$(a_0, a_1, \ldots, a_{N-1}) <_W (b_0, b_1, \ldots, b_{N-1})$ if
$\exists i$ with $0 \leq i \leq N - 1 :$ $(a_i < b_i \wedge \forall j$ with $0 \leq j < i :$ $a_j = b_j)$.
As the a_i and b_i are non-negative integers, this order relation on W is well founded. The function $F = (f_0, f_1, \ldots, f_{N-1})$ from the system-state to W is usually such that a coordinate f_k stands for a linear combination of numbers of processes in a certain state and numbers of (a certain type of) messages under way.

The proof method of assertional verification by system-wide invariants is firmly founded in the Temporal Logic of linear time; see e.g. [MP88]. Temporal Logic contains, apart from the operators from predicate logic, operators for expressing relations in time, such as *until, next,* and *eventually.* In Temporal Logic, it is assumed that programs are executed in a fair way. However, it is not necessary to restrict oneself to the formalism of Temporal Logic to give a proof of partial correctness for a distributed algorithm.

The design and proof system for parallel programs UNITY proposed by Chandy and Misra [CM88] is also based on Temporal Logic. Minor differences from our model can be found in the use of guards and flow control. In the model of Chandy and Misra, an operation is always enabled, while in our model an operation can also be disabled. Consider however the operation B:

B: $\{ g \}$ **begin** A **end**

This is equivalent to operation C:

C: **begin if** g **then** A **else** skip **fi end**

which is always enabled. However, a fairness rule might have to be phrased differently for the respective formulations.

As for flow control, Chandy and Misra only allow assignment statements in their programs, which can be multiple assignments and/or conditional assignments. We allow control flow statements like **if**-clauses and **do**-loops. In general, we use very little control flow in the basic protocol skeletons, and more in the refinements. However, an **if**-clause can be rewritten as a conditional assignment, and a loop like "**forall** neighbors **do** ... **od**" is actually a multiple assignment. We feel that rewriting protocols in terms of multiple conditional assignments unnecessarily obscures the protocol for the reader.

In UNITY, a strict separation of concerns is made between *what* should be done, described in the program, and *when*, *where*, and *how* it should be done, described in a so-called *mapping*, i.e., a description of how the program is executed on a specific architecture. The main difference between our proof method and UNITY has already been mentioned: UNITY adopts a fairness rule, while we do not. This makes our method less powerful in general but, in those places where we feel the need for an assumption like "fairness", we explicitly state the necessary assumption in the theorems (see chapter 4). Finally, the UNITY method is more completely developed as a formal proof system.

Joseph *et al.* [JRT86] presented a proof method based upon a combination of the analysis of finite-state machines and assertional verification. They demonstrate the method for variants of some of the protocols we present in chapter 2.

Since 1984 Halpern and others [HM84, HF85, HZ87] have developed a theory of so-called *knowledge-based protocols*, i.e., protocols which explicitly develop and test for "system knowledge". They argue that knowledge-based protocols provide much more insight into what happens in the protocols than traditionally stated protocols where the correctness proofs do not contribute to a better understanding of "why what action is taken when". Some of the protocols which we present in chapter 2 were formulated and proved as knowledge-based protocols by Halpern and Zuck [HZ87]. In the correctness proof of a knowledge-based protocol the assertions can contain so-called *knowledge operators*, i.e., logical operators with the meaning: "a processor knows". Apart from this, it is just another form of assertional verification.

The *action systems* introduced by Back and Sere [BS89] are very similar to our concept of a protocol skeleton. Back and Sere use action systems to stepwise derive a parallel program from a sequential program, thereby preserving the correctness of the latter. They are mainly interested in total correctness.

The tradition in assertional verification of parallel programs was started by Owicki and Gries [OG76] and can best be described as the *quest for compositionality* (see [dR85, HdR86] for an overview). Suppose one has a program consisting of several components, and separate proofs that these components satisfy their specifications. Then the goal is to derive a correctness proof for the composite program by using as little information about the inner structure of the components as possible. If it is possible to derive a correctness proof which only uses the specifications of the components, then the proof method is called *compositional*. Owicki and Gries use the concept of *"interference freedom of proofs"* and thus their method is not compositional. Lamport introduced "concurrent Hoare logic" [Lam80] which is compositional, but has the disadvantage that the specifications of the components must be equal to the specifications of the composite program.

Over the years, numerous proof systems for concurrent programs have been devised, with more emphasis on the theoretical properties of such proof systems, e.g. compositionality, than on their practical applicability for actual program verification. Examples can be found in the works of Zwiers [Zwi88] and Gerth [Ger89]. It is interesting to note that for a practical application, namely the verification of the distributed minimum spanning tree algorithm of Gallager, Humblet, and Spira [SdR87], a system-wide invariant is again introduced. This is done in spite of the effort made in decomposing the algorithm into components and combining the component proofs into a verification of the whole algorithm, and Temporal Logic is used. This suggests that, for our present understanding of the verification of distributed algorithms, the non-compositional method is easier for use in practical situations. It remains to be seen whether this is still the case for really large and complex distributed algorithms.

Another method used for verification is by means of *process algebra* (see e.g. [BK88]). The idea is to capture both the specification of a composite program and the specifications of the component processes in sets of equations. From the latter set a set of equations is then constructed which describes the behavior of the composite program in terms of its components, and a proof is given that this set of equations is equivalent to the set for the specification of the composite program. This is done by means of algebraic formula manipulation; unfortunately the formulas tend to explode and only simple protocols have been verified by this method so far. The alternating bit protocol is treated for example in [BK86, BK88, Wei89], and a sliding window protocol with a window size of 1 in [Vaa86].

2

Link-level Protocols

In this chapter we consider some link-level protocols and show their partial correctness by assertional verification. Link-level protocols, i.e., protocols residing in the data link layer, are designed to control the exchange of information between two computing stations, e.g. computers or processors over a full-duplex link. They should guard against the loss of information when the transmission medium is unreliable. We only discuss transmission errors that occur while the link is up, and thus use the model of a static network consisting of two nodes i and j, and a bidirectional link (i, j). We will not deal with the problems caused by links or nodes going down, nor with the termination of a protocol. In a different context, these issues will be dealt with in later chapters.

In section 2.1 we discuss a generalization of the sliding window protocol. This protocol is meant to control the exchange of messages in an asynchronous environment. Although sliding window protocols belong to the data link layer, we will see in chapter 4 that the generalization can also be used as a basis for connection management, which belongs to the transport layer. We show that the alternating bit protocol and the "balanced" two-way sliding window protocol are instances of this one general protocol skeleton, that contains several further parameters to tune the simultaneous transmission of data over a full-duplex link. After proving the partial correctness of the protocol skeleton, we discuss the dependence of the optimal choice of the parameters on the propagation delay of the link, the transmission speed of the senders, and the error rate of the link.

In section 2.2 we discuss another version of the sliding window protocol: the "block acknowledgment protocol". Brown et al. [BGM91] have redesigned the sliding window protocol such that it tolerates both message loss and message disorder, while using only bounded sequence numbers. Both safety and liveness are proven for this protocol (skeleton) in [BGM91]. We investigate the consequences of an implementation of this protocol with timers and show how easily one loses either the safety or the liveness in an implementation. We give the (total) correctness proof of a version of the protocol using timers. This section illustrates how intricately the safety and liveness properties of a protocol (skeleton) can be related.

In section 2.3 we discuss some protocols devised by Aho *et al.* [AWYU82] to transmit a sequence of bits in a synchronous environment. Although this might seem to be a problem which is more low-level than the previous one, we will discuss it as if it were just a special instance of it – special because of the restricted message size (one bit) and the environment (synchronous) of the problem. We show that assertional verification can be applied for proving the protocols partially correct.

2.1 A Balanced Link-level Protocol

Several link-level protocols exist to control the exchange of messages (sometimes called frames in this context) when the transmission medium is unreliable (cf. Tanenbaum [Tan88, ch. 4], and Sloman and Kramer [SK87, ch. 8]). The *alternating bit protocol* (Lynch [Lyn68], Bartlett *et al.* [BSW69]) is a classic example of a protocol that works on a frame-by-frame basis. The *sliding window protocol* (Cerf and Kahn [CK74]) controls the transfer of "windows" of messages or frames from processor i to processor j, with acknowledgements being transmitted from j to i. The windows for i and j, respectively, correspond to the range of outstanding messages, i.e., messages sent but not yet acknowledged, and the range of acceptable messages. An extended (symmetric or "balanced") version of the sliding window protocol for the two-way simultaneous transfer of data between two processors was discussed by e.g. Bochmann [Boc75] and Carlson [Car82].

In this section we show that the alternating bit protocol and the "balanced" two-way sliding window protocol are instances of one general protocol skeleton, that facilitates a mathematical analysis of the correctness and the performance of the protocols. The result substantiates and generalizes the common belief that the alternating bit protocol is "a (balanced) sliding window protocol with window size $= 1$". However, it is not a special instance of the balanced sliding window protocols described by e.g. Bochmann [Boc75] or Carlson [Car82], since in those protocols separate sequence numbers are used for the messages sent and the piggy-backed acknowledgements as opposed to one bit, serving both purposes, in the alternating bit protocol.

In section 2.1.1 we present the general protocol skeleton (SW) together with its system-wide invariants. In section 2.1.2 we discuss the effect of several choices of the parameters, the first result being that the alternating bit protocol is a special case of protocol skeleton SW. By other choices of the parameters we can tune the performance of the protocol, depending on the propagation delay of the link, the processing speed of the senders, and the error rate of the link.

2.1.1 The protocol skeleton

In the sequel we give a protocol skeleton for communicating sequences of messages between processors i and j over the bidirectional link (i, j). We recall that we use the model of a static network with send and receive procedures as in chapter 1. Although it is usually assumed for communication on this level that links behave as FIFO queues, we will defer this assumption until after theorem 2.1.3, as protocol skeleton SW will be used in another context in chapter 4, where we cannot make this assumption.

As the protocol skeleton is completely symmetric, we will only state it for processor i. The text of the operations for j can be obtained by interchanging all i's and j's. Likewise, all system-wide invariants occur in symmetric pairs, too, hence we will only state and prove one of both assertions of a symmetric pair.

We assume that the only transmission errors possible are deletion errors, modeled by the operations E_{ij}^l and E_{ji}^l, defined in section 1.2.1.2. We assume that, due to the physical layer, a garbled message is considered lost by the link layer.

For ease of notation we suppose that the sequence of messages that i should transmit is in $sstring_i$, and that the sequence of messages it receives from j is written in $rstring_i$. As we allow messages to be sent out of order, we include a sequence number in the frame containing the message. Thus messages sent, i.e., the frames, are of the form $<x, n>$ where x is the contents of the message and n the sequence number. No separate acknowledgements will be exchanged, not even by "piggy-backing" acks on messages. Instead, when a message $<x, n>$ is sent by i to j, its sequence number n is used as an implicit acknowledgement for all messages from j up to a certain number, say, $n - w_{ji}$. Thus $<x', 0>$, $<x'', 1>$, ..., $<x''', n - w_{ji}>$ are all received by i when it sends $<x, n>$. Likewise, if i receives a message $<x, n>$ it interprets it as an implicit acknowledgement from j for, say, the first $n - w_{ij} + 1$ messages that it sent. Because of this interpretation, we demand that $w_{ij} \geq 0$ and $w_{ji} \geq 0$. The parameters w_{ij} and w_{ji} are global constants both known to i and j. Note that j uses w_{ji} and w_{ij} as i uses w_{ij} and w_{ji}. In addition to the global constants w_{ij} and w_{ji}, i needs two local variables:

$acked_i$ = the number of consecutive messages for which i has received an acknowledgement from j: thus j has received and stored at least $rstring_j[0 : acked_i - 1]$,

$stored_i$ = the number of consecutive messages that i has received and stored: i has received and stored at least $rstring_i[0 : stored_i - 1]$.

Likewise, j needs the variables $acked_j$ and $stored_j$. We get the following protocol skeleton.

Protocol skeleton SW:

Initially $Q\,[i,j] = Q\,[j,i] = \emptyset$, $acked_i = -w_{ij}$, $stored_i = 0$,
$\qquad \forall n \geq 0: \quad sstring_i[n] \neq nil, \quad rstring_i[n] = nil$.

S_i^{SW} : $\{stored_i + w_{ji} > 0\}$
$\qquad$ **begin** choose $n \geq 0$ such that
$\qquad\qquad\qquad \min\{acked_i, stored_i + w_{ji} - 1\} \leq n < stored_i + w_{ji}$;
$\qquad\qquad$ send $<sstring_i[n], n>$ to j
$\qquad$ **end**

R_i^{SW} : $\{Q\,[j,i] \neq \emptyset\}$
$\qquad$ **begin** receive $<x, n>$ from j; $rstring_i[n] := x$;
$\qquad\qquad$ **if** $n - w_{ij} + 1 > acked_i$ **then** $acked_i := n - w_{ij} + 1$ **fi**;
$\qquad\qquad$ $stored_i := \max\{a \mid \forall b < a: rstring_i[b] \neq nil\}$
$\qquad$ **end**

S_j^{SW} and R_j^{SW} : defined similarly, and

E_{ij}^l and E_{ji}^l : defined as in section 1.2.1.2.

For protocol skeleton SW we can prove the following invariants.

Lemma 2.1.1 *Using protocol skeleton SW, the following assertions hold invariantly for all $n \geq 0$:*
(1) $acked_i$ *and* $stored_i$ *are non-decreasing,*
(2) $rstring_i[n] \neq nil \Rightarrow acked_i \geq n - w_{ij} + 1$,
(3) $acked_i \geq stored_i - w_{ij}$,
(4) $<x, n> \in Q\,[i,j] \Rightarrow x = sstring_i[n] \wedge n < stored_i + w_{ji}$,
(5) $acked_i \leq stored_j$,
(6) $rstring_i[n] \neq nil \Rightarrow rstring_i[n] = sstring_j[n]$.

Proof. (1) and (2) follow directly from the protocol skeleton.
(3). Use (2) and the definition of $stored_i$ in operation R_i^{SW}.
(4). The premise is rendered true by operation S_i^{SW} together with the conclusion of the assertion. An increase in $stored_i$ in operation R_i^{SW} does not falsify the conclusion. Operations R_j^{SW} and E_{ij}^l can only falsify the premise.
(5). Initially the assertion holds. An increase in $stored_j$ in operation R_j^{SW} does not falsify the assertion. When $acked_i$ is increased in R_i^{SW}, it is increased to $n - w_{ij} + 1$ upon receipt of a message $<x, n>$. By assertion (4) with i and j interchanged we

have $n < stored_j + w_{ij}$. Hence assertion (5) is kept invariant.

(6). As initially $rstring_i[n]$ is *nil* for all values of n, and it is only changed upon receipt of a message, we have by assertion (4) that the correct value is written in $rstring_i[n]$.   □

Theorem 2.1.2 *Using protocol skeleton SW, the following assertion holds:*
$$sstring_i[0 : stored_j - 1] = rstring_j[0 : stored_j - 1].$$

Proof. Initially the assertion holds for the empty strings. As $stored_j$ is increased in operation R_j^{SW}, it follows from lemma 2.1.1(4) that the assertion remains true.
                                                                            □

Thus protocol skeleton SW is partially correct. It is clear that this protocol skeleton is too general to be able to prove termination. However, we can specify in which circumstances it is free from deadlock.

Theorem 2.1.3 *Using protocol skeleton SW, there is no deadlock if and only if* $w_{ij} + w_{ji} \geq 1$.

Proof. For the if-part we have to prove that there is always at least one operation that is enabled in the case that the parameters have values that satisfy the constraint. As $w_{ij} + w_{ji} \geq 1$ and both parameters are non-negative, at least one of them is ≥ 1. Hence one of the operations S_i^{SW} or S_j^{SW} is enabled. Without loss of generality, let it be S_i^{SW}. Then in the statement: "choose $n \geq 0$ such that $\min \{acked_i, stored_i + w_{ji} - 1\} \leq n < stored_i + w_{ji}$" in S_i^{SW}, it is always possible to choose, as $n = stored_i + w_{ji} - 1 \geq 0$ is a permissible value. As $stored_i$ and $stored_j$ are non-decreasing, this remains the case. Conversely, if $w_{ij} = w_{ji} = 0$, we have that initially R_i^{SW}, R_j^{SW}, E_{ij}^l, and E_{ji}^l are disabled because the message queues are empty, while S_i^{SW} and S_j^{SW} are disabled because their guards are false. Thus we have deadlock.   □

Note that until now we have not used the assumption that the message queues behave as FIFO queues and that we have let the sequence numbers n of the messages grow arbitrarily large. We will now prove that in the case of FIFO message queues sequence numbers can be kept bounded.

Lemma 2.1.4 *Using protocol skeleton SW, the following assertions hold invariantly for all $n \geq 0$ and $n' \geq 0$:*
  (1) $<x, n> \in Q[i, j] \Rightarrow n \geq acked_j - w_{ij}$,
  (2) $<x', n'>$ behind $<x, n> \in Q[i, j] \Rightarrow n < n' + w_{ij} + w_{ji}$.

Proof. We prove the assertions by simultaneous induction. Initially the message queues are empty, hence the assertions hold. Operation S_i^{SW} adds a message, say $<x, n>$, at the end of queue $Q[i, j]$. We know that min $\{acked_i, stored_i + w_{ji} - 1\}$ $\leq n < stored_i + w_{ji}$ holds. In case $n \geq acked_i$, we have by lemma 2.1.1(3) that $n \geq stored_i - w_{ij}$. In case $n \geq stored_i + w_{ji} - 1$, we can use $w_{ij} + w_{ji} \geq 1$ to get the same result. Hence we have by lemma 2.1.1(5) that $n \geq acked_j - w_{ij}$. For a message $<x', n'> \in Q[i, j]$ before $<x, n>$, we have by lemma 2.1.1(4) that $n' < stored_i + w_{ji}$ holds. As $stored_i \leq n + w_{ij}$, we have $n' < n + w_{ij} + w_{ji}$. Thus operation S_i^{SW} leaves the assertions true. Operation R_j^{SW} can increase $acked_j$ on receipt of some message $<x'', n''>$. Let $<x', n'> \in Q[i, j]$. Then assertion (2) held before the operation with $<x, n>$ replaced by $<x'', n''>$, and $n' > n'' - w_{ij} - w_{ji} = acked_j - 1 - w_{ij}$. Hence assertion (1) still holds for messages in $Q[i, j]$ after $acked_j$ is increased. As the other operations can only falsify the premise of the assertions, these assertions remain invariant. □

Theorem 2.1.5 *Using protocol skeleton SW, the following assertion holds for all $n \geq 0$:*

$$<x, n> \in Q[i, j] \implies stored_j - w_{ij} - w_{ji} \leq n < stored_j + w_{ij} + w_{ji}.$$

Proof. This follows immediately from lemmas 2.1.1 and 2.1.4. □

Hence it is sufficient to communicate sequence numbers modulo m, where m is some fixed number with $m \geq 2(w_{ij} + w_{ji})$. The chosen m is called the *window size*. Thus we get the following protocol skeleton.

Protocol skeleton *SW*1:

Initially $Q[i, j] = Q[j, i] = \emptyset$, $acked_i = -w_{ij}$, $stored_i = 0$,
$\qquad \forall n \geq 0: \quad sstring_i[n] \neq nil, \quad rstring_i[n] = nil.$

$S_i^{SW1} : \{stored_i + w_{ji} > 0\}$
$\qquad$ **begin** choose $n \geq 0$ such that
$\qquad\qquad\qquad$ min $\{acked_i, stored_i + w_{ji} - 1\} \leq n < stored_i + w_{ji}$;
$\qquad\qquad$ send $<sstring_i[n], n \bmod m>$ to j
$\qquad$ **end**

$R_i^{SW1} : \{Q[j, i] \neq \emptyset\}$
$\qquad$ **begin** receive $<x, b>$ from j;
$\qquad\qquad$ $n := m.\lfloor (stored_i + w_{ij} + w_{ji} - b - 1)/m \rfloor + b$; $rstring_i[n] := x$;
$\qquad\qquad$ **if** $n - w_{ij} + 1 > acked_i$ **then** $acked_i := n - w_{ij} + 1$ **fi**;
$\qquad\qquad$ $stored_i := \max \{a \mid \forall b < a : rstring_i[b] \neq nil\}$
$\qquad$ **end**

S_j^{SW1} and R_j^{SW1} : defined similarly, and

E_{ij}^l and E_{ji}^l : defined as in section 1.2.1.2.

Corollary 2.1.6 *Protocol skeleton SW1 is partially correct.*

Proof. As $b = n \bmod m$, we know that $n - b = 0 \bmod m$. As by theorem 2.1.5 $stored_i - w_{ij} - w_{ji} \le n < stored_i + w_{ij} + w_{ji}$, we have $n - b \le stored_i + w_{ij} + w_{ji} - b - 1 < n - b + m$. Thus $n - b = m.\lfloor (stored_i + w_{ij} + w_{ji} - b - 1)/m \rfloor$, and protocol skeleton $SW1$ is a refinement of protocol skeleton SW.   □

2.1.2 The window size

In this section we discuss the effect of the choice of the window size, i.e., the choice of the parameters w_{ij} and w_{ji}, on protocols which are refinements of protocol skeleton SW from the previous section. We begin by considering the minimum window size, namely $w_{ij} + w_{ji} = 1$, and show that the alternating bit protocol falls into this category. Next we discuss how to choose the parameters in relation to processing speeds and propagation delays. In both cases we use protocol skeleton SW in the analysis because that simplifies the formulation of the results. However, the results hold for bounded sequence numbers (protocol skeleton $SW1$) as well.

2.1.2.1 A window size of 1.
Setting the window size to the minimum value of 1 has the effect that the protocol skeleton becomes simpler, in the sense that we need fewer local variables and that, for example, in operation S_i^{SW} the value of n is uniquely determined. This is formalized in the next lemma.

Lemma 2.1.7 *Using protocol skeleton SW with $w_{ij} + w_{ji} = 1$, the following assertion holds invariantly: $acked_i = stored_i - w_{ij}$.*

Proof. Initially the assertion holds. Both $acked_i$ and $stored_i$ are only changed in operation R_i^{SW} on receipt of some message $<x, n>$. By theorem 2.1.5 we have that $stored_i - 1 \le n \le stored_i$. As the assertion held beforehand, neither $acked_i$ nor $stored_i$ is changed if $n = stored_i - 1$ because then $n - w_{ij} + 1 = acked_i$. On the other hand, both variables are increased by 1 if $n = stored_i$. Thus the assertion is invariant.   □

The alternating bit protocol [Lyn68, BSW69] was devised for a slightly different model of computation and for a half-duplex link. It was assumed that most errors consisted of messages being garbled, and that this always could be detected. The alternating bit protocol is a message-driven protocol, where the receipt of a message triggers the next send operation. To deal with lost messages, a message is also sent upon a *timeout*. A timeout can be viewed as a timer going off. If a message is sent, a timer is set for that message and, if no reply is received within a certain predetermined time interval, a timeout occurs and a retransmission of that message might be necessary.

Theorem 2.1.8 *The alternating bit protocol is a refinement of protocol skeleton SW1 with $w_{ij} + w_{ji} = 1$.*

Proof. We argue that the send and receive operations are the same, by the following discussion. According to lemma 2.1.7 one variable can be eliminated, say $acked_i$. The choice in messages to send in operation S_i^{SW} is restricted to the one message with sequence number $stored_i - w_{ij}$. The test in operation R_i^{SW}, whether the received message is a retransmission or a new message, reduces to $n = stored_i$. As sequence numbers modulo 2 suffice (theorem 2.1.5), we need only one bit for this number, and thus the test in R_i^{SW1} can be reformulated as $b = stored_i$ mod 2. The asymmetry in the alternating bit protocol between the processor which initiates sending and the one which follows suit corresponds to the asymmetry in the parameters w_{ij} and w_{ji}. If $w_{ij} = 1$ and $w_{ji} = 0$, then j is the initiator and i the follower. $\square$

We conclude with the alternating bit protocol in our notation, adding the "garble" operation E^g, and a test in operation R_i^{AB} on garbled messages. We recall that a garbled message is denoted by $<\lambda>$. We do not specify the timeout mechanism, but refer to [JRT86] for a correctness proof of the alternating bit protocol with timeouts.

Protocol skeleton AB:

Initially $Q[i,j] = Q[j,i] = \emptyset$, $stored_i = 0$,
$\qquad\qquad \forall n \geq 0: \quad sstring_i[n] \neq nil$, $rstring_i[n] = nil$.

$R_i^{AB} : \{Q[j,i] \neq \emptyset\}$
$\qquad$ **begin** receive $<x,b>$ from j;
$\qquad\qquad$ **if** $<x,b> \neq <\lambda>$
$\qquad\qquad$ **then if** $b = stored_i$ mod 2
$\qquad\qquad\qquad$ **then** $rstring_i[stored_i] := x$; $stored_i := stored_i + 1$
$\qquad\qquad\qquad$ **fi**
$\qquad\qquad$ **fi**; $n := stored_i - w_{ij}$;
$\qquad\qquad$ **if** $n \geq 0$ **then** send $<sstring_i[n], n$ mod $2>$ to j **fi**
$\qquad$ **end**

S_i^{AB} :{$stored_i + w_{ji} > 0 \ \wedge$ timeout}
      begin $n := stored_i - w_{ij}$; send $< sstring_i[n], n \bmod 2 >$ to j **end**

S_j^{AB} and R_j^{AB} : defined similarly,

E_{ij}^g, E_{ji}^g, E_{ij}^l, and E_{ji}^l : defined as in section 1.2.1.2.

Thus the alternating bit protocol is partially correct as it is a refinement of protocol skeleton $SW1$. We refer to Yemini and Kurose [YK82] for a discussion of the total correctness of this protocol.

2.1.2.2 *Window size and processing speed.*

It is clear that a successful exchange of messages depends not only on the choice of the parameters w_{ij} and w_{ji} and on the error rate of the link over which the messages are sent, but also on a sensible choice and timing of the send and receive operations for i and j. On the other hand, the choice of w_{ij} and w_{ji} will depend on things like: the rate at which messages can be sent or received, determined by either the characteristics of the link or the processing speed of sender and receiver; and the propagation delay on the link. For a more detailed (but still approximate) analysis we define the following quantities:

d_{ij} (d_{ji}) = propagation delay from i to j (from j to i),

s_i (s_j) = minimum time between two S_i^{SW1} operations (two S_j^{SW1} operations), and

r_i (r_j) = minimum time between two R_i^{SW1} operations (two R_j^{SW1} operations).

To simplify the formulas we define the following abbreviations: $w = w_{ij} + w_{ji}$, $mtime = \max \{s_i, s_j, r_i, r_j\}$, and $d = (d_{ij} + d_{ji})/mtime$.

We allow the minimum time between S_i^{SW1} and R_i^{SW1} and between S_j^{SW1} and R_j^{SW1}, respectively, to be zero. Hence we neglect the time to perform the operations, or rather, the execution times are assumed to be contained in s_i, s_j, r_i, and r_j. The times s_i, s_j, r_i, and r_j typically are more or less constant during one connection, and could be provided by i, j, and the network when the actual connection is set up. To simplify matters, we assume that the propagation delay as well as the times s_i, s_j, r_i, and r_j are indeed constants (for the duration of the connection). A message on a link may encounter an additional delay apart from the propagation delay, namely if it arrives at a moment when the receiver is not ready to receive. We will term this extra delay *queuing delay*. We begin by assuming that there are no transmission errors and that no messages are lost, and investigate how fast messages can get through if we do not lose time in retransmissions. To keep track of the sequence number of the next message to send, the processors i and j need variables $next_i$ and $next_j$, initialized at 0. We define the following strategy for the order of the operations S_i^{SW1} and R_i^{SW1}.

Definition 2.1.1 Strategy I *is the order of operations determined by the following program for i where all statements are executed as soon as possible, depending on s_i and r_i, and the corresponding program for j:*
Strategy I:

Initially $next_i = 0$.

while no termination
do   **if** $Q[j, i] \neq \emptyset$ **then** R_i^{SW1} **fi**;
    if $next_i < stored_i + w_{ji}$ **then** S_i^{SW1} for $n = next_i$; $next_i := next_i + 1$ **fi**
od

Thus messages are sent in the right order and exactly once.

Definition 2.1.2 *The* communication time *for i is the maximum of the time between two consecutive S_i^{SW1} operations and the time between two consecutive R_i^{SW1} operations.*

Theorem 2.1.9 *If no messages are lost and there are no transmission errors, and i and j operate under Strategy I, then i and j eventually have a communication time of mtime if and only if $w_{ij} + w_{ji} \geq (d_{ij} + d_{ji})/mtime$.*

Proof. Let the message with sequence number n be sent from i to j at time t. At what time (say t') can i send the message with sequence number $n + 2w$? For two simple examples, see figure 2.1.

As i has to do $2w$ S_i^{SW1} operations, $t' \geq t + w.s_i$. But we also know that the sending window must be shifted far enough, i.e., $stored_i > n + 2w - w_{ji} = n + w + w_{ij}$. Thus the message from j with sequence number $n + w + w_{ij}$ is received by i. This can be sent only if $stored_j$ is large enough: $stored_j > n + w + w_{ij} - w_{ij} = n + w$. Thus j has received the message from i with number $n + w$. Thus we can also say that $t' \geq t + w.s_i + d_{ij} + d_{ji}$: the time to send messages n up to $n + w$ to j, the propagation delay of the latter to j, and the propagation delay of message $n + w + w_{ij}$ from j to i.

We do not know exactly how many R_i^{SW1} operations are done by i between times t and t', but at least the receipt of message $n + w_{ij}$ from j up to the message with sequence number $n + w + w_{ij}$ falls between t and t', because message $n + w_{ij}$ is the acknowledgement for message n from i. Thus $t' \geq t + d_{ij} + d_{ji} + w.r_i$: the sum of the propagation delay for message n to j, the propagation delay for message $n + w_{ij}$

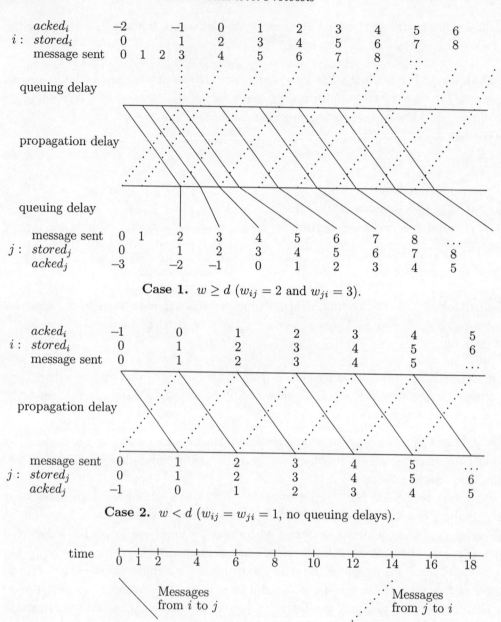

Case 1. $w \geq d$ ($w_{ij} = 2$ and $w_{ji} = 3$).

Case 2. $w < d$ ($w_{ij} = w_{ji} = 1$, no queuing delays).

(only the sequence numbers of messages are shown)
$s_i = s_j = 1$, $r_i = r_j = 2$, ($mtime = 2$), $d_{ij} = d_{ji} = 3$, ($d = 3$).

Figure 2.1 COMMUNICATION WITH STRATEGY I (NO LOSSES).

to i, and the receipt of w messages. But we also know that after time $t + d_{ij}$, j has to do w operations R_j^{SW1} (for messages n up to $n + w$), and w operations S_j^{SW1} (for messages $n + w_{ij}$ up to $n + w + w_{ij}$ to i). Hence $t' \geq t + d_{ij} + \max\{s_j, r_j\}\, w + d_{ji}$.

Combining these inequalities, we get that $t' - t \geq (d + w)mtime$, and averaging over the $2w$ S_i^{SW1} operations, this leads to a communication time of at least $(d + w)mtime/2w$. Thus for values of d that are $> w$, a communication time of $mtime$ is not possible. Note that the same holds for processor j.

Now assume that $d \leq w$. We use induction to prove that a communication time of $mtime$ is indeed reached in this case. As $d \leq w$, we know that either $d_{ij} \leq w_{ij}.mtime$ or $d_{ji} \leq w_{ji}.mtime$ holds. Assume that the former holds. Initially, the sequence numbers 0 up to $w_{ji} - 1$ are within the sending window of processor i. Because $mtime \geq s_i$, processor i sends these messages consecutively, each within $mtime$ time. Thus they arrive at j between d_{ij} and $d_{ij} + w_{ji}.mtime$. As message 0 from i is the first message to arrive at j it can be received immediately, and the next messages up to $w_{ji} - 1$ within $d_{ij} + w_{ji}.mtime$, as $mtime \geq r_j$. Now j sends messages 0 up to $w_{ij} - 1$ within $(w_{ij} - 1).mtime$, and as by $w_{ij}.mtime$ message 0 is received from i because $d_{ij} \leq w_{ij}.mtime$, we know $stored_j \geq 1$, Hence j continues sending at intervals of $\geq mtime$ messages w_{ij} up to $w - 1$ because the first w_{ji} messages from i arrive and are received in time.

Now consider message w_{ji} from i to j. This is the acknowledgement for message 0 from j. It is sent by i at time $\max\{d_{ji}, w_{ji}.s_i\} \leq \max\{d_{ji}, w_{ji}.mtime\}$. Thus it arrives at j at time $d_{ij} + \max\{d_{ji}, w_{ji}.mtime\} \leq w.mtime$. As message $w_{ji} - 1$ from i was received within $(w_{ji} - 1)mtime$, message w_{ji} is received within $d_{ij} + (w_{ji} - 1)mtime \leq (w - 1)mtime$, message w_{ji} is received within $w.mtime$, and hence $stored_j \geq w_{ji}$. We conclude that j sends message n within time $n.mtime$ for $0 \leq n \leq w + 1$. The induction step is the following :

Let j send message n at time t, and the next w messages $n + k$ within time $t + k.mtime$ for $1 \leq k \leq w$. Then j sends messages $n + k$ within $t + k.mtime$ time for $w \leq k \leq 2w$.

Proof. Message n arrives at $t + d_{ji}$ at i. When it is received, $stored_i := n + 1$. Thus message $n + w_{ji}$ to j can only be sent hereafter, say at time t'. But as message $n + w$ to i is sent within $t + w.mtime$, $stored_j n + w_{ji}$, hence message $n + w_{ji}$ was sent before $t + w.mtime - d_{ij}$. Thus $t + d_{ji} \leq t' \leq t - d_{ij} + w.mtime$. Hence messages $n + k$ to i for $0 \leq k \leq w$ are received before $t' + k.mtime$ such that $stored_i = n + k$. As message $n + w_{ji}$ to j is sent at t', messages $n + w_{ji} + k$ to j are sent within $t' + k.mtime$ for $0 \leq k \leq w$ and arrive at j within $d_{ij} + t' + k.mtime \leq t + (w + k)mtime$. As message $n + w$ is sent to i within $t + w.mtime$, messages $n + w + k$ are sent within $t + (w + k)mtime$.

Thus we conclude that j communicates in time *mtime*, and it is clear from the proof that i does also.   □

Since the protocol forces i and j to operate with intervals of length *mtime*, we may as well assume that i and j determine the value when the connection is set up, and do their send and receive operations with intervals of *mtime*. Thus we avoid the creation of a queue at the slower receiver.

Let us now consider what happens if an occasional transmission error occurs and a message is lost or garbled. We have to extend Strategy I to ensure the possible retransmission of messages.

Definition 2.1.3 Strategy II *is the order of operations determined by the following program for i where all statements are executed as soon as possible, depending on s_i and r_i, and the corresponding program for j:*
Strategy II:

Initially $next_i = 0$.

while no termination
do   **if** $Q[j,i] \neq \emptyset$ **then** R_i^{SW1} **fi**;
      if $next_i = stored_i + w_{ji} > 0$
      then S_i^{SW1} for the n with
                    $\min \{acked_i, stored_i + w_{ji} - 1\} \leq n < stored_i + w_{ji}$
                    and which is the sequence number of the message that
                    was last sent the longest ago
      else S_i^{SW1} for $n = next_i$; $next_i := next_i + 1$
      fi
od

Note that in the case that there are no errors and $w_{ij} + w_{ji} \geq (d_{ij} + d_{ji})/mtime$, Strategy II defines the same order as Strategy I. Also note that in the case of errors, Strategy II implicitly defines a timeout mechanism. If i cannot shift its sending window because a message was lost, a retransmission of old messages will occur.

Lemma 2.1.10 *Let i and j operate under Strategy II with one cycle in mtime and with windows such that $w_{ij} + w_{ji} \geq (d_{ij} + d_{ji})/mtime$. Let exactly one message get lost. Then the loss of time for both i and j is $w.mtime$.*

Proof.   Assume the message from i to j with sequence number x is lost. It was sent at time $x.mtime$. See figure 2.2 for an example.

Processor j can send consecutive messages until time $(x + w_{ij} - 1).mtime$, but

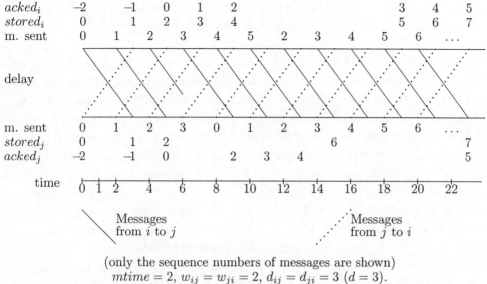

$acked_i$	-2	-1	0	1	2					3	4	5
$stored_i$	0	1	2	3	4					5	6	7
m. sent	0	1	2	3	4	5	2	3	4	5	6	...

delay

m. sent	0	1	2	3	0	1	2	3	4	5	6	...
$stored_j$	0		1	2					6			7
$acked_j$	-2		-1	0		2	3	4				5

time   0 1 2   4   6   8   10   12   14   16   18   20   22

＼ Messages from i to j ⋰ Messages from j to i

(only the sequence numbers of messages are shown)
$mtime = 2$, $w_{ij} = w_{ji} = 2$, $d_{ij} = d_{ji} = 3$ ($d = 3$).
The message from i to j with sequence number 2 is lost,
leading to a loss of $w.mtime = 8$ time units.

Figure 2.2 COMMUNICATION WITH STRATEGY II (ONE LOSS).

at time $(x + w_{ij}).mtime$ j cannot send the message with sequence number $x + w_{ij}$ because that would be an implicit acknowledgement for the lost message. Thus i cannot shift its sending window at time $(x + w).mtime$ because it did not receive the ack for the lost message. Thus i will retransmit the lost message at time $(x + w).mtime$. Hence j can increase $stored_j$ and send the message with sequence number $x + w_{ij}$ at time $(x + w + w_{ij}).mtime$. Thus at time $(x + 2w).mtime$ i can shift its sending window and transmit the new message with sequence number $x + w$. As a consequence, i has retransmitted messages with sequence numbers x, $x + 1$, ..., $x + w - 1$ in the time between $(x + w).mtime$ and $(x + 2w - 1).mtime$. Likewise, due to this one error, j has retransmitted the messages with sequence numbers $x - w_{ji}$ up till $x + w_{ij} - 1$. After $w.mtime$ time, communication is resumed as if nothing had happened. □

Thus one error costs $w.mtime$ in extra transmission time. But note that any number of errors inside one time-slot of length $w.mtime$ still only costs $w.mtime$ extra time. Hence the total time to exchange two sequences of n messages between the processors does not depend on the actual number of errors, but only on whether there are errors in time intervals of length $w.mtime$ or not. We now use an approximation for the expected value of this total exchange time to determine how we might choose w_{ij} and w_{ji} depending on the values of $d_{ij} + d_{ji}$, *mtime*, and the error rate, assuming that i and j operate under Strategy *II* with one cycle in *mtime*.

Let the probability of errors in one message be given by a Poisson process with parameter λ for intervals of length *mtime*. We view the problem from the standpoint of i only, and make no distinction between the loss of a message from i to j, and the loss of its acknowledgement from j to i, as the difference between the two cases is not observable for i, and the effect in the loss of transmission time is the same. As we assume that both processors operate with intervals of length *mtime* we have no queuing delays, and the time that one message or its ack is subject to errors is $d_{ij} + d_{ji}$. Let P$[k, t]$ denote the probability of k errors in one message in an interval of length t. Then P$[0, mtime] = e^{-\lambda}$ and hence P[one message and its ack are not lost] = P$[0, d.mtime] = e^{-d\lambda}$. For the case that $w \geq d$, we know that one or more errors in an interval of length $w.mtime$ leads to an extra transmission time of $w.mtime$. In the case that $w < d$, it takes $d.mtime$ to transmit w messages. The loss of a single message leads to an extra transmission time of $w.mtime$ because there is time left for $d - w$ retransmissions, while errors in more messages in an interval of length $d.mtime$ can lead to an extra time of $d.mtime$. We approximate the loss in time by $d.mtime$ for no other reason than that approximation by $w.mtime$ does not lead to an analytical solution. As an approximation, we now consider fixed intervals of length $\max\{w, d.mtime\}$. In both cases, we know that the sending window may be shifted by w if w messages are not lost. Assuming that errors in different messages are independent, we have P[w messages and their acks are not lost] = (P$[0, d.mtime])^w = e^{-wd\lambda}$. If in some fixed interval of $\max\{w, d.mtime\}$ there are errors and the sending window is not shifted, we retransmit messages, in our simplification for a fixed interval of $\max\{w, d.mtime\}$, again with a certain probability that this time the lost messages come through. This probability lies somewhere between $e^{-wd\lambda}$ (for high error rates or small windows), and 1 (for low error rates and large windows). We approximate the probability by $e^{-wd\lambda}$ as it can be easily shown that in the latter case the minimal expected total transmission time is reached for the same value of w. Thus we model the transmission of a sequence of n messages as a sequence of Bernoulli trials:

- if no error occurs in a time interval of length $\max\{w, d.mtime\}$ we succeed and the sending window is shifted by w;
- if one or more errors occur in a time interval of length $\max\{w, d.mtime\}$ the sending window is not shifted and we have a failure;
- and with the probability of success equal $e^{-wd\lambda}$.

Thus the time necessary to transmit sequences of n messages in the presence of errors can be considered as the waiting time for $r = n/w$ successes, where the probability of success p is $e^{-wd\lambda}$. This is the negative binomial distribution [Fel68], and the expectation of the waiting time is $r + r(1-p)/p = r/p$. Thus the expected total waiting time T is here $T = \max\{w, d.mtime\}.e^{wd\lambda}.n/w$. Note that we have implicitly assumed that $r \geq 1$ and $n \geq w$.

Case 1: $d \leq w$. Then $T = n.mtime.e^{wd\lambda}$, and T is minimal for minimal w, hence we choose $w = \max\{1, d\}$.

Case 2: $d > w$. Then $T = mtime.e^{wd\lambda}.dn/w$. Differentiation by w gives $T' = mtime.(wd\lambda - 1).e^{wd\lambda}.dn/w^2$, hence T has a minimum for $w = 1/(d\lambda)$. It depends on the relative values of d and λ how to choose w, as $1 \leq w \leq d$.

Case 2.1: $1/(d\lambda) < 1$. Thus we have to choose $w = 1$ in the case that P[a message and its ack are not lost] $= e^{-d\lambda} < e^{-1}$.

Case 2.2: $1 \leq 1/(d\lambda) \leq d$. Or otherwise stated, $1/d \leq d\lambda \leq 1$. Thus we choose $w = 1/(d\lambda)$, while $e^{-1} \leq$ P[a message and its ack are not lost] $\leq e^{-1/d}$.

Case 2.3: $1/(d\lambda) \geq d$. Then T is decreasing for values of w with $w \leq d$, hence we choose $w = d$, unless $d < 1$, in which case we choose 1.

Of course we always have to round values found, as w must be an integer. Hence we propose to choose w as follows:

$$
\begin{array}{llll}
\max\{1, d\} & \text{if} & \text{P[a message or its ack is lost]} \leq 1 - e^{-1/d}, \\
1/(d\lambda) & \text{if} \quad 1 - e^{-1/d} \leq \text{P[a message or its ack is lost]} \leq 1 - e^{-1}, \\
1 & \text{if} \quad 1 - e^{-1} \leq \text{P[a message or its ack is lost]}.
\end{array}
$$

We do not claim that Strategy *II* is the best; it was just chosen as an obvious strategy. Trying out some examples shows that when $d \geq 2w$, it works better to send two copies of each message one immediately after the other, thus effectively decreasing the error rate, as we assumed that the bandwidth used is no cost criterion.

In the preceding part of this chapter we have shown what protocol results if we extend the well-known alternating bit protocol to larger windows. The advantage of this protocol over sliding window protocols with piggy-backed acknowledgements is obviously that the actual numbers of the acks are not sent, thus decreasing message length. However, since the information flow in the two directions is coupled, one error will not only cause the retransmission of a whole window in one direction, but also in the other. Thus it should only be used with low error rates.

2.2 Block Acknowledgement Protocols

The protocols of the preceding section cannot tolerate the reordering of messages, while the protocol of Stenning [Ste76], which tolerates both message loss and re-ordering of messages, uses unbounded sequence numbers. Brown, Gouda, and

Miller [BGM91] redesigned the window protocol to be able to tolerate both message loss and reordering of messages, where sequence numbers are bounded. We use this so-called *block acknowledgement protocol* to illustrate the difficulties that arise if one wants to give an implementation of a protocol (skeleton) that retains the safety and liveness properties of the original protocol. In [BGM91], the safety and liveness of the block acknowledgement protocol are proved and an implementation is suggested by means of timers. Due to the dependency between the safety and liveness properties of the protocol, we have to adapt the protocol slightly to arrive at an implementation that is both safe and alive.

As the protocol tolerates message loss, it contains a possibility for retransmission of messages upon *timeout*. The condition derived for "timeout" ensures a correct operation of the protocol; however, whether the boolean expression defined as "timeout" evaluates to true or not is not directly observable for the sender process. The authors propose an implementation of the timeout condition by means of timer(s) in the sender process only. We show that several attempts at such an implementation have drawbacks, such as losing liveness, losing safety, or a severe restriction in retransmission facilities. Hence we suggest implementations with additional timer(s) in the receiver process. Moreover, we have changed the specification of the protocol slightly by relaxing the timeout condition to arrive at a protocol that can be implemented by means of timers. We then prove that this implementation is partially correct by means of an invariant, and show that progress is always possible. We will use unbounded sequence numbers in this section for clarity's sake, as the transition to bounded sequence numbers is independent of the implementation of "timeout" and completely analogous to the transition from protocol skeleton SW to $SW1$ in section 2.1. The block acknowledgement protocol with bounded sequence numbers can be found in [BGM91].

The remainder of the section is structured as follows. We give a short overview of the original protocol together with the invariant that implies its safety in subsection 2.2.1. Subsection 2.2.2 discusses several implementations of the protocol with timers in the sender process only, and their respective drawbacks. occur if one tries to implement the protocol with timers. Finally, subsection 2.2.3 contains the proposed changes which lead to a slightly different protocol, and a proof that the proposed implementation with timers of the repaired protocol is correct.

2.2.1 The original block acknowledgement protocol

The window protocol described by Brown, Gouda, and Miller in [BGM91] is based on a new method of acknowledgement, called *block acknowledgement*: one acknowledgement message acknowledges a block of data messages. Unlike in the previous section, it is a unidirectional sliding window protocol, that is, the data messages all go from one processor, the sender i, to the other processor, the receiver j, and all acknowledgements go from j to i. As the protocol is thus asymmetric, and the sender and receiver have different variables, we delete the subscripts denoting to which processor a variable belongs. Each new data message is assigned a new sequence number from the natural numbers, and as we are not interested in the actual data transferred, a data message is identified with its sequence number. A block acknowledgement message $<x, y>$ has two numbers x and y to acknowledge all data messages with sequence numbers ranging from x to y.

The following variables are used in the protocol. We assume that i has an infinite boolean array $ackd[0\ldots]$ in which it records which data messages have been acknowledged by j. We assume that j has an infinite boolean array $rcvd[0\ldots]$ in which it records which data messages it has received. The sender i maintains a window of messages in transit, which has a maximum size of w (some predefined constant). It is bounded by na, the next message to be acknowledged, and ns, the next message to send. The receiver j maintains the number of the next message to receive and acknowledge in nr. The variable vr is used to determine how many data messages can be acknowledged in one acknowledgement message. As we assume that links may lose or reorder messages, we add the operations E_{ij}^d, E_{ji}^d, E_{ij}^r, and E_{ji}^r to the protocol skeletons. Thus we can think of the message queues $Q[i, j]$ and $Q[j, i]$ as multisets.

As we will also consider liveness properties of the protocol, we assume that enabled operations are executed atomically and in a fair way. We will call the unbounded version of the original protocol $B0$. The protocol is as follows:

Protocol skeleton $B0$:

Initially $Q[i, j] = Q[j, i] = \emptyset$,
$\qquad$ **In** i : $na = ns = 0$, $\forall n \geq 0$: $ackd[n] = false$,
$\qquad$ **In** j : $nr = vr = 0$, $\forall n \geq 0$: $rcvd[n] = false$,

S_i^{B0}: $\{\ ns < na + w\ \}$ **begin** send $<ns>$; $n\dot{s} := ns + 1$ **end**

R_i^{B0}: $\{\ Q[j, i] \neq \emptyset\ \}$
$\qquad$ **begin** receive $<x, y>$ from j; $l := x$;
$\qquad\qquad$ **while** $l \leq y$ **do** $ackd[l] := true$; $l := l + 1$ **od**;
$\qquad\qquad$ **while** $ackd[na]$ **do** $na := na + 1$ **od**
$\qquad$ **end**

T_i^{B0}: $\{\ \texttt{timeout}(k)\ \}$ send $<k>$

R_j^{B0}: $\{\ Q\,[i,j] \neq \emptyset\ \}$
    begin receive $<v>$;
        if $v < nr$ **then** send $<v,v>$ **else** $rcvd[v] := true$ **fi**
    end

I_j^{B0}: $\{\ rcvd[vr]\ \}$ $vr := vr + 1$

S_j^{B0}: $\{\ nr < vr\ \}$ **begin** send $<nr, vr-1>$; $nr := vr$ **end**

E_{ij}^l, E_{ji}^l, E_{ij}^r, and E_{ji}^r : defined as in section 1.2.1.2.

The boolean expression $\texttt{timeout}(k)$ is defined as follows:

$$\texttt{timeout}(k) \overset{\text{def}}{=} \begin{aligned}&(na \leq k \wedge k < ns \wedge \neg ackd[k]) \wedge (^{\#}L_{ij}(k) = 0) \wedge\\ &(k < nr \vee \neg rcvd[k]) \wedge (^{\#}L_{ji}(k) = 0)\end{aligned}$$

    where

    $^{\#}L_{ij}(k) \overset{\text{def}}{=}$ number of messages with sequence number k in $Q\,[i,j]$

    $^{\#}L_{ji}(k) \overset{\text{def}}{=}$ number of messages $<p,q>$ with $p \leq k \leq q$ in $Q\,[j,i]$.

The safety of the protocol follows from the invariant which is the conjunct of the assertions in the following theorem, due to Brown, Gouda, and Miller [BGM91].

Theorem 2.2.1 *Using protocol skeleton $B0$, the following assertions hold invariantly for all $n \geq 0$:*

  (1) $na \leq nr \leq vr \leq ns \leq na + w$,
  (2) $(n < na \Rightarrow ackd[n]) \wedge (ackd[n] \Rightarrow n < nr) \wedge \neg ackd[na]$,
  (3) $(rcvd[n] \Rightarrow n < ns) \wedge (n < vr \Rightarrow rcvd[n])$,
  (4) $^{\#}L_{ij}(n) + {}^{\#}L_{ji}(n) \leq 1$,
  (5) $^{\#}L_{ij}(n) > 0 \Rightarrow n < ns \wedge \neg ackd[n] \wedge (n < nr \vee \neg rcvd[n])$,
  (6) $^{\#}L_{ji}(n) > 0 \Rightarrow n < nr \wedge \neg ackd[n]$,
  (7) $^{\#}L_{ij}(n) > 0 \Rightarrow nr - w \leq n < nr + w$,
  (8) $^{\#}L_{ji}(n) > 0 \Rightarrow na \leq n < na + w$.

Assertions (7) and (8) establish that it is safe to use sequence numbers and arrays modulo m if $m \geq 2w$: thus the protocol skeleton with bounded sequence numbers is defined as protocol skeleton $B0$ with all unbounded numbers and arrays taken modulo some $m \geq 2w$. This transformation is the same as the one from protocol skeleton SW to $SW1$ in section 2.1.1, hence we will not show it here.

The authors suggest that the timeout condition mentioned in the protocol be implemented by means of timers in the sender process only.

2.2.2 Original suggested implementation

2.2.2.1 Derivation of the protocol. In protocol skeleton $B0$ it is possible to resend all unacknowledged data messages, i.e., with sequence numbers from na to ns. The timeout condition for a message with sequence number k is given in section 2.2.1. However, while this condition ensures correct operation of the protocol, as is shown in [BGM91], only the tests of whether the number k lies in the right range and is not acknowledged yet can be evaluated directly by i. Hence it is necessary to supply i with a test which implies $\texttt{timeout}(k)$ if it evaluates to true. The authors suggest implementing this timeout condition by local timers in the sender i, one timer for each outstanding message. Additionally, they suggest a mechanism for aging messages in transit, to ensure that messages are eventually discarded if not received. The goal is to deduce the value of the other conjuncts of $\texttt{timeout}(k)$ from the timer values. Thus we shall now develop an implementation $B1$ of protocol skeleton $B0$. A formal modeling of the suggestions above, in a notation which fits the rest of the protocol, is the following.

We add to the code of i a local (infinite) array of timers, one ($tmi[n]$) for each data message, with the meaning that the "timer goes off" in case $tmi[n] \leq 0$. (In the version with bounded sequence numbers, this reduces to w timers for i.) Thus we get

in T_i^{B0}: $\texttt{timeout}(k)$ is replaced by $(na \leq k < ns) \wedge (tmi[k] \leq 0) \wedge \neg ackd[k]$

To set the timer tmi when it sends a message (either in operation S_i^{B1} or in operation T_i^{B1}), i needs a constant tp, the timeout period. To implement the aging of messages in transit, we add to each message a timer field tf as first field, which is set when the message is sent. Thus both i and j need a constant mdi and mdj (not necessarily the same) to set the timer field in the messages they send. These values mdi and mdj can be thought of as the maximum delay of a message from i to j, and from j to i, respectively. Thus we get

in S_i^{B0}:	send $<ns>$	is replaced by	send $<mdi, ns>$; $tmi[ns] := tp$
in T_i^{B0}:	send $<k>$	is replaced by	send $<mdi, k>$; $tmi[k] := tp$
in R_j^{B0}:	send $<v, v>$	is replaced by	send $<mdj, v, v>$
in S_j^{B0}:	send $<nr, vr - 1>$	is replaced by	send $<mdj, nr, vr - 1>$

To simulate the progress of time, we add operation TIME which decreases all timers, in processors and messages, by the same positive amount (see section 1.2.1.5). To discard messages that are "too old", we test the decreased timer field in messages and delete outdated messages from the links in the operation TIME. This now becomes as follows:

TIME: **begin** choose $\delta \in \mathbb{N}^+$;
        forall messages $<tf, v> \in Q\,[i,j]$
        do $tf := tf - \delta$; **if** $tf < 0$ **then** delete $<tf, v>$ from $Q\,[i,j]$ **fi od**;
        forall messages $<tf, x, y> \in Q\,[j,i]$
        do $tf := tf - \delta$; **if** $tf < 0$ **then** delete $<tf, x, y>$ from $Q\,[j,i]$ **fi od**;
        forall $n \geq 0$ **do** $tmi[n] := tmi[n] - \delta$ **od**
   end

Note that it is not the case that the new guard of operation T_i^{B1} (i.e., $(na \leq k < ns) \wedge (tmi[k] \leq 0) \wedge \neg ackd[k])$ implies $\texttt{timeout}(k)$. First we have to derive what the relation is between the constants we defined. It is clear that the condition $^\#L_{ij}(k) = 0$ is implied by $tmi[k] \leq 0$ if we choose the constants tp and mdi such that $tp > mdi$. For acknowledgements $<tf, k, k>$ sent in operation R_j^{B0} immediately upon receipt of a data message with number $k < nr$, we know that they have disappeared from $Q\,[j,i]$ within $mdi + mdj$ time since the data message was sent. Hence we demand $tp > mdi + mdj$. However, the condition $^\#L_{ji}(k) = 0$ is *not* implied by $tmi[k] \leq 0$ if we choose tp, mdi, and mdj such that $tp > mdi+mdj$. This is the case because although messages sent in operation R_j^{B0} are sent "immediately" upon receipt of a message from i (operation R_j^{B0} is defined as an atomic operation), messages sent in operation S_j^{B0} may be sent an arbitrary time after the last receipt operation. Thus we cannot derive any bound on the value of tp. To enable i to use timers anyway, we demand that if j sends a message in operation S_j^{B1}, it does so immediately upon receipt of a message from i. (Without a timer, j cannot measure any other time than "0".)

Second, there is a comparable problem with the conjunct $\neg rcvd[k]$ of $\texttt{timeout}(k)$. Its value is directly observable only for j. What we can try to do is to take care that this conjunct *always* holds, by formulating operation I_j^{B0} as a loop, always adding operation S_j^{B0}, and doing this as soon as a new message is received in R_j^{B0}. The result is that the protocol for j now consists of only one atomic operation:

R_j^{B1}: $\{\ Q\,[i,j] \neq \emptyset\ \}$
    begin receive $<tf, v>$;
        if $v < nr$ **then** send $<mdj, v, v>$
        else $rcvd[v] := true$; **while** $rcvd[vr]$ **do** $vr := vr + 1$ **od**;
            if $nr < vr$ **then** send $<mdj, nr, vr - 1>$; $nr := vr$ **fi**
        fi
   end

We call the protocol skeleton which is the result of all these changes (i.e., the implementation of protocol skeleton $B0$) protocol skeleton $B1$.

2.2.2.2 *The problem.* Unfortunately, for values of k with $na < k < ns$, it is *not* the case that $\neg ackd[k] \wedge (tmi[k] \leq 0)$ implies $\texttt{timeout}(k)$. The problem lies in the clause "$(k < nr) \vee \neg rcvd[k]$". This more or less requires i to "know" whether data message $<k>$ arrived or not. Consider the following two scenarios that are indistinguishable for i.

Processor i sends data messages $<0>$, $<1>$, $<2>$, and $<3>$, and receives acknowledgements $<0,0>$ and $<1,1>$. Processor i resends data message $<2>$. At this point, the variables of i have the following values: $ns = 4$, $na = 2$, $j = 1$, $i = 2$, $ackd[0] = ackd[1] = true$, $ackd[2] = ackd[3] = false$. Let i time out for data message $<3>$ now.

In the first scenario, processor j has received data messages $<0>$, $<1>$, $<3>$, and $<2>$ (in this order), and thus has sent acknowledgements $<0,0>$, $<1,1>$, and $<2,3>$. The variables of j have the following values: $nr = vr = 4$, $v = 2$, $rcvd[0] = rcvd[1] = rcvd[2] = rcvd[3] = true$. Acknowledgement $<2,3>$ is lost. When processor i times out for data message $<3>$, it is indeed the case that $\texttt{timeout}(3)$ holds, as $3 < nr = 4$.

In the second scenario, processor j has received data messages $<0>$, $<1>$, and $<3>$, data message $<2>$ is lost, and thus j has sent acknowledgements $<0,0>$ and $<1,1>$. The variables of j have the following values: $nr = vr = 2$, $v = 3$, $rcvd[0] = rcvd[1] = rcvd[3] = true$, and $rcvd[2] = false$. When processor i times out for data message $<3>$, it is *not* the case that $\texttt{timeout}(3)$ holds, as $3 \not< 2$ and $rcvd[3] = true$. Thus assertion (5) of theorem 2.2.1: $^{\#}L_{ij}(n) > 0 \Rightarrow n < ns \wedge \neg ackd[n] \wedge (n < nr \vee \neg rcvd[n])$ is violated for $n = 3$. Assertion (5) is part of the invariant which implies the safety of the block acknowledgement protocol (see section 2.2.1). We have only shown that, in the second scenario, it is possible that the invariant of the protocol which implies its safety is violated. As such, this does not necessarily mean that the protocol operates incorrectly. In the versions of the protocol that we discussed so far, we used unbounded sequence numbers, and hence each message is uniquely identified by its number. It is only when we convert the protocol to a version which uses finite sequence numbers that we can pinpoint an erroneous execution where one message is mistaken for another. Hence we will proceed to show that this can actually happen if the second scenario as sketched above occurs.

We define the remaining constants as follows. Let $mdi = mdj = 1$ and $tp = 3$. Let $w = 2$ and $m = 4$. It is shown in [BGM91] that it is possible to use sequence numbers and to do all computations mod m when $m \geq 2w$. In processor j, the sequence number v of a received data message is expected to lie between $nr - w$ (inclusive) and $nr + w$ (exclusive). Thus we show an execution in Figure 2.3 where the illegal retransmission of data message $<3>$ is considered as a receipt of data

"time"	i operation	na	links receipt	j (mess. sent)	nr
0	send $<1,0>$	0	receive $<1,0>$	$(<1,0,0>)$	1
	send $<1,1>$	0	receive $<1,1>$	$(<1,1,1>)$	2
	receive $<1,0,0>$	1			
		TIME with $\delta = 1$			
1	send $<1,2>$	1	**lost**		
	receive $<0,1,1>$	2			
		TIME with $\delta = 1$			
2	send $<1,3>$	2	receive $<1,3>$		2
		TIME with $\delta = 2$			
4	resend $<1,2>$	2	receive $<1,2>$	$(<1,2,3>)$	4
		TIME with $\delta = 1$			
5	**resend $<1,3>$**	2			
	receive $<0,2,3>$	4			
	send $<1,0>$ $(=4)$	4	receive $<1,0>$ $(=4)$	$(<1,0,0>)$	5
	send $<1,1>$ $(=5)$	4	receive $<1,1>$ $(=5)$	$(<1,1,1>)$	6
			receive $<1,3>$ $(\neq 7)$		6
		TIME with $\delta = 1$			
6	receive $<0,0,0>$	5			

Executions of operations are ordered from top to bottom, and within one line from left to right. The send and receive action that give rise to the actual error are shown in bold.

Figure 2.3 AN ERRONEOUS EXECUTION.

message $<7>$ by j ($3 = 7 \bmod m$). This will be the case if $nr - w = 4$ and thus if $nr = 6$. As a consequence of the illegal timeout, data message $<3>$ is on its way to j, while in the mean time, when j receives the also resent data message $<2>$, acknowledgement $<2,3>$ is sent to i. If it is received, na is increased to 4 and i sends the next two data messages $<4>$ and $<5>$, with 0 and 1 as sequence numbers. These arrive fast at j, before the resent message $<3>$. As data message $<3>$ had already been received by j before, j increments nr to 5 and 6 upon receipt of messages $<0>$ (i.e., 4) and $<1>$ (i.e., 5). When the resent data message $<3>$ is received by j, nr has the value of 6, and as j expects that the sequence number of a received message lies between $nr - w$ and $nr + w$, that is, between

4 and 8 in this case, j considers this to be the message with sequence number 7. Thus this execution with bounded sequence numbers is erroneous.

We conclude that it is indeed *necessary* to keep the assertion $^\#L_{ij}(n)+^\#L_{ji}(n) \leq 1$ always true for all n.

2.2.2.3 *Possible solutions.*

Is it possible to prevent a situation like this, i.e., that $tmi[k] < 0$ while $\neg\texttt{timeout}(k)$, from occuring in the protocol? The problem lies in the timeout condition for the data message with number k in case i has not received an acknowledgement yet for messages numbered $k-1$ and higher. The condition $k < nr \vee \neg rcvd[k]$ requires i to decide whether the acknowledgement $<k-1,k>$ was lost (timeout warranted) or data message $<k-1>$ was lost while data message $<k>$ was received (timeout *not* warranted). We now will list a number of (attempts at) solutions together with the disadvantages that are the consequences.

The first trivial solution is to prevent any timeout happening by setting the constant tp to ∞. This is safe, but unless there are no communication errors and all messages are sent in the right order, the progress of the protocol is violated.

Another trivial solution is to prevent message $<k>$ from being sent if message $<k-1>$ is not acknowledged yet. This amounts to setting $w = 1$, and reduces to the alternating bit protocol (with longer acknowledgements). This is a safe and alive restriction of the block acknowledgement protocol. However, the use of block acknowledgements does not make any sense any more.

The third solution is to prevent message $<k>$ from being *resent* if message $<k-1>$ is not acknowledged yet. This amounts to a simpler protocol where only one outstanding message of the sending window can be retransmitted. This has the disadvantage that if a number of consecutive data messages are lost, the retransmissions of those data messages all have to be separated by a full timeout period. (In this case, the timeout condition would become $(na \neq ns) \wedge (Q[i,j] = Q[j,i] = \emptyset) \wedge \neg rcvd[nr]$, while the message that is possibly resent has sequence number na.)

Let the receiver j send an acknowledgement for $<k>$ if $<k-1>$ is not received yet. Unfortunately, this is not in accordance with the specification of the protocol. The consequence is that all messages will have to be acknowledged separately again, and the concept of a block acknowledgement is lost altogether.

Try using timers in j also. We began our attempt to implement the protocol with timers in i only, but would it help to use any additional timers? The only use we can make of timers is to prohibit the execution of an otherwise enabled operation subject to a certain condition on the value of a timer. We need to distinguish between two different situations: in both, message $<k>$ is received by j, while in one all acknowledgements of $<k>$ and $<k-1>$ are lost, and in the other, all (re)transmissions of $<k-1>$ are lost. However, both situations can exist for an arbitrary time (i.e., finite but unbounded). (Note that the assumption of *fairness* only states that messages that are sent infinitely often will eventually be received, not that this will happen within some bounded time.) This means that we cannot use the concept of time to discriminate them.

We thus conclude that an implementation of the block acknowledgement protocol with full retransmission capabilities is *not* possible in this way.

2.2.3 Our implementation

As we showed above that it is not observable for i whether $k < nr \vee \neg rcvd[k]$ holds in j, we will have to ensure that a situation as sketched above cannot occur any more. Thus we will now ensure that j does not send an acknowledgement for a data message that might be retransmitted by i because its timer goes off. Hence we again introduce a "maximum reply time", now for each data message separately, and only allow j to send one block acknowledgement for several data messages at once if the maximum reply time is not exceeded for any of them. Hence we supply j with a timer for each possible data message. As for the possibility of using only one timer in j instead of one for each data message, this leads to an unacceptable performance. (We do not consider the possibility of simulating m timers by one timer, which is of course possible.)

2.2.3.1 The protocol skeleton.
We assume that process j has an infinite array of timers tmj. (This reduces to $2w$ timers in the version with bounded sequence numbers.) The timer $tmj[n]$ is used to measure whether the maximum reply time mrt has elapsed or not since j received (the last occurrence of) data message $<n>$, in order to decide whether j can send an acknowledgement for $<n>$ or not. Thus $tmj[n]$ has to be set upon receipt of data message $<n>$ and operation R_j^{B2} of j becomes as follows:

R_j^{B2}: $\{\, Q\,[i,j] \neq \emptyset \,\}$
   begin receive $<tf,v>$; $tmj[v] := mrt$;
       if $v < nr$ **then** send $<mdj,v,v>$ **else** $rcvd[v] := true$ **fi**
   end

We have to choose the timeout period tp in i accordingly, such that tp is strictly larger than $mdi + mdj + mrt$. As we now have to check all timer values $tmj[vr]$ of those values vr that are candidates to be included in a block acknowledgement sent in operation S_j^{B0}, we include operation I_j^{B0} in the new operation S_j^{B2}, subject to the values in the relevant timers. (As a consequence nr always equals vr outside an operation.) Thus we have to change the guard of the operation to the condition that ensures that vr will indeed be increased inside the new operation S_j^{B2}. This condition is $rcvd[nr] \wedge tmj[nr] > 0$. Hence operation S_j^{B2} of j becomes as follows:

S_j^{B2}: $\{ \ rcvd[nr] \wedge tmj[nr] > 0 \ \}$
 begin while $rcvd[vr] \wedge tmj[vr] > 0$ **do** $vr := vr + 1$ **od**;
  send $< mdj, nr, vr - 1 >$; $nr := vr$
 end

Of course, in the operation TIME we have to decrease $tmj[n]$ by the same amount as all other timers, hence we add the statement "**forall** $n \geq 0$ **do** $tmj[n] := tmj[n] - \delta$ **od**".

For ease of reference, we now give the complete code of the protocol as derived above.

Protocol skeleton $B2$:

Initially $Q[i, j] = Q[j, i] = \emptyset$,
  In i : $na = ns = 0$, $\forall n \geq 0 : ackd[n] = false$, $tmi[n] = 0$,
  In j : $nr = vr = 0$, $\forall n \geq 0 : rcvd[n] = false$, $tmj[n] = 0$.

S_i^{B2}: $\{ \ ns < na + w \ \}$
 begin send $< mdi, ns >$; $tmi[ns] := tp$; $ns := ns + 1$ **end**

R_i^{B2}: $\{ \ Q[j, i] \neq \emptyset \ \}$
 begin receive $< tf, x, y >$ from j; $l := x$;
   while $l \leq y$ **do** $ackd[l] := true$; $l := l + 1$ **od**;
   while $ackd[na]$ **do** $na := na + 1$ **od**
 end

T_i^{B2}: $\{ \ (na \leq k < ns) \wedge (tmi[k] \leq 0) \wedge \neg ackd[k] \ \}$
 begin send $< mdi, k >$; $tmi[k] := tp$ **end**

R_j^{B2}: $\{ \ Q[i, j] \neq \emptyset \ \}$
 begin receive $< tf, v >$; $tmj[v] := mrt$;
   if $v < nr$ **then** send $< mdj, v, v >$ **else** $rcvd[v] := true$ **fi**
 end

S_j^{B2}: $\{ \ rcvd[nr] \wedge tmj[nr] > 0 \ \}$
 begin while $rcvd[vr] \wedge tmj[vr] > 0$ **do** $vr := vr + 1$ **od**;
  send $< mdj, nr, vr - 1 >$; $nr := vr$
 end

TIME: **begin** choose $\delta \in \mathbb{R}^+$;

        forall messages $<tf, n> \in Q[i, j]$

        do $tf := tf - \delta$; **if** $tf < 0$ **then** delete $<tf, n>$ from $Q[i, j]$ **fi od**;

        forall messages $<tf, n, m> \in Q[j, i]$

        do $tf := tf - \delta$; **if** $tf < 0$ **then** delete $<tf, n, m>$ from $Q[j, i]$ **fi od**;

        forall $n \geq 0$ **do** $tmi[n] := tmi[n] - \delta$; $tmj[n] := tmj[n] - \delta$ **od**

  end

E^l_{ij}, E^l_{ji}, E^r_{ij}, and E^r_{ji} : defined as in section 1.2.1.2.

Although we now have formulated a correct protocol as we will show below, it is not a strict implementation of the block acknowledgement protocol from [BGM91] as our timeout condition for operation T_i^{B2}: $(na \leq k < ns) \wedge (tmi[k] \leq 0)$ does *not* imply `timeout`(k). It is however based on the same principle, namely to keep the assertion $^\#L_{ij}(n) + {}^\#L_{ji}(n) \leq 1$ always true for all values of n. If we consider again the erroneous execution in subsection 2.2.2, i still "illegally" times out for data message $< 3 >$ (as $(3 \not< nr) \wedge rcvd[3]$), but the acknowledgement $< 2, 3 >$ would not have been sent (in the execution of Figure 2.3, as $tp = 3$, mrt must be chosen < 1 and thus $tmj[3] < -1$ at the moment j receives data message $< 2 >$ and considers sending acknowledgement $< 2, 3 >$), and hence $^\#L_{ij}(n) + {}^\#L_{ji}(n)$ remains ≤ 1 for $n = 3$.

2.2.3.2 *Proof of safety.*

In view of the fact that the changed protocol is not a strict implementation of the original version, it perhaps not surprising that we need a slightly different invariant to prove the safety of the changed protocol. The invariant for (the original) protocol skeleton $B0$ is given in theorem 2.2.1, and is the conjunct of 8 assertions (for all values of n). Of these, we can slightly strengthen assertion (1), while assertions (2) to (4) remain the same. We have to weaken assertion (5) because the clause $n < nr \vee \neg rcvd[n]$, which ensures that j will not send an acknowledgement for data message $<n>$, does not hold any more. It is replaced by $tmj[n] \leq 0$, which has the same effect.

For a safe transition to bounded sequence numbers and finite arrays, we need assertions (7) and (8), which hold for both the original ($B0$) and the changed protocol ($B2$). (We do not show the actual transition here; it is done in the same way as in section 2.1, and is given in [BGM91].)

For the proof of the safety of protocol $B2$ we need additional assertions that relate the values of the timers in the protocol to the other variables. Let $tf(n)$ denote the value of the timer field of the message in transit concerning n if it exists. We know by assertion (4) that there is at most one message concerning n. We can now state the theorem.

Theorem 2.2.2 *Using protocol skeleton B2, the following assertions hold invariantly for all $n \geq 0$:*

(1) $na \leq nr = vr \leq ns \leq na + w$,

(2) $(n < na \Rightarrow ackd[n]) \wedge (ackd[n] \Rightarrow n < nr) \wedge \neg ackd[na]$,

(3) $(rcvd[n] \Rightarrow n < ns) \wedge (n < vr \Rightarrow rcvd[n])$,

(4) $\#L_{ij}(n) + \#L_{ji}(n) \leq 1$,

(5) $\#L_{ij}(n) > 0 \Rightarrow n < ns \wedge \neg ackd[n] \wedge tmj[n] \leq 0$,

(6) $\#L_{ji}(n) > 0 \Rightarrow n < nr \wedge \neg ackd[n]$,

(7) $\#L_{ij}(n) > 0 \Rightarrow nr - w \leq n < nr + w$,

(8) $\#L_{ji}(n) > 0 \Rightarrow na \leq n < na + w$,

(9) $tmi[n] \leq 0 \Rightarrow \#L_{ij}(n) = 0 \wedge tmj[n] \leq 0 \wedge \#L_{ji}(n) = 0$,

(10) $\#L_{ij}(n) > 0 \Rightarrow tmi[n] > mrt + mdj + tf(n)$,

(11) $tmj[n] > 0 \Rightarrow \#L_{ij}(n) = 0 \wedge tmi[n] > mdj + tmj[n]$,

(12) $\#L_{ji}(n) > 0 \Rightarrow tmi[n] > tf(n)$.

Proof. It is easy to verify that all assertions hold for the initial values of the variables. Furthermore, note that operations E_{ij}^d and E_{ji}^d can only invalidate the premise of some assertions, thereby leaving the assertion itself valid. Operations E_{ij}^r and E_{ji}^r have no influence on the assertions whatsoever.

(1). From operation R_i^{B2} we know that once na is strictly positive, $ackd[na - 1]$ holds and thus by assertion (2) $na - 1 < nr$, hence $na \leq nr$. An increase in nr cannot invalidate this. Only in operation S_j^{B2} are nr and vr changed, and the last statement is $nr := vr$. Hence they are the same outside all operations. Furthermore, once $vr > 0$, it is clear that $rcvd[vr - 1]$ holds, and thus with (3) $vr - 1 < ns$, hence $vr \leq ns$. An increase in ns cannot invalidate $vr \leq ns$. Operation S_i^{B2} ensures that $ns \leq na + w$, and an increase in na cannot invalidate this.

(2). The variable $ackd[n]$ is only set to *true* upon receipt of a message $< tf, x, y >$ where $x \leq n \leq y$ in operation R_i^{B2}. This implies that before the operation, $\#L_{ji}(n) > 0$, and thus with (6) that $n < nr$. As nr can only be increased, a change in nr cannot invalidate $n < nr$. The variable na is only increased by 1 if $ackd[na]$ holds, hence for all $n < na$, $ackd[n]$ holds. As the increase is done until $ackd[na]$ does not hold any more, we know that $\neg ackd[na]$. Notice that $ackd[n]$ is never set to *false* again once it is set to *true*.

(3). In operation R_j^{B2}, the variable vr is only increased (one by one) when $rcvd[vr]$ holds. Thus $rcvd[n]$ holds for all $n < vr$. Furthermore, $rcvd[n]$ is only set to *true* on receipt of a message $< tf, n >$. Hence before the receipt we had $\#L_{ij}(n) > 0$.

With (5) we have $n < ns$. An increase in ns leaves the $n < ns$ valid. Also for $rcvd[n]$ it is the case that it is never set to *false* again.

(4). First note that a message concerning n from i to j is only sent once in operation S_i^{B2}, and from j to i only once in operation S_j^{B2}. A message only exists with a non-negative timer field, due to operation TIME. Once $^{\#}L_{ij}(n) + {}^{\#}L_{ji}(n) = 1$, we know by assertions (10) and (12) that operation T_i^{B2} is disabled and hence cannot add another message concerning n. If a message is sent in operation R_j^{B2} then $^{\#}L_{ij}(n)$ is decreased before $^{\#}L_{ji}(n)$ is increased by 1, hence the sum stays the same. By assertion (11) we have that operation S_j^{B2} is only enabled if $^{\#}L_{ij}(n) = 0$ and operation T_i^{B2} is disabled for n. By assertion (9) we have that operation T_i^{B2} is only enabled if there are no messages concerning n on their way and operations S_j^{B2} and R_j^{B2} are disabled. Thus there can be only one message on its way concerning n.

(5). If the send operation that caused the premise to become true was S_i^{B2}, then we know that before the operation, $n = ns$. Hence afterwards $n < ns$ holds, and as beforehand $\neg rcvd[ns]$ held (by (3)), we have with (2) that $\neg ackd[ns]$ held, and thus afterwards $\neg ackd[n]$. As $tmj[n]$ is only set to a value > 0 upon receipt of a message, i.e. if $rcvd[n]$ holds, we know $tmj[n] \leq 0$. On the other hand, if the send operation was T_i^{B2}, then the guard of the timeout operation ensured that assertion (5) holds (if we use (11)). The variable ns can only be increased, thus the assertion remains valid. If $tmj[n]$ is set to a positive value in operation R_j^{B2}, that is because of the receipt of message $<n>$, and hence with (4) $^{\#}L_{ij}(n)$ is now 0 and the premise of (5) invalidated. Likewise, if $ackd[n]$ is set to *true*, that must happen in operation R_i^{B2}, and hence we had beforehand $^{\#}L_{ji}(n) = 1$ and $^{\#}L_{ij}(n) = 0$.

(6). It is clear from operations R_j^{B2} and S_j^{B2} that when an acknowledgement is sent and $^{\#}L_{ji}(n)$ becomes > 0 that $n < nr$. As nr can only be increased, the inequality continues to hold. A message to i can only be sent within mrt time of a receipt of a message from i in operation R_j^{B2}, and we know by assertion (5) that $ackd[n]$ did not hold then. By assertion (4) we know that before the receipt operation $^{\#}L_{ji}(n) = 0$, hence we know that as long as $n \geq nr$ and no acknowledgement for n is sent, $ackd[n]$ remains *false* as operation R_i^{B2} is disabled. Thus $\neg ackd[n]$ holds when $^{\#}L_{ji}(n)$ becomes 1 and can only be set to *true* when the premise is invalidated by operation R_i^{B2}.

(7). That $n < nr + w$ follows from assertions (5) and (1). By assertion (5) we have that $\neg ackd[n]$ and hence with (2) and (1) that $n \geq nr - w$.

(8). By assertion (6) we have $\neg ackd[n]$ and thus with (2) $n \geq na$. Likewise, we have by (6) that $n < nr$ and thus with (1) that $n < na + w$.

(9). With the observation that operation TIME ensures that $^{\#}L_{ij}(n) > 0$ implies $tf(n) \geq 0$, and $^{\#}L_{ji}(n) > 0$ implies $tf(n) \geq 0$, this assertion follows directly from the assertions (10), (11), and (12).

(10). In operation S_i^{B2}, when a message $<t, n>$ is sent, $^{\#}L_{ij}(n)$ becomes 1, $tmi[n]$ becomes tp and $t = tf(n) = mdi$. Thus $tmi[n] = tp > mdi + mdj + tf(n)$. Operation TIME decreases $tmi[n]$ and $tf(n)$ by the same amount, hence the inequality remains valid. Operation T_i^{B2} sets the timers as in operation S_i^{B2}, hence the same inequality holds afterwards. Operation R_i^{B2} invalidates the premise.

(11). The timer $tmj[n]$ is only set in operation R_j^{B2} upon receipt of a message $<n>$. As a consequence, we have by (4) that $^{\#}L_{ij}(n) = 0$ and that $rcvd[n]$ holds and thus $n < ns$. By applying assertion (10) to the situation before the receipt, we know that $tmj[n]$ is set such that $tmi[n] > mdj + tmj[n]$ holds. Operation TIME decreases both timers by the same amount, hence the inequality remains to hold. As long as $tmj[n] > 0$ we know that operation T_i^{B2} is disabled, hence $^{\#}L_{ij}(n) = 0$ continues to hold.

(12). If $^{\#}L_{ji}(n) > 0$ is validated by operation R_j^{B2} then we know by assertion (10) that before the operation $tmi[n] > mrt + mdj$. As the timer field of the acknowledgement message is set to mdj, we know that $tmi[n] > tf(n)$ now holds. If however $^{\#}L_{ji}(n) > 0$ is validated by operation S_j^{B2}, we know that $tmj[n]$ was > 0, and as $tf(n)$ is set to mdj, we know by (11) that $tmi[n] > tf(n)$. Operation TIME decreases both timers by the same amount, and invalidates the premise if $tf(n)$ becomes negative. Operation R_i^{B2} invalidates the premise. $\qquad \square$

As the assertions of theorem 2.2.2 are invariant under operations E_{ij}^d, E_{ji}^d, E_{ij}^r, and E_{ji}^r, the proof of fault tolerance is included in the proof of safety.

2.2.3.3 *Progress.* To prove progress, it is sufficient to show that na is incremented infinitely often. This is the case because nr and ns remain within a distance w of na by assertion (1) of theorem 2.2.2. First consider the case that there are no losses of messages. We then have a sequence of enabled operations whose execution enables other operations (shown in Figure 2.4). Note that the sending of data message $<na>$ is enabled infinitely often. By operations E_{ij}^d, E_{ji}^d, and TIME the operations R_j^{B2} and R_i^{B2} can be disabled, but with the assumption of *fairness* they will eventually be executed, and na increased. Thus na is increased infinitely often. As we know by assertions (1), (2) and (3) that all messages with a sequence number $<na$ are received by j, infinitely many (new) messages are received.

2.3 Synchronous Link-level Protocols

Aho *et al.* [AWYU82] consider the problem of sending a sequence of bits over an error-prone link in a synchronous environment. They distinguish different classes of possible errors, and try to devise protocols of minimum complexity for the different

enabled operation	$S_i(na) \vee T_i(na) \vee$ TIME; $T_i(na)$	
execution results in	${}^{\#}L_{ij}^{na} = 1$	
enabled operation	$R_j(na)$	
execution results in	case 1: $na = nr$ $tmj[nr] > 0$	case 2: $na < nr$ ${}^{\#}L_{ji}^{na} = 1$
enabled operation	$S_j(na)$	$\vdots$
execution results in	${}^{\#}L_{ji}^{na} = 1$	$\vdots$
enabled operation	$R_i(na)$	
execution results in	$na := na + 1$	

The superscript $B2$ is deleted for brevity. Enabled operations are ordered from top to bottom. Below each enabled operation the value that results from execution of that operation is given.

Figure 2.4 CYCLE OF OPERATIONS THAT ENSURES PROGRESS.

classes that would ensure the full transmission of a sequence. The protocols that Aho *et al.* devise are stated in terms of finite-state automata. This is a way of precisely formulating a protocol, and has the advantage of providing a measure for the complexity of the protocol, namely the number of states of the automata. Aho *et al.* first prove that if all errors are allowed, no correct protocol is possible. Next they consider protocols for the case that the communication link only admits deletion errors. They begin by proving that one-state automata do not suffice for a correct protocol. We feel however that the proof is not completely fair, as connection-management issues are used in a counterexample. Halpern and Zuck [HZ87] give a knowledge-based protocol of which they claim that it contains all protocols defined by Aho *et al.*, together with a correctness proof.

The disadvantage of a correctness proof in terms of finite-state automata is that all possible state transitions have to be checked. Considering the protocols of Aho *et al.*, the question arose whether it is possible to give a correctness proof making use of system-wide invariants (and thus by assertional verification). However, a main assumption in this proof method is that only one atomic action takes place at a time, while in the protocols proposed by Aho *et al.* synchronicity is assumed, i.e., operations of sender and receiver take place at the same time. Also, information is derived from things *not* happening at a certain time. Hence, to make the protocols amenable to assertional verification, we lessen the constraint of synchronicity slightly, while retaining the correctness of the protocols. Chandy and Misra [CM88] use a different approach for an assertional verification of a synchronous program. They lump all atomic actions located at the different processors which are supposed to be executed at the same time together into one large action which is considered to be atomic.

In the next section we give both the model of Aho *et al.* and the model which we use for the correctness proofs. Section 2.3.2 presents the actual protocols in our notation together with the correctness proofs. For one of the protocols only the ideas were sketched in [AWYU82]. The (non-trivial) details are shown in section 2.3.2.3.

2.3.1 The models

We first give a synopsis of the model used by Aho *et al.* (details can be found in [AWYU82]). We then give the modifications which lead to our model, and state the necessary assumptions.

2.3.1.1 The original model.
Aho *et al.* considered the situation of two processors i and j, connected by an unreliable communication link, where a sequence of bits must be transmitted from i to j. Actions to be taken by the processors are described in terms of finite automata. Processors i and j operate in a synchronous fashion. At each time step, they both do one move. A move of the sender i is based upon its current state, the symbol received over the communication link, and the symbol to transmit. It can consist of a change in state, sending a symbol over the link, and possibly advancing its input (reading the next bit of the input). A move of receiver j is based on its current state and the symbol received over the link. It can consist of a change in state, sending a symbol over the link, and possibly writing a 0 or a 1 on the output (i.e., appending it to the bit sequence that it is accumulating).

The types of information that can be exchanged over the communication link, in each direction per "time step", are the bits 0 and 1, and "nothing", which is represented by the symbol λ. The following transmission errors are considered:
- *deletion errors*, in which a 0 or 1 is sent, but λ is received;
- *mutation errors*, in which a 0 or 1 sent is received as a 1 or 0, respectively; and
- *insertion errors*, where a λ sent is received as a 0 or 1.

2.3.1.2 Our model.
In the model of Aho *et al.*, the non-arrival of a physical bit in a time step was modeled as the arrival of a λ. Thus we must assume in our model that messages can contain three different symbols: 0, 1, and λ. When we write $<\lambda>$ we mean: a physical message with empty contents. We need physical

messages in our model to render the guard of the receive operation true: "a message
has arrived".

As outlined in chapter 1 we model the different transmission errors by operations
acting on the "contents" of the communication link. The error operations we
consider are:

$$E_{ij}^g \ : \ \{ \ \exists <x> \in Q\,[i,j] \ \} \ \textbf{begin} \ <x> := <\lambda> \ \textbf{end} \qquad\qquad \text{(deletion)}$$

$$E_{ij}^m \ : \ \{ \ \exists <x> \in Q\,[i,j] \ \text{with} \ x \neq \lambda \ \} \qquad\qquad\qquad \text{(mutation)}$$
$$\qquad \textbf{begin if} \ x = 0 \ \textbf{then} \ <x> := <1> \ \textbf{else} \ <x> := <0> \ \textbf{fi end}$$

$$E_{ij}^i \ : \ \{ \ \exists <\lambda> \in Q\,[i,j] \ \} \ \textbf{begin} \ \text{choose} \ x \in \{0,1\}; \ <\lambda> := <x> \ \textbf{end} \quad \text{(insertion)}$$

and the corresponding operations E_{ji}^g, E_{ji}^m, and E_{ji}^i for messages in $Q\,[j,i]$. By
statements of the sort $<x> := <y>$ we mean: change only the contents and not
the position or the existence of the message in the queue. Note that the deletion
operation E_{ij}^g really is the "garble" operation from section 1.2.1.2, but we retain the
terminology of Aho *et al.* here. Thus we have made the following extra assumption
about the system of processors and the communication link.

Assumption 2.3.1 *Transmission delays are sufficiently bounded such that the
arrival of an empty message (i.e., the non-arrival of a bit) can be inferred.*

In synchronous computation it is usually assumed that messages are transmitted
with a fixed delay, but assumption 2.3.1 is sufficient to make the transition from the
synchronous model where the non-arrival of a message is used as information to an
asynchronous model which is driven by the arrival of (possibly empty) messages.
The assumption is not necessary if we allow messages with three possible contents,
forgetting the original meaning. However, these three different contents cannot be
represented by a single bit any more.

In the model of Aho *et al.*, the class of an error is defined by the relation between
the symbol sent and the symbol received. In our model an error is an operation
upon the contents of a message queue. These different viewpoints lead to a dis-
crepancy for the case of deletion and insertion errors. This is discussed further in
section 2.3.2.3.

As we want to model a synchronous system, we include one send and one receive
action of one processor into one operation. Thus the operation will consist of
the work to be done by one processor in "one time step". The operation will be
guarded by the arrival of a message. The assumption that the link has the FIFO
property is not meaningful in the original synchronous model, but is necessary now.

To see this, consider the case that $Q[i,j]$ and $Q[j,i]$ both contain one message, and that processor i receives one message from j. It then also sends a message to j. Hence $Q[i,j]$ now contains two messages. If these messages were reordered, j would receive the second message first. This clearly could never happen in the synchronous model of Aho *et al.*, hence we have to exclude this possibility here.

To start the protocols, we assume that both $Q[i,j]$ and $Q[j,i]$ initially contain one empty message. This is done to remain close to the model of Aho *et al.*, otherwise we would have to introduce a separate starting operation to send the first message. We denote the assertion "there is exactly one message in $Q[i,j]$ which is empty" as $<\lambda> \in! Q[i,j]$. Thus we get as a general synchronous protocol skeleton:

Protocol skeleton SP:

Initially $<\lambda> \in! Q[i,j]$ and $<\lambda> \in! Q[j,i]$.

$\text{R}_i^{SP} : \{ Q[j,i] \neq \emptyset \}$
      begin receive $<m>$ from j; compute; send $<x>$ to j **end**

R_j^{SP} : defined similarly, and

E_{ij}^g, E_{ji}^g, E_{ij}^i, E_{ji}^i, E_{ij}^m, and E_{ji}^m : as defined above.

Given protocol skeleton SP, we are now ready to prove the first invariant.

Lemma 2.3.1 *Using protocol skeleton SP, the number of messages in $Q[i,j]$ and $Q[j,i]$ together is 2.*

Proof. Initially this is true. Recall that operations are considered to be atomic actions, hence the assertion has to reflect the state of the queues only after completion of an operation. The error operations do not change the number of messages in the queues, only their contents. Hence these operations do not falsify the assertion. In operation R_i^{SP} the number of messages in $Q[j,i]$ is decreased by 1, while the number of messages in $Q[i,j]$ is increased by 1. Hence the total number stays the same. For operation R_j^{SP} the same holds with i and j interchanged. Thus the assertion is kept invariant by all possible operations.   □

Let the *system state* be the entity consisting of the set of values of the local variables and the contents of message queues. We now define the concept of a *balanced state*, which corresponds to the states that can occur in the synchronous model of Aho *et al.*

Definition 2.3.2 *A system state is* balanced *if the number of messages in $Q\,[i,j]$ is equal to the number of messages in $Q\,[j,i]$.*

Lemma 2.3.2 *Using protocol skeleton SP, the following assertions hold invariantly:*

    (1) in a balanced state both R_i^{SP} and R_j^{SP} are enabled,

    (2) in an unbalanced state one of R_i^{SP} and R_j^{SP} is enabled, the other is disabled,

    (3) operation R_i^{SP} transforms a balanced state in an unbalanced one and vice versa, as does operation R_j^{SP},

    (4) starting from a balanced state, a sequence of two consecutive R^{SP}-operations can only consist of R_i^{SP} and then R_j^{SP}, or R_j^{SP} and then R_i^{SP}, and in both cases this leads to a balanced state.

Proof. Obvious from the definition and the protocol skeleton. $\square$

Hence we can restrict ourselves to balanced states and need not worry whether it was $\mathrm{R}_i^{SP}; \mathrm{R}_j^{SP}$ or $\mathrm{R}_j^{SP}; \mathrm{R}_i^{SP}$. (This is the case under the assumption that R_i^{SP} and R_j^{SP} are independent, i.e., the action that i takes does not depend on the value of a local variable of j. This should be the case in any protocol.)

Thus the artificial difference that we created in this model between "R_i^{SP} before R_j^{SP}" and "R_i^{SP} after R_j^{SP}" in contrast with "R_i^{SP} at the same time as R_j^{SP}" in the original model can be overlooked if we confine ourselves to balanced states.

2.3.2 Assertional proofs of the protocols of Aho et al.

In this section we specify refined skeletons for the protocols of Aho *et al.* for different (combinations of) errors. The partial correctness proofs more or less follow the transitions of the product automata of the protocols. In section 2.3.2.1 we discuss the protocol for the case of deletion errors only. In section 2.3.2.2 we consider deletion and mutation errors, while the combination of deletion and insertion errors is discussed in section 2.3.2.3.

First we give some general notation. The sequence of bits that i has to transmit to j is in $string_i$, and j stores it in $string_j$. For sake of notation and easy formulation of invariants, we consider the sequences as arrays which are subscripted by n_i and n_j, respectively, to give the current position. Hence a statement like "advance the input" is encoded as $n_i := n_i + 1$. However, we nowhere make use of any further properties of arrays, and we could as well use a one-way tape with one head.

The states of i and j are recorded in the variables $state_i$ and $state_j$, respectively. For the values of the variable $state$ we use numbers: for 2-state automata we use numbers modulo 2, and for 3-state automata we use numbers modulo 3, respectively. As the actions of the protocol skeleton differ for i and j, we will denote their actions as S_i^D and R_j^D. As superscript we use a code for the class of errors allowed.

2.3.2.1 *Deletion errors only.* The protocol Aho *et al.* give for the case of deletion errors only can be viewed as a special implementation of the alternating bit protocol, in which the control bit is not sent, but "signaled" by the sending of non-λ symbols at either odd or even time steps. The protocol takes the following form in our model and notation.

Protocol skeleton D:

Initially $state_i = state_j = 0$, $n_i = n_j = 1$, $<\lambda> \in! \, Q\,[i,j]$, $<\lambda> \in! \, Q\,[j,i]$.

$S_i^D : \{\, Q\,[j,i] \neq \emptyset \,\}$
    begin receive $<x>$ from j;
        if $state_i = 0 \wedge x = \lambda$ **then** send $<string_i[n_i]>$ to j; $state_i := 1$
        elif $state_i = 0 \wedge x \neq \lambda$ **then** send $<\lambda>$ to j; $n_i := n_i + 1$
        else send $<\lambda>$ to j; $state_i := 0$
        fi
    end

$R_j^D : \{\, Q\,[i,j] \neq \emptyset \,\}$
    begin receive $<x>$ from i;
        if $x = \lambda$ **then** send $<\lambda>$ to i; $state_j := state_j + 1 \bmod 2$
        else send $<1>$ to i;
            if $state_j = 1$ **then** $string_j[n_j] := x$; $n_j := n_j + 1$
            else $state_j := 1$
            fi
        fi
    end

E_{ij}^g and E_{ji}^g as in section 2.3.1.2.

For this protocol we can derive the following invariants.

Lemma 2.3.3 *Using protocol D, the following assertions hold invariantly:*
(1) $state_i = 0 \Rightarrow <\lambda>$ *tail of* $Q\,[i,j] \vee Q\,[i,j] = \emptyset$,
(2) $state_j = 0 \Rightarrow <\lambda>$ *tail of* $Q\,[j,i] \vee Q\,[j,i] = \emptyset$,
(3) $<x>$ *tail of* $Q\,[i,j] \wedge x \neq \lambda \Rightarrow x = string_i[n_i] \wedge state_i = 1$,
(4) $<x>$ *tail of* $Q\,[j,i] \wedge x \neq \lambda \Rightarrow state_j = 1$.

Proof. (1). Initially $state_i = 0$ and $<\lambda> \in Q[i,j]$ is the last (and only) message, hence the assertion holds. Operation E_{ij}^g cannot change the content of an empty message. Operation R_j^D receives a message and deletes it from $Q[i,j]$. If it was the last one, then $Q[i,j] = \emptyset$ now holds; if it was not, then $<\lambda>$ remains the last message in $Q[i,j]$. Operation S_i^D can send a message such that the last message in $Q[i,j]$ does not contain λ any more; however, then $state_i$ is changed to 1. If S_i^D renders the premise true by setting $state_i = 0$, then i sends $<\lambda>$ to j. Hence the assertion is kept invariant by all possible operations.

(2). Initially the assertion holds. Likewise, in R_j^D, if $state_j$ is set to 0, $<\lambda>$ is sent to i. If j sends a non-λ symbol, $state_j$ is set to or remains 1. Operation S_i^D does not affect the last message of $Q[j,i]$ unless it empties the queue.

(3). Initially the premise is false, hence the assertion holds. In operation S_i^D, if i sends a non-λ message $<x>$, then $x = string_i[n_i]$ and i sets $state_i$ to 1. When n_i is increased, another message is sent to j and $<x>$ is no longer the last message. Operation E_{ij}^g on the last message in $Q[i,j]$ falsifies the premise, as does operation R_j^D if the last message from $Q[i,j]$ is received.

(4). Initially the premise is false. If in operation R_j^D $<1>$ is sent to i, $state_j$ becomes or remains 1. If in R_j^D $state_j$ is set to 0, $<\lambda>$ is sent, hence $<1>$ is no longer the last message in $Q[j,i]$. Operation E_{ji}^g may falsify the premise, and so does S_i^D if the last message is received. $\square$

Lemma 2.3.4 *Using protocol D, the following assertions hold invariantly:*
   (1)   the state is balanced and $state_i = state_j \Rightarrow n_i = n_j$,
   (2)   the state is balanced and $state_i \neq state_j \Rightarrow n_i = n_j - 1$.

Proof. We prove the assertions by simultaneous induction. By lemma 2.3.2 we know that we reach a balanced state from another balanced state by one operation S_i^D and one operation R_j^D in an arbitrary order, as the code of the operations is indeed independent. Initially $state_i = state_j = 0$ and $n_i = n_j = 1$. If the state is balanced and $state_i = state_j = 0$, we know by lemmas 2.3.3 and 2.3.1 that the first message in both queues is $<\lambda>$, hence the next balanced state will be $state_i = state_j = 1$. As neither n_i nor n_j is changed upon receipt of $<\lambda>$, $n_i = n_j$ still holds. If $state_i = 1$, then the next $state_i = 0$ and n_i is not changed. If $state_j = 1$, then either n_j is increased by 1 and $state_j$ remains 1, or n_j is not changed but $state_j$ is set to 0. Hence the next balanced state has $state_i = state_j = 0$ and $n_i = n_j$ or $state_i = 0$, $state_j = 1$, and $n_i = n_j - 1$. From this last case, we get in the next state $state_j = 0$ and n_j unchanged because $<\lambda>$ was received. Operation S_i^D either sets $state_i$ to 1 and leaves n_i unaltered, or increases n_i by 1 and leaves $state_i = 0$. Hence the next balanced state has either $state_i = 1$, $state_j = 0$, and

$n_i = n_j - 1$; or $state_i = state_j = 0$ and $n_i = n_j$. From the first case we get $state_i = 0$ and n_i unchanged because we had $<\lambda> \in Q[j,i]$, and from $state_j = 0$ we get $state_j = 1$ and n_j unchanged, hence we get $state_i = 0$, $state_j = 1$, and $n_i = n_j - 1$. This exhausts all possibilities. □

Theorem 2.3.5 *Using protocol D, $string_i[1 : n_j - 1] = string_j[1 : n_j - 1]$.*

Proof. Initially n_j is 1, and the strings are both empty. The only operation which affects the assertion is R_j^D, when n_j is increased. This is only done if $state_j$ was 1 and $<x> \in Q[i,j]$ with $x \neq \lambda$ held. Thus the last balanced state was $state_i = state_j = 1$ and hence $n_i = n_j$. By lemma 2.3.3 we have that for this received message $<x>$, $x = string_i[n_i]$ and hence $x = string_i[n_j]$. As x is written in $string_j[n_j]$ and n_j is increased afterwards in R_j^D, we now have $string_i[n_j - 1]$ $= string_j[n_j - 1]$. As the assertion held for the old value of n_j, we now have $string_i[1 : n_j - 1] = string_j[1 : n_j - 1]$ for the new value. □

This concludes the assertional proof of the partial correctness of protocol D for the case of deletion errors only.

2.3.2.2 Deletion and mutation errors. We now assume that deletion and mutation errors can occur, but no insertion errors. As the difference between the bits 0 and 1 can now be obscured by mutation errors, another way is needed to distinguish them. In protocol D an alternation between odd and even time steps marked the difference between retransmissions and new values sent, while now an "alternation" between time steps that are 0, 1, and 2 modulo 3 distinguishes between retransmissions, a new 0, and a new 1. The protocol proposed by Aho *et al.* is as follows.

Protocol skeleton *DM*:

Initially $state_i = state_j = 0$, $n_i = n_j = 1$, $<\lambda> \in ! \, Q[i,j]$, $<\lambda> \in ! \, Q[j,i]$.

```
S_i^DM : { Q[j,i] ≠ ∅ }
      begin receive <x> from j;
            if state_i = 0 then send <1> to j; state_i := 1
            else send <λ> to j;
                 if state_i = 2 ∧ x ≠ λ
                 then if string_i[n_i] = 1 then state_i := 1 fi; n_i := n_i + 1
                 else state_i := state_i + 1 mod 3
                 fi
            fi
      end
```

$\mathrm{R}_j^{DM} : \{\, Q\,[i,j] \neq \emptyset \,\}$
    begin receive $<x>$ from i;
        if $x = \lambda$ **then** send $<\lambda>$ to i; $state_j := state_j + 1 \bmod 3$
        else send $<1>$ to i;
            if $state_j = 0$ **then** $string_j[n_j] := 1$; $n_j := n_j + 1$
            elif $state_j = 2$ **then** $string_j[n_j] := 0$; $n_j := n_j + 1$
            fi; $state_j := 2$
        fi
    end

E_{ij}^g, E_{ji}^g, E_{ij}^m, and E_{ji}^m as in section 2.3.1.2.

For protocol DM we can derive the following invariants.

Lemma 2.3.6 *Using protocol DM, the following assertions hold invariantly:*
  (1) $state_i = 0 \vee state_i = 2 \;\Rightarrow\; <\lambda>$ tail of $Q\,[i,j] \vee Q\,[i,j] = \emptyset$,
  (2) $state_j = 0 \vee state_j = 1 \;\Rightarrow\; <\lambda>$ tail of $Q\,[j,i] \vee Q\,[j,i] = \emptyset$,
  (3) $<x>$ tail of $Q\,[i,j] \wedge x \neq \lambda \;\Rightarrow\; state_i = 1$,
  (4) $<x>$ tail of $Q\,[j,i] \wedge x \neq \lambda \;\Rightarrow\; state_j = 2$.

Proof. Obvious from the protocol and the allowed error operations.   □

Lemma 2.3.7 *Using protocol DM, the following assertions hold invariantly:*
  (1) *the state is balanced and* $state_i = state_j \Rightarrow$
        $n_i = n_j \wedge string_i[n_j - 1] = string_j[n_j - 1]$,
  (2) *the state is balanced and* $state_i = state_j - 1 \bmod 3 \Rightarrow$
        $n_i = n_j + 1 \wedge string_i[n_j] = 0$,
  (3) *the state is balanced and* $state_i = state_j + 1 \bmod 3 \Rightarrow$
        $n_i = n_j + 1 \wedge string_i[n_j] = 1$.

Proof. We will prove the three assertions by simultaneous induction. Again we can use lemma 2.3.2 to observe that in going from one balanced state to the next we need to consider one S_i^{DM} and one R_j^{DM} operation in arbitrary order. Initially $state_i = state_j = 0$ and $n_i = n_j = 1$, hence the strings are equal, as they are both empty. By lemma 2.3.6 we have that both queues contain $<\lambda>$, hence in the next balanced state $state_i = state_j = 1$ and n_i and n_j are unchanged. From this state we get $state_i = state_j = 2$ and n_i and n_j remain unaltered. As $state_i = 2$ implies that $<\lambda> \in Q\,[i,j]$, we have $state_j := 0$ and n_j unchanged. In operation S_i^{DM} three things can happen. First, $state_i := 0$ and n_i remains unchanged; secondly, $state_i := 1$, n_i is increased by 1, and $string_i[n_i - 1] = string_i[n_j] = 1$, rendering assertion (3) true; and thirdly, $state_i$ remains 2, n_i is increased by 1 and $string_i[n_i - 1]$

$= string_i[n_j] = 0$, rendering assertion (2) true. Starting from the balanced state $state_i = 2$, $state_j = 0$, $n_i = n_j + 1$, and $string_i[n_j] = 0$, we have $<\lambda> \in Q[i, j]$, hence the next $state_j = 1$, next $state_i = 0$, and n_i and n_j unchanged. Again, $<\lambda>$ is in both queues, hence the next balanced state is $state_i = 1$ and $state_j = 2$ with n_i and n_j unchanged. As in operation R_j^{DM} the message $<\lambda>$ was received, $<\lambda>$ was sent to i, also. Hence $state_i$ becomes 2 with n_i unchanged. From $state_j = 2$ now two things can happen: either $<\lambda>$ is received, $state_j := 0$, and n_j is unchanged, leaving assertion (2) true; or a non-λ symbol is received causing a 0 to be written in $string_i[n_j]$ and causing n_j to be increased, thus rendering assertion (1) true. Starting from the balanced state $state_i = 1$, $state_j = 0$, $n_i = n_j + 1$, and $string_i[n_j] = 1$, we have $<\lambda> \in Q[j, i]$ and next $state_i = 2$ with n_i unchanged. In R_j^{DM} two things can happen: $string_i[n_j] := 1$, n_j is increased by 1, and $state_j := 2$, rendering assertion (1) true, or $state_j := 1$ and n_j is unchanged, leaving assertion (3) true. As $<\lambda>$ is in both queues, the next balanced state is $state_i = 0$ and $state_j = 2$ with n_i and n_j unchanged. The next state is $state_i = 1$, $state_j = 0$, with n_i and n_j unchanged, which completes all possibilities. $\square$

Theorem 2.3.8 *Using protocol DM, $string_i[1 : n_j - 1] = string_j[1 : n_j - 1]$.*

Proof. Follows from lemma 2.3.7. $\square$

This concludes the assertional verification of the safety of protocol DM.

2.3.2.3 Deletion and insertion errors. In case deletion and insertion errors (only) can arise, we encounter the problem that modeling errors by operations acting on the contents of the message queues, i.e., the contents of the link, leads to a difference with the model of Aho *et al.* In our model, operations can be executed in any order and as often as wished, as long as their guards are true. Thus, for a message $<0> \in Q[i, j]$ we can have a deletion error, changing this message to $<\lambda> \in Q[i, j]$. But nothing now prevents an insertion error, changing it to $<1> \in Q[i, j]$. Thus we have produced a mutation error, in the terminology of Aho *et al.*, as in their case the kind of error is determined by the relation between the symbol sent and the symbol received. One way to restore the correspondence between the model of Aho *et al.* and ours is to restrict errors: to demand that a message in a queue is subject to an error operation only once. Another, easier, way is to use the fact that the protocols of Aho *et al.* for deletion and insertion errors avoid insertion errors by never sending λ: as λ is never sent, insertion errors in fact do not occur. Thus by leaving out the insertion error operations in the protocol skeletons for the case of deletion and insertion errors and not sending λ, we model the same situation as Aho *et al.*

Aho *et al.* gave two protocols for the case of deletion and insertion errors, but only in words. Although the idea upon which the first protocol ($DI1$) is based is simple, its actual code is not as simple as that of the previous protocols, at least if "simple" is defined as: consisting of only a few states. Our translation of the idea for the protocol needs four states for the sender and even six states for the receiver, although we are not sure this is the minimum number necessary with the idea of this protocol. The problem can be solved by a protocol with fewer states, as the second protocol ($DI2$) in this section demonstrates. The idea used in protocol $DI1$ is to distinguish new bits being sent and retransmissions of old bits of the string by a parity bit, as in the alternating bit protocol. However, the need to remember the current parity increases the number of states by a factor of 2. In stating the protocol we will not do this, but write n_i mod 2 to denote the parity, since we feel that it is more clear in this way. However, if one wants to state the protocol as a finite state automaton in the model of Aho *et al.*, each state has to be replaced by two states, one where the parity is odd, and one for an even parity. The protocol sends the bit to transmit in odd time steps and the control bit in even time steps. The straightforward transcription of this idea leads to the following protocol.

Protocol skeleton $DI1$:

Initially $state_i = state_j = 0$, $n_i = n_j = 1$, $<\lambda> \in! Q\,[i,j]$, $<\lambda> \in! Q\,[j,i]$.

$S_i^{DI1} : \{\ Q\,[j,i] \neq \emptyset\ \}$
    begin receive $<x>$ from j;
        if $x \neq \lambda \wedge x \neq n_i$ mod 2 **then** $n_i := n_i + 1$ **fi**;
        if $state_i = 0$ **then** send $<n_i$ mod 2$>$ to j
        else send $<string_i[n_i]>$ to j
        fi; $state_i := state_i + 1$ mod 2
    end

$R_j^{DI1} : \{\ Q\,[i,j] \neq \emptyset\ \}$
    begin receive $<x>$ from i;
        if $x \neq \lambda \wedge state_j = 0$ **then** $string_j[n_j] := x$; $n_j := n_j + 1$ **fi**;
        if $state_j = 2 \vee state_j = 1 \wedge x \neq \lambda \wedge x = n_j$ mod 2
        then $state_j := state_j - 1$
        else $state_j := state_j + 1$
        fi; send $<n_j$ mod 2$>$ to i
    end

E_{ij}^g and E_{ji}^g as in section 2.3.1.2.

Processor j needs three states apart from the parity, because two states are used for remembering whether to expect a parity bit or a bit with string information, while the third is used for the case "a string bit is coming but it is probably a retransmission". The trick of repeatedly writing retransmitted values in the same position of $string_j$ does not work, as it might also be a new value that is sent, but the receiver has no way of "knowing" that, and the old value would be lost.

Lemma 2.3.9 *Using protocol DI1, the following assertions hold invariantly:*
(1) $state_i = 0 \land <x>$ *tail of* $Q[i,j] \land x \neq \lambda \Rightarrow x = string_i[n_i]$,
(2) $state_i = 1 \land <x>$ *tail of* $Q[i,j] \land x \neq \lambda \Rightarrow x = n_i \bmod 2$,
(3) $<x>$ *tail of* $Q[j,i] \land x \neq \lambda \Rightarrow x = n_j \bmod 2$.

Proof. Obvious from the protocol skeleton and the allowed error operations. □

Lemma 2.3.10 *Using protocol DI1, the following assertions hold invariantly:*
(1) *the state is balanced* $\Rightarrow state_i = state_j \lor state_i = 0 \land state_j = 2$,
(2) *the state is balanced and* $state_j = 0 \Rightarrow$
$$n_i = n_j \land string_i[n_j - 1] = string_j[n_j - 1],$$
(3) *the state is balanced and* $(state_j = 1 \lor state_j = 2) \Rightarrow$
$$(n_i = n_j \lor n_i = n_j - 1) \land string_i[n_j - 1] = string_j[n_j - 1].$$

Proof. (1). Obvious from the protocol skeleton. We prove assertions (2) and (3) by simultaneous induction. Initially (2) holds. As in a balanced state $state_i$ is determined by $state_j$ according to (1), we will only state the value of $state_j$ in the sequel. From assertion (2), the next balanced state has $state_j = 1$. As before this transition we had $n_i = n_j$, we have by lemma 2.3.9(3) that n_i is unchanged. In R_j^{DI1} two things can happen. First, if the symbol received was not λ, we have by lemma 2.3.9(1) that n_j is increased such that $n_i = n_j - 1$ and the new value is $string_j[n_j - 1] = string_i[n_j - 1]$. Secondly, if the symbol received was λ, then n_j remains unchanged. Hence assertion (3) is rendered true. From this balanced state with $n_i = n_j - 1$, if a non-λ symbol is received in S_i^{DI1}, then it was $n_j \bmod 2$ by lemma 2.3.9(3), hence n_i is increased such that $n_i = n_j$ holds again. Otherwise, n_i remains $n_j - 1$. In operation R_j^{DI1} we have by lemma 2.3.9(2) that the next $state_j = 2$ with n_j unchanged. From the balanced state with $state_j = 1$ and $n_i = n_j$, we get n_j unchanged and next $state_j$ is either 0 or 2. In S_i^{DI1} n_i remains unchanged because of lemma 2.3.9(3). Thus assertion (3) remains true or (2) is rendered true. From the balanced state with $state_j = 2$ and $n_i = n_j - 1$ we get that the next $state_j = 1$, n_j unchanged, and in S_i^{DI1} n_i can remain unchanged or is increased such that $n_i = n_j$. Hence assertion (3) remains true. From the balanced state with $state_j = 2$ and $n_i = n_j$ we get next $state_j = 1$, n_j unchanged, and n_i unchanged, too. Thus assertion (3) remains true. This completes all possible transitions. □

Theorem 2.3.11 *Using protocol DI1, we have*

$$string_i[1 : n_j - 1] = string_j[1 : n_j - 1].$$

Proof. Initially this is true because the strings are empty. By lemma 2.3.10 the assertion remains true as n_j is increased.   □

The second idea for a protocol for the case of deletion and insertion errors is based on protocol DM for the case of deletion and mutation errors in section 2.3.2.2. This latter protocol is based on the fact that the symbol λ cannot be changed by the error operations to a symbol $\neq \lambda$. If we allow only deletion and insertion errors, we know that the symbol 0 is never changed into the symbol 1. Thus we can use the same protocol in this case, if replace all symbols appropriately: "λ" by "0", and "$\neq \lambda$" by "1". Hence we get the following protocol.

Protocol skeleton $DI2$:

Initially $state_i = state_j = 0$, $n_i = n_j = 1$, $<0> \in! Q[i,j]$, $<0> \in! Q[j,i]$.

$$S_i^{DI2} : \{ \, Q[j,i] \neq \emptyset \, \}$$
   begin receive $<x>$ from j;
      if $state_i = 0$ **then** send $<1>$ to j; $state_i := 1$
      else send $<0>$ to j;
            if $state_i = 2 \wedge x = 1$
            then if $string_i[n_i] = 1$ **then** $state_i := 1$ **fi**; $n_i := n_i + 1$
            else $state_i := state_i + 1 \bmod 3$
            fi
      fi
   end

$$R_j^{DI2} : \{ \, Q[i,j] \neq \emptyset \, \}$$
   begin receive $<x>$ from i;
      if $x \neq 1$ **then** send $<0>$ to i; $state_j := state_j + 1 \bmod 3$
      else send $<1>$ to i;
            if $state_j = 0$ **then** $string_j[n_j] := 1$; $n_j := n_j + 1$
            elif $state_j = 2$ **then** $string_j[n_j] := 0$; $n_j := n_j + 1$
            fi; $state_j := 2$
      fi
   end

E_{ij}^g and E_{ji}^g as in section 2.3.1.2.

Now we can derive the following invariants.

Lemma 2.3.12 *Using protocol DI2, the following assertions hold invariantly:*

(1) $state_i = 0 \vee state_i = 2 \Rightarrow \;<x>\;$ tail of $Q\,[i,j] \wedge x \neq 1 \vee Q\,[i,j] = \emptyset$,

(2) $state_j = 0 \vee state_j = 1 \Rightarrow \;<x>\;$ tail of $Q\,[j,i] \wedge x \neq 1 \vee Q\,[j,i] = \emptyset$,

(3) $<1>$ tail of $Q\,[i,j] \Rightarrow state_i = 1$,

(4) $<1>$ tail of $Q\,[j,i] \Rightarrow state_j = 2$.

Proof. Obvious from the protocol skeleton and the allowed error operations. □

Corollary 2.3.13 *Using protocol DI2, we have*

$$string_i[1 : n_j - 1] = string_j[1 : n_j - 1].$$

Proof. This follows from lemma 2.3.12, the correspondence with operations S_i^{DM} and R_j^{DM}, and theorem 2.3.8. □

Similarly, this protocol can be used for the remaining possibilities of classes of errors.

3

Minimum-hop Route Maintenance

A basic problem that must be addressed in any design of a distributed network is the routing of messages. That is, if a node in the network wants to send a message to some other node in the network or receives a message destined for some other node, a method is needed to enable the node to decide over which outgoing link it has to send this message. Algorithms for this problem are called *routing algorithms.* In the sequel we will only consider *distributed* routing algorithms which are determined by the cooperative behavior of the local routing protocols of the nodes in order to guarantee effective message handling and delivery.

Desirable properties of routing algorithms are for example correctness, optimality, and robustness. *Correctness* seems easy to achieve in a static network, but the problem is far less trivial in case links and nodes are allowed to go down and come up as they can do in practice. *Optimality* is concerned with finding the "quickest" routes. Ideally, a route should be chosen for a message on which it will encounter the least delay but, as this depends on the amount of traffic on the way, such routes are hard to predict and hence the goal is actually difficult to achieve. A frequent compromise is to minimize the number of *hops*, i.e., the number of links over which the message travels from origin to destination. We will restrict ourselves to *minimum-hop routing. Robustness* is concerned with the ease with which the routing scheme is adapted in case of topological changes.

Our aim in this chapter is twofold. First we present a systematic development of a number of distributed algorithms for minimum-hop route determination and maintenance, including a reappraisal of several existing methods for static networks and a detailed analysis of some dynamic algorithms. Secondly, we present assertional correctness proofs for these algorithms, which have not been presented before in most cases that we consider. This applies in particular to the interesting distributed algorithm for minimum-hop route maintenance due to Chu [Chu78] (see also [Tan88] and [Sch80]), for which we will develop both a complete protocol skeleton and a correctness proof.

The chapter is organized as follows. We first concentrate on computing minimum-hop distances in a static network (section 3.1). We begin by deriving general properties of distributed minimum-hop algorithms, and then discuss different ways – related to different modes of computation – for deciding whether an estimate of a minimum-hop distance is correct (section 3.1.1). We conclude this section with the correctness proof of the minimum-hop route determination algorithms proposed by Gallager and Friedman [Fri78] (section 3.1.2).

In section 3.2 we consider the problem of maintaining routes in dynamic networks, i.e., networks with links going down and coming up. A general acquaintance with the contents of sections 3.1.1 and 3.1.2.1 is assumed here. In section 3.2.1 we discuss some typical problems in adapting distributed algorithms for static networks to distributed algorithms for dynamic networks, both in general and specifically for minimum-hop route maintenance. We present the well-known dynamic routing algorithm of Tajibnapis [Taj77, Lam82] for comparison in section 3.2.2, and in section 3.2.3 the dynamic routing algorithm of Chu [Chu78] is developed. The latter was presented as an improvement of the algorithm of Tajibnapis by Tanenbaum [Tan88] and Schwartz [Sch80] but, while Tajibnapis' algorithm has been proved correct by Lamport [Lam82], it is not clear at all that the algorithm of Chu is correct. Moreover, the presentation of Chu's algorithm in the original report is very imprecise. In section 3.2.3 we give a complete specification of Chu's algorithm and a correctness proof.

3.1 Minimum-hop Distances in a Static Network

In chapter 1 the assumptions were stated that we use when we are concerned with the network layer. We assume that the underlying communication protocols ensure that no messages are lost, garbled, duplicated, or delayed infinitely long. We also assume that messages are not reordered, and thus that the links behave like FIFO queues. Hence the context is that of a fault-free static network (section 1.2.1.1), and we do not have to add any error operation to the protocol skeletons. For the message-driven and the simulated synchronous mode of computation we need the additional assumption that in each connected component a node awakens spontaneously. Finally, in the synchronous mode of computation, every node must awaken spontaneously.

We begin by applying the most general protocol skeleton of chapter 1 (section 1.1.2) to the computation of minimum-hop distances. That is, we specify the contents of a message, we define variables to record computed values, and we specify the computation which has to be performed. After investigating what can be derived about estimated distances which are obtained in this way, we show in section 3.1.1 how to arrive at minimum-hop distances if we refine the protocol skeletons P, M, SS, and S defined in chapter 1 in this way. In section 3.1.2 we discuss some algorithms due to Gallager and Friedman [Fri78].

We assume that a message contains the identity of some destination node together with the estimated distance between the sender of the message and the destination. So messages (denoted as $<x, l>$) consist of two fields: the destination is in the first field and the (estimated) distance of the sender of the message to the destination is in the second field. We assume that each node maintains an array D with (estimated) distances to all nodes. If we want to use the minimum-hop distance for routing, we also need to remember the neighbor which sent a node the estimated minimal distance. This will be maintained in *dsn* (for *downstream neighbor*). (If the routing tables are filled and used for the routing of messages, one can visualize a "stream" of messages for a fixed destination, where with each hop in the routing algorithm messages get further downstream towards their destination.) The following protocol skeleton gives the basic framework for the computation of minimum-hop distances.

Protocol skeleton *MH*:

Initially $\forall i$: $D_i[i] = 0$ and $\forall x \neq i$: $D_i[x] = \infty$, $dsn_i[x] = $ none.

S_i^{MH} : **begin forsome** x **do** send $<x, D_i[x]>$ to some neighbor j **od end**

R_i^{MH} : { $\exists j : Q[j, i] \neq \emptyset$ }
     begin receive $<x, l>$ from j;
         if $l + 1 < D_i[x]$ **then** $D_i[x] := l + 1$; $dsn_i[x] := j$ **fi**
    end

Although it is not really necessary, we suppose for ease of notation that the set of all nodes in the (static) network is known a priori to every node.

We can already derive some meaningful statements about the relation between the values in $D_i[x]$ and the real (minimum-hop) distance between i and x, which is denoted by $d(i, x)$.

Lemma 3.1.1 *Using protocol skeleton MH, the following assertions hold invariantly for all x and i:*
   (1) $D_i[x]$ *is not increasing,*
   (2) $<x, l> \in Q[j, i] \Rightarrow l \geq D_j[x]$,
   (3) $D_i[x] \geq d(i, x)$.

Proof. (1), (2). Obvious from protocol skeleton *MH*.

(3). This is initially true, as $d(i,i) = D_i[i] = 0$ and $d(i,x) \leq \infty$ for all x. If a message $<x,l>$ is sent by j, j sends its value $D_j[x]$ as l. Hence by assertion (3) for j and x, $l \geq d(j,x)$ for messages sent by j. In case i receives a message $<x,l>$ from j and adjusts $D_i[x]$, we know by the triangle inequality that $d(i,x) \leq d(i,j)+d(j,x)$ $= 1 + d(j,x)$ and thus $1 + d(j,x) \leq 1 + l = D_i[x]$.   □

Lemma 3.1.2 *Using protocol skeleton MH, the following assertion holds invariantly for all i and x with $x \neq i$:*

$$D_i[x] = k < \infty \Rightarrow \text{ there is a path from } i \text{ to } x \text{ of at most } k \text{ hops via } dsn_i[x] \text{ and}$$
$$D_{dsn_i[x]}[x] \leq k - 1.$$

Proof. Consider operation R_i^{MH}, and let the message received be $<x,l>$. Then $l \geq D_j[x]$ by lemma 3.1.1(2). If $l = \infty$, i does not change $D_i[x]$ because $1 + \infty \not< D_i[x]$ always. Thus if i changes $D_i[x]$ and sets $dsn_i[x]$ to j, $l < \infty$. We distinguish two cases.

Case 1: $l = 0$. As $l \geq d(j,x)$ we know $d(j,x) = 0$ and hence $j = x$. Thus x is neighbor of i and there is a path of one hop to x. Then $D_i[x]$ is set to 1 and $dsn_i[x] = j$ while $D_j[x] \leq 1 - 1 = 0$.

Case 2: $l > 0$. As $D_j[j]$ is equal to 0 initially and is never changed (lemma 3.1.1), $l > 0$ implies $x \neq j$. Hence we can use the induction hypothesis for j and conclude that there is a path of $\leq l$ hops to x from j. We have $l \geq D_j[x]$, $dsn_i[x]$ is set to j, and $D_i[x]$ to $l+1$ while there is a path of $\leq l+1$ hops via j to x from i.

Thus in both cases there is such a path.   □

Baran's *perfect learning algorithm* [Bar64] is essentially identical to protocol skeleton *MH*. On messages sent for other reasons, a hop count of the distance traveled is piggybacked. This hop count is used by the receiver of the message to adjust its distance table in the manner described above. This distance table is then used in routing, without bothering whether the distances recorded are minimum distances.

3.1.1 Structuring the protocol skeleton

From the preceding section we conclude that any protocol which sends (estimates of) minimum-hop distances to neighbors, and adjusts distances upon receipt of messages in this way, yields estimates which are upper bounds on the real minimum distances, provided the initial values were upper bounds. In general however, one would like to know when the upper bounds are equal to the minima. Clearly, one has to send "enough" values around. Thus the problem reduces to deciding for each node when it can stop sending values of distances because all nodes (including the node itself) have the correct values. The way to achieve this is to add extra structure to the protocol skeleton. Both with phasing and in the message-driven mode one can decide when the distance tables are correct.

3.1.1.1 Phasing. The idea of phasing was explained in section 1.1.2.2. In order to distinguish messages of different phases, messages will now get a third field containing the current phase of the sender. All the work of one phase in this case consists of gathering all information about nodes which lie at a distance of $phase_i + 1$, and sending this information on in the next phase. We refine protocol skeleton P of chapter 1 to protocol skeleton $P1$.

Protocol skeleton $P1$:

Initially $\forall\, i\colon D_i[i] = 0$, $phase_i = 0$, $\forall\, x \neq i\colon D_i[x] = \infty$, $dsn_i[x] = $ none.

S_i^{P1}: **begin forsome** x **do** send $<x, D_i[x], phase_i>$ to some neighbor j **od end**

R_i^{P1}: $\{\, \exists j\colon Q[j,i] \neq \emptyset \,\}$
       begin receive $<x, l, p>$ from j;   record it as received for phase $= p$;
            if $l + 1 < D_i[x]$ **then** $D_i[x] := l + 1$; $dsn_i[x] := j$ **fi**
       end

P_i^{P1}: {all messages of phase $= phase_i$ from all neighbors have been received}
       begin $phase_i := phase_i + 1$ **end**

The guard of operation P_i^{P1} still is rather informally stated. It depends on the actual implementation how this statement should be formulated exactly. For example, the guard could be "from all neighbors j and about all destinations x a message of $phase_i$ has been received". We assume that at least the messages about those destinations x are included that would have a distance field of $phase_i$. We are not interested in how this could be implemented, we only assume that a node can somehow decide this question.

Note that in operation R_i^{P1} we did not test the phase number p of the received message against the phase number $phase_i$ of the node i. Whether a message is buffered until i has reached the corresponding phase or is processed directly, or even is thrown away, is immaterial for the partial correctness of the protocol skeleton, as we will see. Thus we did not impose an extra restriction on R_i^{P1}.

As this protocol skeleton is also a refinement of protocol skeleton *MH*, lemmas 3.1.1 and 3.1.2 still hold.

Lemma 3.1.3 *Using protocol skeleton $P1$, the following assertions hold invariantly for all i and x:*

(1) phase$_i$ is not decreasing,
(2) $d(i,x) > phase_i \lor d(i,x) \geq D_i[x]$,
(3) $<x,l,p> \in Q[i,j] \land l \leq p \Rightarrow l = D_i[x] = d(i,x)$.

Proof. (1). Obvious from protocol skeleton $P1$.

(2). Initially $d(i,x) > phase_i = 0$ for $i \neq x$ and $d(i,i) = D_i[i] = 0$. We also note the following. First, operation S_i^{P1} does not change any variables. Second, operation R_i^{P1} can only decrease $D_i[x]$, hence the assertion remains true. Third, consider operation P_i^{P1}. We only need to consider the case that $phase_i$ is increased to the value that happens to be $d(i,x)$. Thus assume $d(i,x) = k \geq 1$. Hence there is a path of k hops from i to x. Let j be the first node after i on this path. Thus $d(j,x) = k-1$. As the operation is enabled, i has received a message $<x,l,p>$ from j with $p = k-1$. Together with the induction hypothesis we have $d(j,x) > p$ or $d(j,x) \geq l$. As $d(j,x) = k-1$, we know $k-1 \geq l$. In R_i^{P1} the result of receiving $<x,l,p>$ is that $D_i[x] \leq l+1$, whether or not $D_i[x]$ is adjusted. As $D_i[x]$ is not increasing, this is still the case. Hence $D_i[x] \leq l+1 \leq k = d(i,x)$.

(3). By lemma 3.1.1(3) and assertion (2) we have $d(i,x) > phase_i \lor d(i,x) = D_i[x]$. Hence operation S_i^{P1} has the effect that for the message $<x,l,p>$ sent, $d(i,x) > p$ or $d(i,x) = l = D_i[x]$. Thus for values of l such that $l \leq p$ we have that the latter clause holds, as $l \leq d(i,x)$ by lemma 3.1.1. As $D_i[x]$ is not changed any more when it has reached the correct value, the assertion continues to hold. $\square$

Now it is clear from operation R_i^{P1} that if two messages $<x,l,p>$ and $<x,l,p'>$ are received from j, the second one has no effect whatsoever upon the distance table D_i. Hence it is not necessary for j to send the second message, as long as i is able to determine when it has received "all" messages of a phase. Likewise, if a message $<x,\infty,p>$ is received from j in operation R_i^{P1}, there is no effect upon the distance table D_i, but only upon the administration of "received messages of phase p". Thus this message could be deleted, if i can correctly decide the guard of operation P_i^{P1} in that case. This could be implemented for example by letting j send the total number of messages of each phase to be expected, or sending all messages over one link inside one large message per phase. The proof of lemma 3.1.3 is easily adjusted for the set of atomic operations where this different definition of "all messages per phase" is used in the guard of operation P_i^{P1}. This will be discussed in more detail in section 3.1.3.

Theorem 3.1.4 *Using protocol skeleton $P1$, the following assertions hold for all i and x:*
(1) $d(i,x) \leq phase_i \Rightarrow D_i[x] = d(i,x)$,
(2) $D_i[x] \leq phase_i \Rightarrow D_i[x] = d(i,x)$.

Proof. Follows directly from lemma 3.1.3 combined with lemma 3.1.1(3). $\qquad\square$

Thus we know on the one hand that i knows the correct distance to all nodes x that have a distance less than or equal to the current phase number from i, and on the other hand that, if the value that i has for the distance to x is less than or equal to the current phase number, then this value is correct.

Corollary 3.1.5 *Using protocol skeleton $P1$, the following assertion holds for all i:* $\qquad phase_i > \max_x\{D_i[x] \mid D_i[x] < \infty\} \Rightarrow \forall x: D_i[x] = d(i,x).$

Proof. By theorem 3.1.4 we have that for all x with $d(i,x) \leq phase_i$, $D_i[x] = d(i,x)$. For those x with $d(i,x) = \infty$ we have by lemma 3.1.1 that $D_i[x] = d(i,x)$. Assume there is an x with $d(i,x) = k > phase_i$, and $d(i,x) < \infty$. Then there is a path of length k from i to x. Thus on this path, there must be a node y with $d(i,y) = phase_i$. By lemma 3.1.3 we know $d(i,y) = D_i[y] < phase_i$, which contradicts the premise. Thus for all nodes x we have $D_i[x] = d(i,x)$. $\qquad\square$

Hence a node can decide when all its distance values are correct. In an actual algorithm for computing minimum-hop distances this can be used as a stop criterion in the algorithm. Note that the protocol skeleton as given here is too general for being able to prove that it terminates and does not deadlock or generates messages forever.

3.1.1.2 Message-driven computation.
In this case structure is added in the order of computation by specifying which messages are to be sent if a certain message is received. If the receipt of a message from a neighbor leads to an adjustment in the distance table, this "news" is sent to all other neighbors. We obtain the following protocol skeleton.

Protocol skeleton $M1$:

Initially $\forall i$: $awake_i = false$, $D_i[i] = 0$, $\forall x \neq i$: $D_i[x] = \infty$, $dsn_i[x] = $ none.

$A_i^{M1} : \{\neg awake_i\}$
    begin $awake_i := true$; **forall** neighbors j **do** send $<i,0>$ to j **od end**

$R_i^{M1} : \{ \exists j: Q[j,i] \neq \emptyset \}$
    begin receive $<x,l>$ from j; **if** $\neg awake_i$ **then** do A_i^{M1} **fi**;
        if $l+1 < D_i[x]$
        then $D_i[x] := l+1$; $dsn_i[x] := j$;
            forall neighbors k with $k \neq j$ **do** send $<x,D_i[x]>$ to k **od**
        fi
    end

As this protocol skeleton is a refinement of skeleton *MH*, lemmas 3.1.1 and 3.1.2 still hold.

Lemma 3.1.6 *Using protocol skeleton M1, the following assertion holds invariantly for all links (i,j) and all nodes x:*

$$awake_i \wedge D_i[x] < \infty \Rightarrow <x, D_i[x]> \in Q[i,j] \vee D_j[x] \leq D_i[x] + 1.$$

Proof. Initially the premise is false. We consider the effect of any of the permitted operations that can influence the assertion.

– Operation A_i^{M1}. When i awakens, only $D_i[i]$ is set to a value $< \infty$. But then $<i,0>$ is sent to j in the same operation, hence $<i,0> \in Q[i,j]$.

– Operation R_i^{M1}. Here a $D_i[x]$ can be changed. If it is, it is done upon receipt of some message $<x,l>$ from some node k, not necessarily over the same link (i,j) as mentioned in the assertion, and $D_i[x]$ is set to $l + 1$. We distinguish two cases.

Case 1: $j = k$. By lemma 3.1.1 we have $l \geq D_k[x]$, thus $D_j[x] \leq l \leq D_i[x] + 1$.

Case 2: $j \neq k$. Then the message $<x, D_i[x]>$ is sent to j, and $<x, D_i[x]> \in Q[i,j]$.

– Operation R_j^{M1}. It can falsify the assertion $<x, D_i[x]> \in Q[i,j]$ by causing j to receive this specific message, but then the result is $D_j[x] \leq D_i[x] + 1$. If this last assertion holds, it can not be falsified by an R_j^{M1} operation because $D_j[x]$ is not increasing (lemma 3.1.1). $\qquad\square$

Lemma 3.1.7 *Using protocol skeleton M1, the following assertion holds for all nodes i and x:*

$$d(i,x) = D_i[x] \vee$$
$$(d(i,x) < D_i[x] \wedge$$
$$\quad \exists j : (d(i,j) = 1 \wedge d(i,x) = d(j,x) + 1 \wedge$$
$$\quad\quad ((d(j,x) = D_j[x] \wedge (<x, D_j[x]> \in Q[j,i] \vee (\neg awake_j \wedge x = j))) \vee$$
$$\quad\quad d(j,x) < D_j[x]))).$$

Proof. In case $d(i,x) < D_i[x]$ it follows that $i \neq x$ and $d(i,x) < \infty$. It is a property of minimum-hop distances that i has a neighbor j as specified on a path to x. By lemma 3.1.1 we have $d(j,x) \leq D_j[x]$. In case $d(j,x) = D_j[x]$ the remaining part of the assertion follows from lemma 3.1.6. $\qquad\square$

Lemma 3.1.8 *The number of messages sent in protocol skeleton M1 is finite.*

Proof. First note that in any message $<x,l>$ which is sent, $0 \leq l < \infty$. Secondly, let N be the total number of nodes in the network. Then $l < N$ in any message $<x,l>$ (use lemma 3.1.2). Moreover, for every two messages $<x,l>$ and $<x',l'>$ that are sent in the same direction over a link, either $x \neq x'$ or $l \neq l'$. This gives the desired result. $\qquad\square$

Theorem 3.1.9 *Using protocol skeleton* $M1$, $TERM \Rightarrow \forall i, x: D_i[x] = d(i, x)$.

Proof. Use lemmas 3.1.6 and 3.1.7. □

Corollary 3.1.10 *Protocol skeleton* $M1$ *is correct if enabled operations are performed within finite time.*

Proof. As messages can always be received when they arrive, and delays are finite, this protocol skeleton can terminate in finite time. It follows from theorem 3.1.9 that all distance tables contain the correct values upon termination. □

The only problem now left is that a node i cannot see from the values of its variables whether there is termination or not, and hence whether its distance table is correct. Unless we make further assumptions about the network such as: all messages have only a bounded delay, we need to add a so-called termination detection algorithm to be able to detect that all activity of the protocol skeleton has ceased (see e.g. [Tel91]).

3.1.1.3 Simulated synchronous computation. In this mode, phasing is incorporated in the message-driven mode of computation, as discussed in chapter 1. We obtain the following protocol skeleton if we refine protocol skeleton SS from section 1.1.2.4 with the computation of the distances.

Protocol skeleton $SS1$:

Initially $\forall i$: $awake_i = false$, $phase_i = 0$, $D_i[i] = 0$,
$\qquad\qquad \forall x \neq i$: $D_i[x] = \infty$, $dsn_i[x] = none$, $\forall$ neighbors j: $rec_i[j] = false$.

R_i^{SS1} : $\{ \exists j: Q[j,i] \neq \emptyset \wedge \neg rec_i[j]\}$
$\quad$ **begin** receive $<x, l, p>$ from j; **if** $\neg awake_i \wedge p = 0$ **then** do A_i^{SS1} **fi**;
$\qquad\quad$ **if** $awake_i \wedge p = phase_i$
$\qquad\quad$ **then if** $l + 1 < D_i[x]$ **then** $D_i[x] := l + 1$; $dsn_i[x] := j$ **fi**;
$\qquad\qquad\quad$ **if** this was j's last message in $phase_i$ **then** $rec_i[j] := true$ **fi**;
$\qquad\qquad\quad$ **if** $\forall$ neighbors k: $rec_i[k]$
$\qquad\qquad\quad$ **then** $phase_i := phase_i + 1$;
$\qquad\qquad\qquad\quad$ **forall** neighbors k
$\qquad\qquad\qquad\quad$ **do** $rec_i[k] := false$;
$\qquad\qquad\qquad\qquad\quad$ **forall** nodes x **do** send $<x, D_i[x], phase_i>$ to k **od**
$\qquad\qquad\qquad\quad$ **od**; **if** $\neg \exists x$ with $D_i[x] = phase_i$ **then** $awake_i := false$ **fi**
$\qquad\qquad\quad$ **fi**
$\qquad\quad$ **fi**
$\quad$ **end**

A_i^{SS1} : $\{\neg awake_i\}$
    begin $awake_i := true$;
        forall neighbors j
        do forall nodes x **do** send $<x, D_i[x], phase_i>$ to j **od od**
    end

Note that protocol skeleton $SS1$ is also a refinement of protocol skeleton $P1$. Hence lemma 3.1.3, theorem 3.1.4, and corollary 3.1.5 hold for $SS1$.

In protocol skeleton $SS1$ a lot of information turns out to be redundant. Hence we proceed to prove assertions between the variables involved in order to arrive at a simpler protocol skeleton whose correctness follows from the correctness of skeleton $SS1$. Note that the guard of operation R_i^{SS1} does not contain the test $p = phase_i$, contrary to R_i^{SS}. The next theorem states that this test is indeed not necessary.

Lemma 3.1.11 *Using protocol skeleton SS1, the following assertions hold invariantly for all links (i,j), all nodes x, and all integers $h \geq 0$:*

(1) $<x', l', p'>$ *behind* $<x, l, p> \in Q[i,j] \Rightarrow p' \geq p$,

(2) $\exists <x, l, p> \in Q[i,j]$ *with* $p = h \Rightarrow$
        $phase_i \geq h \;\wedge\; (phase_j < h \;\vee\; (phase_j = h \;\wedge\; rec_j[i] = false))$,

(3) $(((awake_i \;\wedge\; phase_i = h = 0) \;\vee\; 0 < h \leq phase_i) \;\wedge$
        $\neg\exists <x, l, p> \in Q[i,j]$ *with* $p = h) \Rightarrow$
        $phase_j > h \;\vee\; (phase_j = h \;\wedge\; rec_j[i] = true) \;\vee$
        $(\neg awake_j \;\wedge\; phase_j \geq 1)$,

(4) $((\neg awake_i \;\wedge\; phase_i = h = 0) \;\vee\; h > phase_i) \Rightarrow$
        $\neg\exists <x, l, p> \in Q[i,j]$ *with* $p = h \;\wedge$
        $(phase_j < h \;\vee\; (phase_j = h \;\wedge\; rec_j[i] = false))$.

Proof. (1). Follows from the FIFO property of the message queues and lemma 3.1.3.

We prove the remaining assertions by simultaneous induction. Initially the premises of (2) and (3) are false, and (4) holds for all h, as all queues are empty, and because $phase_j = 0$ and $rec_j[i] = false$, initially. Consider the effects of the different operations upon the assertions.

– Operation A_i^{SS1}. Then the premise of (2) holds for $h = 0$ and $phase_j = 0$ and $rec_j[i] = false$. The premise of (3) is false for $h = 0$. Assertion (4) continues to hold for $h \geq 1$.

– Operation R_i^{SS1}, where $phase_i$ is increased. Assertion (2) continues to hold for $phase_i > h$ as before, and for $h = phase_i$ messages $<x, l, p>$ with $p = h$ are sent to all neighbors including j. As $phase_j \leq phase_i$ before R_i^{SS1}, we must now have $phase_j < h$. Assertion (3) continues to hold for $phase_i > h$ as before, and the premise is false for $h = phase_i$. (4). The premise is falsified for $h = phase_i$ and remains true for $h > phase_i$. As the conclusion of assertion (4) is not influenced by operation R_i^{SS1} it remains true.

– Operation A_j^{SS1}, spontaneously or on receipt of a message from i which was not the last one of the current phase. Hence as a result, $phase_j = 0$ and $rec_j[i] = false$. If (2) held, it still holds. The premise of (3) is false. (4) continues to hold as before.

– Operation R_j^{SS1} on receipt of a message from i which was not the last one of the current phase. Then all assertions remain true as before.

– Operation R_j^{SS1} on receipt of a message $<x,l,p>$ from i which was the last one of the current phase. Then before $rec_j[i] = false$ (assertion (2)). We have two cases.

Case 1: $phase_j$ is not increased. Then $rec_j[i] = true$ and $\neg\exists<x,l,p>\in Q[i,j]$ with $p = phase_j$ holds. An exception is the case where $awake_j$ was *false*, since $rec_j[i] = false$ then.

Case 2: $phase_j$ is increased. Then again $rec_j[i] = false$ and $\neg\exists<x,l,p>\in Q[i,j]$ with $p = phase_j - 1$ now holds. If (2) held before for values of h with $phase_j < h$, then it now holds for $phase_j \leq h$ as $rec_j[i] = false$. In (4) we could not have had $h = phase_j$ before R_j^{SS1}, hence (4) continues to hold now $phase_j$ is increased. If $awake_j$ is set to *false*, $phase_j$ must at least be 1 as $phase_j$ is increased first.

– Operation R_j^{SS1} on receipt of a message from another neighbor than i which results in an increase of $phase_j$. This can only happen if before R_j^{SS1} $rec_j[i] = true$ already, and hence $\neg\exists<x,l,p>\in Q[i,j]$ with $p = phase_j$ before R_j^{SS1}. Afterwards, $rec_j[i] = false$. The premise of (2) only could hold for $h > phase_j$, hence (2) holds afterwards. In (3), $phase_j = h$ and $rec_j[i] = true$ held before, and now $phase_j > h$ holds. In (4), $phase_j = h$ and $rec_j[i] = false$ did not hold, hence increasing $phase_j$ by 1 does not falsify (4).

Hence these assertions remain invariant under all possible operations. $\square$

Theorem 3.1.12 *Using protocol skeleton SS1, the following assertion holds for all links (i,j) and all nodes x:*
$<x,l,p>$ head of $Q[i,j] \Rightarrow (p = phase_j \wedge rec_j[i] = false) \vee$
$\qquad\qquad\qquad\qquad (p > phase_j \wedge (rec_j[i] = true \vee awake_j = false)).$

Proof. Follows directly from lemma 3.1.11(1) and (4), lemma 3.1.11(2) with $h = p$ and lemma 3.1.11(3) with $h \leq p-1$. $\square$

We conclude that the receiver of a message $<x,l,p>$ has no need for the information in the third field. If the receiver is *awake* and the guard is enabled, the message is of the current phase. If the receiver is not *awake*, it is clear from its own phase number (= 0 or > 0) whether it should wake up and start participating in the algorithm or has finished already. In the latter case the message is redundant and can be thrown away. Thus we can omit the third field from the messages. However, there is more information that is redundant.

Lemma 3.1.13 *Using protocol skeleton SS1, the following assertions hold for all links (i, j) and all nodes x:*

(1) $D_i[x] < \infty \Rightarrow D_i[x] \leq phase_i + 1$,

(2) $<x, l, p> \in Q[i, j] \Rightarrow l = \infty \vee l = d(i, x) \leq p$,

(3) $<x, l, p> \in Q[i, j] \wedge l < p = phase_j \Rightarrow D_j[x] = d(j, x)$.

Proof. We prove the first two assertions by simultaneous induction. Initially both are true. If a node awakens, it sends messages of the form $< x, 0, 0 >$ or $<x, \infty, 0>$, which agrees with the second assertion. If in an operation R_i^{SS1} $D_i[x]$ is changed, it is done upon receipt of some message $<x, l, p>$ from, say, j. Then $l \neq \infty$, $p = phase_i$, and $l = d(j, x) \leq phase_i$ by the inductive assumption. As $D_i[x]$ is set to $l + 1$, we have $D_i[x] = d(j, x) + 1 \leq phase_i + 1$. If in operation R_i^{SS1} messages are sent, then $phase_i$ was increased, too. As for those x with $D_i[x] < \infty$, $D_i[x] \leq phase_i + 1$, we have after the increase that $D_i[x] \leq phase_i$ and thus $l \leq p$ in the messages sent, or $l = \infty$. By lemma 3.1.3(3) $l \leq p$ implies $l = d(i, x)$. Hence (1) and (2) remain true.
Assertion (3) follows from the triangle inequality $d(j, x) \leq d(i, x) + 1$ together with (1) and theorem 3.1.4(1). □

Thus the only messages $<x, l, p>$ upon the receipt of which an entry $D_i[x]$ is changed are those with $l = p = phase_i$, and hence $D_i[x]$ is always set to $phase_i + 1$ when it is changed. Necessarily $D_i[x]$ was ∞ beforehand. Thus the test of whether to change $D_i[x]$ or not can be stated differently. Only the name of the node x in a message $<x, l, p>$ is information we need. Now one can do two things. One possibility is to just send messages which only contain the name of a node. The problem with this is that the receiver now has no way of knowing when all messages of one phase have been received, as the number of them is not fixed any more, and even might be zero. The second possibility is to send only one message which contains a (possibly empty) set of node names. Thus we avoid the previous problem, but introduce messages which do not have a fixed length.

We now give the simplified protocol skeleton for the second possibility in skeleton $SS2$, for easy comparison with the synchronous protocol skeleton (see section 3.1.1.4). We use X to denote a set of node names. Note that even now some redundant information is sent. This is exploited in the algorithms of Gallager and Friedman [Fri78]. We refer the reader to section 3.1.2 for more details.

Protocol skeleton $SS2$:

Initially $\forall i$: $awake_i = false$, $phase_i = 0$, $D_i[i] = 0$,
$\qquad\qquad \forall x \neq i$: $D_i[x] = \infty$, $dsn_i[x] = none$,
$\qquad\qquad \forall$ neighbors j: $rec_i[j] = false$.

A_i^{SS2} : $\{\neg awake_i\}$
$\qquad$ **begin** $awake_i := true$; **forall** neighbors j **do** send $<\{i\}>$ to j **od end**

R_i^{SS2} : $\{\ \exists j:\ (\,Q\,[j,i] \neq \emptyset \wedge \neg rec_i[j]\,)\}$
$\qquad$ **begin** receive $<X>$ from j ; **if** $\neg awake_i \wedge phase_i = 0$ **then do** A_i^{SS2} **fi** ;
$\qquad\qquad$ **if** $awake_i$
$\qquad\qquad$ **then** $rec_i[j] := true$;
$\qquad\qquad\qquad$ **forall** $x \in X$
$\qquad\qquad\qquad$ **do if** $D_i[x] = \infty$ **then** $D_i[x] := phase_i + 1$; $\quad dsn_i[x] := j$ **fi od** ;
$\qquad\qquad\qquad$ **if** $\forall$ neighbors k: $rec_i[k]$
$\qquad\qquad\qquad$ **then** $phase_i := phase_i + 1$; $X := \{x \mid D_i[x] = phase_i\}$;
$\qquad\qquad\qquad\qquad$ **forall** neighbors k **do** $rec_i[k] := false$; send $<X>$ to k **od** ;
$\qquad\qquad\qquad\qquad$ **if** $X = \emptyset$ **then** $awake_i := false$ **fi**
$\qquad\qquad\qquad$ **fi**
$\qquad\qquad$ **fi**
$\qquad$ **end**

We now proceed with the issue of correctness of this protocol skeleton, as this does not follow directly from corollaries 3.1.5 and 3.1.10. Since protocol skeleton $SS2$ uses stronger guards, it must be proved that no deadlock can occur. The following lemma establishes that there is always a node with an enabled operation.

Lemma 3.1.14 *Using protocol skeleton SS2, the following assertion holds for all links (i,j):*
$awake_i \wedge rec_i[j] = false \wedge Q\,[j,i] = \emptyset \;\Rightarrow\; (\,phase_j < phase_i \wedge awake_j\,) \;\vee$
$\qquad (\,phase_j = phase_i = 0 \wedge \neg awake_j \wedge Q\,[i,j] \neq \emptyset\,).$

Proof. Using lemma 3.1.11(3) with i and j interchanged and with $h = phase_i$, we get a contradiction. Hence we conclude that $phase_j < phase_i$ or $\neg awake_j \wedge phase_i = phase_j = 0$. In the case of $phase_j < phase_i$, let us assume that $awake_j$ does not hold. Note that j must have awakened for $phase_i$ to get a value greater than $phase_j$. Thus $awake_j$ can only be set to *false* again in an R_j^{SS2} operation. It is clear from the protocol skeleton that this implies that there cannot exist an x with $D_j[x] = phase_j$. Hence there is no node x with $d(j,x) = phase_j$ (theorem 3.1.4). On the other hand, $awake_i$ holds, hence there is some node x with $D_i[x]$

$= d(i, x) = phase_i > phase_j$. This implies that $d(j, x) \geq d(i, x) - 1 \geq phase_j$ because i and j are neighbors, which is a contradiction. Thus $awake_j$ must be true. Upon awakening, i sends a message to j, hence $Q[i, j] \neq \emptyset$. As long as j does not receive the message, $rec_j[i] = false$ and j does not awaken. On the other hand, if j awakens spontaneously, $Q[j, i] = \emptyset$ is falsified. Hence the assertion holds. □

Theorem 3.1.15 *The protocol skeletons $SS1$ and $SS2$ are correct.*

Proof. Lemma 3.1.14 implies that if at least one node in each connected component of the network awakens spontaneously, there is always some node in every connected component which can go on with a next action because its R^{SS1} or R^{SS2} operation is enabled. Thus no deadlock can occur. By corollary 3.1.5 the values in the distance tables are correct. As the number of messages sent is finite, being at most the number of phases (bounded by the diameter of the connected component) times the number of nodes, termination can occur in finite time. □

3.1.1.4 Synchronous computation. In synchronous computation not only are all messages of one phase sent "at the same time", but all messages of one phase are received "at the same time". Refining protocol skeleton S from chapter 1 leads to the following protocol skeleton.

Protocol skeleton $S1$:

Initially $\forall i$: $awake_i = false$, $phase_i = 0$, $D_i[i] = 0$, and
$\qquad\qquad \forall x \neq i$: $D_i[x] = \infty$, $dsn_i[x] = $ none.

A_i^{S1}: $\{\neg awake_i\}$
$\quad$ **begin** $awake_i := true$; **forall** neighbors j **do** send $<\{i\}>$ to j **od end**

R_i^{S1}: $\{\ awake_i \ \wedge \ \forall$ neighbors j: $\ Q[j, i] \neq \emptyset\ \}$
$\quad$ **begin forall** neighbors j
$\qquad\qquad$ **do** $\quad$ receive $<X>$ from j;
$\qquad\qquad\qquad$ **forall** $x \in X$
$\qquad\qquad\qquad$ **do if** $D_i[x] = \infty$ **then** $D_i[x] := phase_i + 1$; $\quad dsn_i[x] := j$ **fi od**
$\qquad\qquad$ **od**; $phase_i := phase_i + 1$; $X := \{x \mid D_i[x] = phase_i\}$;
$\qquad\qquad$ **forall** neighbors j **do** send $<X>$ to j **od**;
$\qquad\qquad$ **if** $X = \emptyset$ **then** $awake_i := false$ **fi**
$\quad$ **end**

Note that protocol skeleton $S1$ is also a refinement of protocol skeleton $SS2$. As the guard of the receive operation in $S1$ is stronger than the corresponding guard in $SS2$, we have to show that in this case also, there is always some operation enabled in some node.

Lemma 3.1.16 *Using protocol skeleton $S1$, the following assertion holds for all links (i, j):*

$$awake_i \wedge Q[j, i] = \emptyset \Rightarrow (phase_j < phase_i \wedge awake_j) \vee$$
$$(phase_j = phase_i = 0 \wedge \neg awake_j \wedge Q[i, j] \neq \emptyset).$$

Proof. Initially the assertion is true. We now consider the relevant operations.
- Operation A_i^{S1} sets $awake_i$ and $Q[i, j] \neq \emptyset$.
- Operations A_j^{S1} and R_j^{S1} falsify the premise.
- Operation R_i^{S1} is only enabled if $Q[j, i] \neq \emptyset$. If afterwards $Q[j, i] = \emptyset$, then $Q[j, i]$ contained exactly one message. By the version of lemma 3.1.11 and theorem 3.1.12 for this protocol skeleton (where messages contain a set of nodes instead of a node, a distance, and a phase number) we know that immediately before execution of an R_i^{S1} operation, $phase_i = phase_j$. As $phase_i$ is increased in the operation, the result is $phase_j < phase_i$. The argument that $awake_j$ holds in the first part of the conclusion is the same as in the proof of lemma 3.1.14.   □

Theorem 3.1.17 *Protocol skeleton $S1$ is correct.*

Proof. Consider the differences between protocol skeletons $S1$ and $SS2$. In operation R_i^{S1} there is no possibility for awakening upon receipt of a message. This is not necessary because of assumption 1.1.3: all nodes awaken spontaneously. The partial correctness follows because protocol skeleton $S1$ is a refinement of protocol skeleton $SS2$. Lemma 3.1.16 implies that there is always a node with a minimal phase number for which some operation is enabled: either awakening or receiving messages over all links. Hence deadlock cannot occur. As the total number of messages sent is finite, this algorithm can terminate in finite time.   □

Although protocol skeleton $S1$ is the straightforward refinement of protocol skeleton $SS2$, it should be noted that the problem we consider, namely computing minimum-hop distances, is not really suitable for a synchronous computation. Ideally, one would not only want all nodes to start simultaneously, but also to finish simultaneously. However, it is inherent to this problem that some nodes have more work to do than others, possibly twice as much. For example, if the network is a path, the nodes at the ends of the path go on twice as long as the one(s) in the middle. Moreover, in the present formulation there are (redundant) messages left in the queues after termination of the algorithm, which is not elegant. It is no problem of course to add some code to receive and purge the remaining messages.

3.1.2 Concrete algorithms

Friedman [Fri78] discussed two algorithms for determining the minimum-hop distances in a static network, which can be viewed more or less as special cases of protocol skeleton $S1$. The first of these algorithms is attributed to Gallager.

3.1.2.1 The algorithm of Gallager.
Gallager noted that in protocol skeleton $S1$ there is still redundant information sent in messages. Consider the case that node i first hears about a node x from its neighbor j. Thus a shortest path from i to x leads via j. However, in the next phase i sends the newly learned identity of x to j too, which clearly is redundant information for j.

Lemma 3.1.18 *Using protocol skeleton $S1$, the following assertion holds for all links (i,j) and all nodes x: $dsn_i[x] = j \Rightarrow D_j[x] = d(j,x)$.*

Proof. Initially the premise is false. If $dsn_i[x]$ is set to some value j in operation R_i^{S1}, then x was included in a message from j. When j sent this message, $D_j[x] = d(j,x)$, and $D_j[x]$ is not changed any more. $\qquad\square$

Thus it is not necessary to include node x in the set X sent to j if $dsn_i[x] = j$. However, from the protocol skeleton it is not clear which neighbor will be chosen as downstream neighbor in case there are more possibilities, as the order of operation in "**forall** neighbors j **do**..." is not specified. For every possibility for j, i.e., every neighbor j with minimal distance to x, it is not necessary to include x in the set X sent to j. Thus, to save messages, the array of single values dsn_i is changed to an array of sets. We now rewrite the protocol in these terms which results (almost) in the algorithm of Gallager as stated by Friedman [Fri78]. There is one difference from the algorithm of Gallager: where we have: "**forall** neighbors j **do** receive $<X>$ from j", Gallager has "receive transmissions from all *active* neighbors". However, we showed in lemma 3.1.14 that all neighbors are *awake* or active long enough and hence this test is unnecessary.

Protocol skeleton G:

Initially $\forall i$: $awake_i = false$, $phase_i = 0$, $D_i[i] = 0$, $dsn_i[i] = \emptyset$, and
$\qquad\qquad \forall x \neq i$: $D_i[x] = \infty$ and $dsn_i[x] = \emptyset$.

A_i^G : $\{\neg awake_i\}$
$\qquad$ **begin** $awake_i := true$; **forall** neighbors j **do** send $<\{i\}>$ to j **od end**

R_i^G : { $awake_i \wedge \forall$ neighbors j : $Q[j,i] \neq \emptyset$ }

    begin forall neighbors j

          do   receive $<X>$ from j ;

                forall $x \in X$

                do   **if** $D_i[x] \geq phase_i + 1$

                      then $D_i[x] := phase_i + 1$; $dsn_i[x] := dsn_i[x] \cup \{j\}$

                      fi

                od

          od ; $phase_i := phase_i + 1$;

          forall neighbors j

          do $X := \{x \mid D_i[x] = phase_i \wedge j \notin dsn_i[x] \}$; send $<X>$ to j **od** ;

          if $\neg \exists x$ with $D_i[x] = phase_i$ **then** $awake_i := false$ **fi**

    end

Corollary 3.1.19 *Protocol skeleton G is correct.*

Proof. Follows from lemma 3.1.18 and theorem 3.1.17. $\square$

As Friedman already noted (without any arguments however) this algorithm can easily be adapted for use in an asynchronous environment. It is a straightforward exercise to incorporate the idea of maintaining sets of downstream neighbors $dsn_i[x]$ in protocol skeleton $SS2$.

3.1.2.2 The algorithm of Friedman. Friedman [Fri78] observed that there is further redundant information sent in the algorithm of Gallager, in the case that the network is not a bipartite graph, i.e., if the network contains cycles of odd length. Consider two neighbors i and j on a cycle of minimal odd length. This means there are nodes (at least one, say x) with the same distance to i and j: $d(i,x) = d(j,x)$. Thus in phase $d(i,x)$ nodes i and j send the name of node x to each other, while this is no new information for them. Friedman tried to adapt the previous algorithm in such a way that this is avoided.

The way he did this is by ensuring that information is not sent in both directions over a link simultaneously. For each link, a HI and a LO end are defined, the number of phases is doubled, and nodes alternately receive and send from LO ends, and receive and send from HI ends. To be able to discuss the relation between the phases in protocol skeleton G and the phases in Friedman's algorithm, we will give the phase-variables in the latter a new name: *Fphase*. In the protocol skeleton we will write in comments what would have happened to the variable *phase*, thus simplifying the formulation of assertions. Note that we cannot always choose HI and LO ends such that nodes have only the HI or only the LO ends of the incident links, because that would mean that the network is bipartite and the problem we want to avoid does not occur.

Hence we distinguish two sets hi_i and lo_i which contain those links for which i is incident to the HI and LO end, respectively. The choice of HI and LO ends is arbitrary, as long as the two ends of a link decide consistently. We assume node names are distinct and can be ordered in some way (lexicographically for example), and we take as HI end for each link the end with the highest node name.

Furthermore, we need some way to remember which node identities were received by LO ends while they were candidates to be sent in the next phase, as those are the identities we want to avoid sending twice. Note that they are not remembered in Gallager's algorithm, because they have a shorter path via another neighbor. We will maintain an array nnn_i (for next nearest neighbor) of sets, where neighbor $j \in nnn_i[x]$ if $d(i, x) = d(j, x)$. If we incorporate these ideas in Gallager's algorithm we get the protocol skeleton below. Lines differing from the algorithm as stated by Friedman himself are marked with an asterisk ($*$) at the beginning of the line. (We will indicate later that the algorithm as stated by Friedman is not correct.)

The operation R_i^G is now split into three different operations: R_i^0, R_i^{odd}, and R_i^{even}. The guards of these operations differ. In R_i^0, messages must have arrived over all links, to receive all of them and decide the HI and LO ends of the links. In R_i^{odd} the *Fphase* number is odd and messages from LO link ends are awaited before the messages of the current phase are sent over these links. If the *Fphase* number is even, messages from HI link ends are awaited in R_i^{even}. In order to be able to state assertions about messages of a certain phase, we first add a second field to messages containing the current *Fphase* number, and insert the corresponding protocol statements in comments in the protocol skeleton. We then prove assertions as if these extended messages were sent and received, and then show that it is indeed not necessary to include the *Fphase* field in the messages.

Protocol skeleton *F*:

Initially $\forall\, i$: $awake_i = false,\ Fphase_i = 0,$ **co** $phase_i = 0$ **co**
          $D_i[i] = 0,\ dsn_i[i] = \emptyset,\ hi_i = \emptyset,\ lo_i = \emptyset,$
          $\forall\, x \neq i$: $D_i[x] = \infty,\ dsn_i[x] = \emptyset,\ nnn_i[x] = \emptyset.$

A_i^F : $\{\neg awake_i\}$
     begin $awake_i := true$;
         forall neighbors j **do** send $<\{i\}>$ to j **od**   **co** send $<\{i\}, 0>$ **co**
     end

R_i^0 : { $awake_i \land Fphase_i = 0 \land \forall$ links $j: Q[j,i] \neq \emptyset$ }
    begin forall links
        do receive $<\{j\}>$ over the link;   **co** receive $<X,f>$ **co**
            $D_i[j]:=1; dsn_i[j]:=\{j\}$;
            if $j<i$ **then** $hi_i := hi_i \cup \{j\}$ **else** $lo_i := lo_i \cup \{j\}$ **fi**
        od ; $Fphase_i := 1$;   **co** $phase_i := 1$ **co**
        forall $j \in hi_i$
*   **do** let $X = \{x \mid D_i[x] = \frac{1}{2}(Fphase_i + 1) \land j \notin dsn_i[x]\}$;
            send $<X>$ to j **co** send $<X, Fphase_i>$ **co**
        od ; **if** $\neg\exists x$ with $D_i[x] = \frac{1}{2}(Fphase_i + 1)$ **then** $awake_i := false$ **fi**
    end

R_i^{odd} : { $awake_i \land odd(Fphase_i) \land \forall j \in lo_i : Q[j,i] \neq \emptyset$ }
    begin forall $j \in lo_i$
        do receive $<X>$ from j;   **co** receive $<X,f>$ **co**
        forall $x \in X$
            do if $D_i[x] \geq \frac{1}{2}(Fphase_i + 3)$
            then $D_i[x] := \frac{1}{2}(Fphase_i + 3)$; $dsn_i[x] := dsn_i[x] \cup \{j\}$
*   **elif** $D_i[x] = \frac{1}{2}(Fphase_i + 1)$
*   **then** $nnn_i[x] := nnn_i[x] \cup \{j\}$
            fi
            od
        od ; $Fphase_i := Fphase_i + 1$;
        forall $j \in lo_i$
*   **do** $X := \{x \mid D_i[x] = \frac{1}{2}Fphase_i \land j \notin dsn_i[x] \land j \notin nnn_i[x]\}$;
            send $<X>$ to j **co** send $<X, Fphase_i>$ **co**
        od
    end

R_i^{even} : { $awake_i \land even(Fphase_i) \land Fphase_i > 0 \land \forall j \in hi_i : Q[j,i] \neq \emptyset$ }
    begin forall $j \in hi_i$
        do receive $<X>$ from j;   **co** receive $<X,f>$ **co**
        forall $x \in X$
            do if $D_i[x] \geq \frac{1}{2}Fphase_i + 1$
            then $D_i[x] := \frac{1}{2}Fphase_i + 1$; $dsn_i[x] := dsn_i[x] \cup \{j\}$
            fi
            od
        od ; $Fphase_i := Fphase_i + 1$;   **co** $phase_i := phase_i + 1$ **co**

> **forall** $j \in hi_i$
>
> *   **do** $X := \{x \mid D_i[x] = \frac{1}{2}(Fphase_i + 1) \ \wedge \ j \notin dsn_i[x] \}$;
>
>   send $<X>$ to j **co** send $<X, Fphase_i>$ **co**
>
>   **od** ;
>
> **if** $\neg \exists x$ with $D_i[x] = \frac{1}{2}(Fphase_i + 1)$
>
> **then** $Fphase_i := Fphase_i + 1$;   **co** send $<\emptyset, Fphase_i>$ **co**
>
>   **forall** $j \in lo_i$ **do** send $<\emptyset>$ to j **od** ; $awake_i := false$
>
> **fi**
>
> **end**

Note that protocol skeleton F is not a refinement of the synchronous or simulated synchronous protocol skeleton because in R_i^{odd} messages of phase $phase_i$ are received while other messages of phase $phase_i$ are sent afterwards in the same operation, whereas in operation R_i^{SS2} all messages of one phase are sent "simultaneously", and messages of that same phase can only be received in a subsequent R_i^{SS2} operation.

Lemma 3.1.20 *Using protocol skeleton F, the following assertions hold for all links (i, j), all nodes x with $x \neq i$, and all integers $k \geq 0$:*

(1) $Fphase_i > 0 \ \Rightarrow \ hi_i \cup lo_i = \{all\ nodes\ j\ incident\ to\ i\} \ \wedge \ hi_i \cap lo_i = \emptyset$,

(2) $Fphase_i > 0 \ \wedge \ Fphase_j > 0 \ \Rightarrow \ (j \in lo_i \wedge i \in hi_j) \ \vee \ (j \in hi_i \wedge i \in lo_j)$,

(3) $<X, f> \in Q\,[i, j] \ \Rightarrow \ f = 0 \ \vee \ (odd(f) \wedge j \in hi_i) \ \vee \ (even(f) \wedge j \in lo_i)$,

(4) $<X, f>$ tail of $Q\,[i, j] \ \Rightarrow \ Fphase_i = f \ \vee \ Fphase_i = f + 1$,

(5) $<X', f'>$ behind $<X, f> \in Q\,[i, j] \ \Rightarrow \ (f = 0 \ \wedge \ f' = 1) \ \vee \ f' = f + 2$,

(6) $<X, f>$ head of $Q\,[i, j] \ \Rightarrow \ f = Fphase_j \ \vee \ f = Fphase_j + 1$,

(7) $phase_i = \lceil \frac{1}{2} Fphase_i \rceil$,

(8) $<X, f> \in Q\,[i, j] \ \wedge \ x \in X \ \Rightarrow \ d(i, x) = D_i[x] = \lceil \frac{1}{2} f \rceil$,

(9) $j \in dsn_i[x] \ \vee \ j \in nnn_i[x] \ \Rightarrow \ D_j[x] = d(j, x)$,

(10) $\neg \exists <X, f> \in Q\,[i, j]$ with $f = k \ \wedge$

         $(k = 0 \ \vee \ (even(k) \ \wedge \ j \in lo_i) \ \vee \ (odd(k) \ \wedge \ j \in hi_i)) \ \Rightarrow$

            $(\neg awake_i \wedge Fphase_i = 0) \ \vee \ Fphase_i < k \ \vee \ Fphase_j > k$.

Proof. (1), (2), and (3) follow directly from the protocol skeleton.

(4). Note that R_i^{odd} and R_i^{even} can only become enabled alternately. If $Fphase_i$ is increased from f to $f + 2$ and hence to a value with the same parity as f, a new last message is sent and the assertion holds for the new message.

(5). Use assertions (3) and (4).

(6). This follows from protocol skeleton F and assertions (4) and (5).

(7). This is clear from protocol skeleton F.

(8). Although F is not a refinement of protocol skeleton SS, we claim that it is a special case of protocol skeleton $P1$. Messages of $phase_i$ (i.e., about nodes x with $d(i,x) = phase_i$) are sent in F when $phase_i = \frac{1}{2}Fphase_i$ and when $phase_i = \frac{1}{2}(Fphase_i + 1)$. As $phase_i = \lceil \frac{1}{2}Fphase_i \rceil$, messages corresponding to phase $phase_i$ are indeed sent in phase $phase_i$. Furthermore we have to show that the guard of operation P_i^{P1} in protocol skeleton $P1$ is true when $phase_i$ is increased in this protocol skeleton. In operation R_i^{even} $phase_i$ is increased. By assertions (2), (3), (4) and (6) we have that $<X,f>$ is received when $f = Fphase_i$. As the messages of $phase_i$ are those with $f = 2.phase_i$ and $f = 2.phase_i - 1$ they have all been received when all messages on the HI links are received in operation R_i^{even}. Thus we can use theorem 3.1.4.

(9). A node j is added to a set $dsn_i[x]$ or $nnn_i[x]$ only upon receipt of a message $<X,f>$ from j where $x \in X$. With (8) we have the desired result.

(10). Initially $\neg awake_i \wedge Fphase_i = 0$ holds. Operation A_i^F falsifies the premise for $k = 0$ and for the other values of k the clause $Fphase_i < k$ now holds. In general, if $Fphase_i < k$ is falsified for some value of k, then the premise is falsified as well: for odd k in R_i^{even} by sending messages over HI link ends, and for even k in R_i^{odd} by sending messages over LO link ends. If the premise is rendered true by the receipt of a message X, k by j, then afterwards $Fphase_j > k$ holds, which cannot be falsified any more. $\square$

It follows from this lemma that if a message is received, it has the expected $Fphase$ value in its second field, and thus that this field can be deleted from all messages. We now have to show that the guards of the operations cannot introduce deadlock, and thus that there is always a node (with a minimal $Fphase$ number) with some operation enabled.

Lemma 3.1.21 *Using protocol skeleton F, the following assertions hold for all links (i,j):*

  (1) $awake_i \wedge Fphase_i = 0 \wedge Q[j,i] = \emptyset \Rightarrow$
          $\neg awake_j \wedge Fphase_j = 0 \wedge Q[i,j] \neq \emptyset,$
  (2) $awake_i \wedge odd(Fphase_i) \wedge j \in lo_i \wedge Q[j,i] = \emptyset \Rightarrow$
          $awake_j \wedge Fphase_j < Fphase_i,$
  (3) $awake_i \wedge even(Fphase_i) \wedge Fphase_i > 0 \wedge j \in hi_i \wedge Q[j,i] = \emptyset \Rightarrow$
          $awake_j \wedge Fphase_j < Fphase_i.$

Proof. (1) follows from lemma 3.1.20(10).

Except for the clause $awake_j$ in the conclusion, (2) and (3) also follow from lemma 3.1.20(10). Let $Fphase_i$ be odd. Then $awake_i$ implies that there is some node x with $d(i,x) = \frac{1}{2}(Fphase_i + 1)$ and hence also a (possibly different) node x with $d(j,x) = \frac{1}{2}(Fphase_i - 1)$. As $Fphase_j < Fphase_i$ we have $awake_j$. On the other hand, let $Fphase_i$ be even. Then $awake_i$ implies that there is some node x with $d(i, x) = \frac{1}{2}Fphase_i$ and hence also a (possibly different) node x with $d(j, x) = \frac{1}{2}(Fphase_i - 2)$. Hence $awake_j$ holds for $Fphase_j \leq Fphase_i - 2$, and as becoming not awake is only done in even $Fphases$, $awake_j$ also holds for the odd $Fphase_j = Fphase_i - 1$, and thus for $Fphase_j < Fphase_i$. $\qquad\square$

Theorem 3.1.22 *Protocol skeleton F is correct.*

Proof. The partial correctness follows from lemma 3.1.20. Freedom from dead-lock is implied by lemma 3.1.21, as the following discussion shows. A node that is not awake initially can always execute operation A_i^F. If node i is awaiting a mes-sage from some neighbor to execute operation R_i^0, then that neighbor can awaken (lemma 3.1.21(1)). If node i is awaiting a message from node j at a LO link end to execute operation R_i^{odd}, then j is awake and has a lower $Fphase$ number (lemma 3.1.21(2)). Likewise, if node i is awaiting a message from a neighbor at a HI link end for operation R_i^{even}, that neighbor has a lower $Fphase$ number (lemma 3.1.21(3)). Thus there is always a node with a minimal $Fphase$ number and an enabled operation. Finally, in this protocol skeleton also, only a finite number of messages is sent. $\qquad\square$

Although protocol skeleton F is based on the ideas of Friedman for his algorithm, it is by no means the same as the algorithm he stated which is as follows:

Step 0:   Node pairs exchange identities and choose HI and LO.
Step l, l odd: All HI nodes broadcast to their corresponding LO neighbors, as in Gallager's algorithm, new identities learned at **Step** $l - 1$.
Step l, l even: All LO nodes broadcast to their corresponding HI neighbors new identities learned at **Step** $l - 2$.
Termination is as in Gallager's algorithm.

It is immediately clear that this cannot be correct, as only new identities learned in even steps are sent through. Hence information received in LO link ends will never be sent through. Moreover, as the algorithm is stated now, information is still sent twice over a link, as executing the algorithm on a cycle of length 3 shows.

3.2 Minimum-hop Distances in a Dynamic Network

In a dynamic network, links can go down and come up, as can the nodes themselves. Hence the minimum-hop distance between two nodes can change in time. We have specified what is meant by "going down" and "coming up" in section 1.2.1.3. We recall that we have the same network assumptions for a dynamic network as for a static network, and that the possible loss of messages when a link goes down is provided for in the send procedure and the operation D_{ij} (see chapter 1). Thus we do not add any error operations, but only the operations for coming up (U_{ij}) and going down (D_{ij}) for every (possible) link (i, j).

In section 3.2.1 we discuss several problems one encounters in algorithm design for dynamic networks. We then give the algorithm of Tajibnapis [Taj77] for comparison in section 3.2.2, and in section 3.2.3 we give a complete formulation and correctness proof of the algorithm of Chu [Chu78].

3.2.1 Comparison with the static case

In protocol skeleton *MH* and all refinements thereof that we have seen for computing minimum-hop distances in the static case, the partial correctness relies heavily on the fact that the $D_i[x]$ are decreasing and approximate $d(i, x)$ from above (lemma 3.1.1). A consequence of this is lemma 3.1.2, which states that a finite entry in $D_i[x]$ reflects the existence of a path from x to i. As the minimum-hop distance of two nodes can increase if a link goes down, the assertion $D_i[x] \geq d(i, x)$ cannot be an invariant any more. In fact, in all algorithms for dynamic networks that we have seen in the literature, it is the case that a node sets $D_i[x]$ to ∞ as soon as it receives information that this assertion might not hold any more.

There are basically two extremes that can be pursued in adapting static algorithms for use in a dynamic network, both with their own advantages and disadvantages. One extreme is to process all new information as it comes in, discarding the old information, and sending it on immediately. Simple though this might seem, it leads to inconsistent information between network nodes, due to the asynchronicity of the network. In the case of minimum-hop routing, it is easy to construct examples such that after some network changes, node i has node j as its downstream neighbor for routing towards x, while node j has node i as its downstream neighbor for x. The problem of avoiding loops by a dynamic network algorithm has received much attention in the literature. A so-called *loop-free* update algorithm is an algorithm where at all times the routing information of all nodes does not contain a loop. The update algorithm of Tajibnapis [Taj77] is an example of an algorithm where during an update, the routing information can contain loops. The algorithm proposed by Chu [Chu78], called the predecessor algorithm by Schwartz [Sch80], is an adaptation of it which avoids some loops, namely those of length 2. Like the algorithm of Tajibnapis, the algorithm of Chu is direct and applicable. As no analysis of the algorithm has appeared after Chu's report and no correctness proof is available, a main aim of section 3.2 will be to provide a correct specification and a correctness proof of this algorithm. On the other hand, even for algorithms which retain loop-freedom during updates, it is always possible to devise a sequence of topological changes which causes messages to loop while the update algorithm is trying to catch up. Thus one should not attach too much importance to the property of loop-freedom.

The other extreme is to first discard all old information in the whole network, reset all nodes to a fresh initial state, and start the static algorithm anew. Clearly this makes routing in the whole network impossible for some time, even in those parts of the network that are not affected by the changes. However, in combination with a minimum-hop algorithm such as that of Gallager, routing is loop free. Of course, any algorithm that defers all routing until lemma 3.1.2 holds again is loop free. Resetting all nodes before restarting could be done by a resynch(ronization) algorithm such as Finn's [Fin79], but usually deferring all routing until the whole network is reset and all routing tables refilled is too slow and too high a price to pay. Therefore attempts have been made to find more economic techniques while retaining loop-freedom.

One approach, suitable for algorithms where updates are performed independently for all destinations, is to limit the resetting of the network and to defer the routing for the affected destinations only. The algorithm of Merlin and Segall [MS79] makes use of this idea. Another approach is to economize on complete resynchronization and only resynchronize partially, by not demanding that all nodes are reset before restarting the minimum-hop algorithm, but only that the neighbors of the node that restarts are. This is done in the fail-safe version of Gallager's algorithm proposed by Toueg [Tou80]. Due to the very special order in which routing tables are filled in this algorithm, it is known during the execution of the algorithm which information is new and which is old.

A basic problem with running different versions of the same algorithm in an asynchronous environment is keeping them apart. One solution, which is usually not chosen, is to defer restarting a new version of the algorithm until the previous one has terminated. A reset algorithm by Afek *et al.* [AAG87] could be used to force termination of the minimum-hop algorithm together with resetting the subnetwork where the minimum-hop algorithm was still in progress. A complete version of this reset algorithm was analyzed and proven correct in [DS88]. The usual solution is to number the different executions ("waves") of the algorithm in some way; see for example Finn [Fin79]. Toueg [Tou80], in his adaptation of Gallager's algorithm, employs logical clocks [Lam78] for it. Both numbering strategies use numbers which are not bounded. Note that algorithms (such as an extension of the Merlin–Segall algorithm, version C in [Seg81]) which rely on Finn's [Fin79] idea of sending (bounded) differences of version numbers are probably not correct. Soloway and Humblett [SH86] showed that this algorithm of Finn is not correct, as it can generate an infinite number of restarts after all topological changes have ceased. However, Soloway and Humblett introduced a new algorithm that does use bounded sequence numbers, based on Gallager's minimum-hop algorithm. As there is an essential difference in the assumptions about the communication in the network, we do not yet know whether this algorithm works in our model as well.

Gafni [Gaf87] discusses a general topology-update scheme based on an algorithm proposed by Spinelli where the topology updated consists of minimum-hop paths (not only distances). The algorithm of Spinelli is of unbounded complexity, which is remedied by Gafni.

Finally, Jaffe and Moss [JM80] presented an algorithm based upon both the algorithm of Merlin and Segall and the algorithm of Tajibnapis, that is still loop free. They observed that the problem of looping only occurs when distances increase. Thus they use the algorithm of Tajibnapis for the case of distance decreases, and the algorithm of Merlin and Segall for the case of distance increases. The algorithm was recently analyzed in detail and proved correct by van Haaften [vH90].

In the sequel we give a general introduction to the algorithm of Tajibnapis, together with the protocol skeleton and the most important invariants for comparison with protocol skeleton $M1$ (section 3.1.1.2). We then proceed with a detailed presentation of the algorithm of Chu. The latter is an extension of the algorithm of Tajibnapis and is proven correct in sections 3.2.3.2 and 3.2.3.3.

3.2.2 The algorithm of Tajibnapis

In protocol skeleton $M1$, if a message $<x, l>$ is received by node i from node j, $D_i[x]$ is recomputed as the minimum of the old value of $D_i[x]$ and $l + 1$. This is due to the fact that we know that the estimate l of $D_j[x]$ is decreasing. In the case that links can go down, however, l might be larger than the previous estimate which i received from j. In this case i cannot recompute a new distance estimate, unless it has stored the latest estimates from its other neighbors to use for the computation also. Hence in the algorithm of Tajibnapis nodes keep track of which distance information was received from which neighbor. Nodes maintain a table $Dtab$, in which $Dtab_i[x, j]$ contains, for every destination $x \neq i$ and every (current) neighbor j of i, the most recent distance information it received from j. Since the set of neighbors of a node i is not fixed any more, this set is maintained in $nbrs_i$.

The algorithm of Tajibnapis contains one other feature, which requires another assumption. It uses that the total number of nodes in the network or, at least, an upper bound of this number is known beforehand.

Assumption 3.2.1 *All nodes in the network know an upper bound of the total number of nodes in the network. We will denote this known number by N.*

The reason why this number is needed is that in the case that the network becomes disconnected, the distances between nodes become infinity. As the algorithm tends to increase the distance estimates with one hop at a time, we need a way to "jump to the conclusion" that the distance is infinity (because the maximum distance less than ∞ has been considered) to prevent that the protocol will never terminate. The underlying observation is that if the total number of nodes is bounded by N, the largest possible finite distance between nodes is bounded by $N - 1$.

We use the symbol ∞ as well as the symbol N for infinite distances. This is to reflect the difference between "throw all information away", e.g. delete column j from the array $Dtab_i$, and "set the value to N", e.g. as initialization for an added column j of the array $Dtab_i$. It depends on the actual implementation whether some variables have to be maintained or whether their value can be deduced from other variables. For example, if obsolete columns of the array $Dtab_i$ are actually thrown away, $nbrs_i$ corresponds to the columns actually present in $Dtab_i$. On the other hand, if the entire column is set to the value N, $j \in nbrs_i$ if and only if $Dtab_i[j, j] = 0$.

Apart from the operations U_{ij} and D_{ij} from section 1.2.1.3, which model link (i, j) coming up or going down, respectively, we add the following extra operations:

RU_i^T : node i receives the message $<up>$, and

RD_i^T : node i receives the message $<down>$.

$<up>$ and $<down>$ will be referred to as *control messages*, all other messages as *non-control messages*. Operation "awaken" A_i^{M1} of section 3.1.1.2 is divided over all links and incorporated in the RU_i^T for each link. Part of the work done in RU_i^T corresponds to what would be done in operation R_i^T if the message received from j were $<j, 0>$. In fact, operations RU_i^T and RD_i^T could be incorporated in R_i^T if $<up>$ is coded as $<j, 0>$ and $<down>$ as $<j, \infty>$, and the necessary code is added for the extra work to be done in the special cases. We feel that this formulation would obscure the special status of these messages. The algorithm of Tajibnapis is specified in the following protocol skeleton.

Protocol skeleton T:

Initially $\forall\, i$: $\quad nbrs_i = \emptyset$, $D_i[i] = 0$,

$\qquad\qquad \forall\, j \neq i$: $\quad linkstate(i, j) = \text{down}$, $Q[i, j] = \emptyset$, $D_i[j] = N$,

$\qquad\qquad\qquad\qquad dsn_i[j] = \text{none}$, $\forall\, x \neq i$: $Dtab_i[x, j] = \infty$.

U_{ij} and D_{ij} from section 1.2.1.3,

RU_i^T : { $\exists j$: $< up >$ head of $Q\,[j,i]$ }

    begin receive $< up >$ from j ; add j to $nbrs_i$; $Dtab_i[j,j] := 0$; $D_i[j] := 1$;

        $dsn_i[j] := j$; **forall** $x \in nbrs_i$ with $x \neq j$ **do** send $<j,1>$ to x **od** ;

        if $|\,nbrs_i\,| = 1$

        then forall x with $x \neq i \,\wedge\, x \neq j$ **do** $D_i[x] := N$; $dsn_i[x] := j$ **od**

        fi ;

        forall x with $x \neq i \,\wedge\, x \neq j$

        do $Dtab_i[x,j] := N$; send $<x, D_i[x]>$ to j **od**

    end

RD_i^T : { $\exists j$: $< down >$ head of $Q\,[j,i]$ }

    begin receive $< down >$ from j ; delete j from $nbrs_i$;

        forall x with $x \neq i$

        do $Dtab_i[x,j] := \infty$;

                if $nbrs_i \neq \emptyset \,\wedge\, dsn_i[x] = j$

                then $olddist := D_i[x]$; choose $ndsn \in nbrs_i$ such that

                        $Dtab_i[x, ndsn] = \min_{a \,\in\, nbrs_i}\{Dtab_i[x,a]\}$;

                    $dsn_i[x] := ndsn$; $D_i[x] := \min\,\{N, 1 + Dtab_i[x, ndsn]\}$;

                    if $olddist \neq D_i[x]$

                    then forall $a \in nbrs_i$ **do** send $<x, D_i[x]>$ to a **od**

                    fi

                elif $nbrs_i = \emptyset$ **then** $D_i[x] := N$; $dsn_i[x] :=$ none

                fi

        od

    end

R_i^T : { $\exists j$: non-control message head of $Q\,[j,i]$ }

    begin receive $<x, l>$ from j ;

        if $x \neq i \,\wedge\, j \in nbrs_i$

        then $Dtab_i[x,j] := l$;

            if $dsn_i[x] = j \,\vee\, l + 1 < D_i[x]$

            then $olddist := D_i[x]$; choose $ndsn \in nbrs_i$ such that

                    $Dtab_i[x, ndsn] = \min_{a \,\in\, nbrs_i}\{Dtab_i[x,a]\}$;

                $dsn_i[x] := ndsn$; $D_i[x] := \min\,\{N, 1 + Dtab_i[x, ndsn]\}$;

                if $D_i[x] \neq olddist$

                then forall $a \in nbrs_i$ **do** send $<x, D_i[x]>$ to a **od**

                fi

            fi

        fi

    end

In the sequel we need to state assertions about the relative positions of control messages in the message queues. There the meaning of the phrase "as last control message" is "the last of the control messages in the queue, but not necessarily the last message of the queue", and the meaning of the phrase "after any control message" is "after the last control message, if there is any".

We now state the basic invariants as proved by Lamport [Lam82] that lead to the partial correctness of this algorithm, for comparison with lemma 3.1.6 and as a precursor of the invariants for the algorithm of Chu.

Theorem 3.2.1 *Using protocol skeleton T, the following assertions hold invariantly for all i, j, and x with $i \neq j$, $x \neq i$, and $x \neq j$:*

(1) $linkstate(i, j) = down \Rightarrow <down> \in Q[j, i]$ *as last control message* $\vee$
$(Dtab_i[x, j] = \infty \wedge Dtab_i[j, j] = \infty)$,

(2) $linkstate(i, j) = up \Rightarrow <up> \in Q[j, i]$ *as last control message* $\vee$
$(Dtab_i[j, j] = 0 \wedge (Dtab_i[x, j] = D_j[x] \vee$
$<x, D_j[x]> \in Q[j, i]$ *after any control message* $))$.

3.2.3 The algorithm of Chu

The problem with the algorithm of Tajibnapis is that, if a node i receives information from a neighbor j that j is l hops away from x, then i has no way of knowing whether this route goes through i itself. This leads to a slow propagation of distance updates in case a link has gone down. The algorithm due to Chu [Chu78] maintains this extra information, thereby maintaining a sink tree for every destination. A *sink tree* for a certain destination is the (directed) tree with as links the links over which messages are routed towards the destination, and as root (or sink) the destination. In the previous algorithms only the outgoing link of the sink tree for a certain destination in a node was maintained, while now the incoming links in a node are maintained also.

3.2.3.1 The algorithm.
In protocol skeleton T $dsn_i[x]$ is maintained, the downstream neighbor to which i should route messages for x. Now we say that j is *upstream* from i for destination x if i is downstream from j for destination x. If i's downstream link for x happens to go down, it is clear that we should not choose an upstream neighbor for x as i's new downstream neighbor, but some other neighbor. If there is no non-upstream neighbor, i sends a message $<x, N, 1>$ upstream saying "help, my route to destination x is blocked" and waits until a route to x is found via another node.

Node i maintains its sink tree information in a table T_i, where $T_i[x, j] = d$ or u

means: neighbor j is downstream or upstream for destination x, respectively, and $T_i[x,j] = n$ means: neighbor j is neither downstream nor upstream for x.

The messages that are sent contain a field to convey this extra information: node i sends messages $<x, D_i[x], 1>$ to j if $T_i[x,j] = d$ (i.e., if j is downstream neighbor) and messages $<x, D_i[x], 0>$ to j if $T_i[x,j] \neq d$. Messages also have to be sent in a situation where algorithm T did not do so. Namely, in the case that the minimum-hop distance to a node x stays the same but the downstream neighbor of a node is changed, the node has to inform the old and new downstream neighbor of this change.

We now give the text of the algorithm of Chu. Aside from denoting it in our own way for comparison to the earlier protocol skeletons, we have had to make some slight changes in order to prove the algorithm correct. These changes are marked with an asterisk ($*$) at the beginning of a line. The assumptions concerning the mode of communication are still the same, hence we add operations D_{ij} and U_{ij} for all i and $j \neq i$ from chapter 1.

Protocol skeleton C:

Initially $\forall\, i$: $\ nbrs_i = \emptyset$, $D_i[i] = 0$,
$\qquad\qquad \forall\, j \neq i$: $\quad linkstate(i,j) = $ down, $Q[i,j] = \emptyset$, $D_i[j] = N$,
$\qquad\qquad\qquad \forall\, x \neq i$: $Dtab_i[x,j] = \infty$, $T_i[x,j] = n$.

RU_i^C : $\{\ \exists j:\ <up>$ head of $Q[j,i]\ \}$
$\qquad$ **begin** receive $<up>$ from j; add j to $nbrs_i$;
$\quad *\qquad$ **if** $|nbrs_i| > 1$
$\qquad\qquad$ **then** let $odsn$ be such that $T_i[j, odsn] = d$; $T_i[j, odsn] := n$
$\qquad\qquad$ **fi**; $T_i[j,j] := d$; $Dtab_i[j,j] := 0$; $D_i[j] := 1$;
$\qquad\qquad$ **forall** $x \in nbrs_i$ with $x \neq j$ **do** send $<j, 1, 0>$ to x **od**;
$\qquad\qquad$ **forall** x with $x \neq i \,\wedge\, x \neq j$
$\qquad\qquad$ **do** $\quad Dtab_i[x,j] := N$;
$\quad *\qquad\qquad$ **if** $|nbrs_i| \neq 1$ **then** $T_i[x,j] := n$; send $<x, D_i[x], 0>$ to j
$\quad *\qquad\qquad$ **else** $T_i[x,j] := d$; $D_i[x] := N$; send $<x, D_i[x], 1>$ to j
$\qquad\qquad\qquad$ **fi**
$\qquad\qquad$ **od**
$\qquad$ **end**

R_i^C : $\{\ \exists j:$ non-control message head of $Q[j,i]\ \}$
$\qquad$ **begin** receive $<x, l, t>$ from j;
$\quad *\qquad$ **if** $x \neq i \,\wedge\, j \in nbrs_i$
$\qquad\qquad$ **then** $olddist := D_i[x]$; let $odsn$ be such that $T_i[x, odsn] = d$;

if $t = 1$
then $Dtab_i[x,j] := l$; $T_i[x,j] := u$;
       if $olddist < N \land odsn = j$
       then if $\exists \, a \in nbrs_i$ with $T_i[x,a] \neq u$
           then choose $ndsn \in nbrs_i$ such that $Dtab_i[x,ndsn] =$
                $\min_{a \in nbrs_i} \{Dtab_i[x,a] \,|\, T_i[x,a] \neq u\}$;
            $T_i[x,ndsn] := d$;
            $D_i[x] := \min\{N, 1 + Dtab_i[x,ndsn]\}$
          elif $|nbrs_i| > 1$
          then choose $ndsn \in nbrs_i$ with $ndsn \neq j$; $D_i[x] := N$;
            $T_i[x,ndsn] := d$; $Dtab_i[x,ndsn] := N$;
            forall $a \in nbrs_i$ with $a \neq ndsn$
            do $Dtab_i[x,a] := N$; $T_i[x,a] := n$ **od**
         else $Dtab_i[x,j] := N$; $T_i[x,j] := d$;
            $D_i[x] := N$; $ndsn := j$
         fi; send $<x, D_i[x], 1>$ to $ndsn$;
         if $D_i[x] \neq olddist$
         then forall $a \in nbrs_i$ with $a \neq ndsn$
            do send $<x, D_i[x], 0>$ to a **od**
         elif $j \neq ndsn$ **then** send $<x, D_i[x], 0>$ to j
         fi
        elif $odsn = j$ **then** $T_i[x,j] := d$; $Dtab_i[x,j] := N$ (*)
       fi
      else $Dtab_i[x,j] := l$; $T_i[x,j] := n$;   **co** $t \neq 1$ **co**
         choose $ndsn \in nbrs_i$ such that $Dtab_i[x,ndsn] =$
          $\min_{a \in nbrs_i} \{Dtab_i[x,a] \,|\, T_i[x,a] \neq u\}$;
         if $Dtab_i[x,ndsn] = Dtab_i[x,odsn]$ **then** $ndsn := odsn$ **fi**;   (*)
         $T_i[x,ndsn] := d$; $D_i[x] := \min\{N, 1 + Dtab_i[x,ndsn]\}$;
         if $odsn \neq ndsn$
         then $T_i[x,odsn] := n$; send $<x, D_i[x], 1>$ to $ndsn$
         fi;
         if $D_i[x] \neq olddist$
         then forall $a \in nbrs_i$ with $a \neq ndsn$
           do send $<x, D_i[x], 0>$ to a **od**
         elif $odsn \neq ndsn$ **then** send $<x, D_i[x], 0>$ to $odsn$
         fi

      fi

  fi
end

RD_i^C : { $\exists j$: $<down>$ head of $Q\,[j,i]$ }

  begin receive $<down>$ from j ; delete j from $nbrs_i$;

    forall x with $x \neq i$

    do $Dtab_i[x,j] := \infty$;

      if $nbrs_i \neq \emptyset \ \wedge \ T_i[x,j] = d$

      then $olddist := D_i[x]$;

        if $\exists a \in nbrs_i$ with $T_i[x,a] \neq u$

        then choose $ndsn \in nbrs_i$ such that $Dtab_i[x,ndsn] =$

            $\min_{a \in nbrs_i} \{Dtab_i[x,a] \,|\, T_i[x,a] \neq u\}$;

          $T_i[x,ndsn] := d$;

          $D_i[x] := \min \{N, 1 + Dtab_i[x,ndsn]\}$

        else choose $ndsn \in nbrs_i$; $Dtab_i[x,ndsn] := N$;

          $T_i[x,ndsn] := d$; $D_i[x] := N$;

          forall $a \in nbrs_i$ with $a \neq ndsn$

          do $Dtab_i[x,a] := N$; $T_i[x,a] := n$ **od**

        fi ; send $<x, D_i[x], 1>$ to $ndsn$;

        if $olddist \neq D_i[x]$

        then forall $a \in nbrs_i$ with $a \neq ndsn$

          do send $<x, D_i[x], 0>$ to a **od**

        fi

 *   **elif** $nbrs_i = \emptyset$ **then** $D_i[x] := N$

      fi ; $T_i[x,j] := n$

    od

  end

U_{ij} and D_{ij} from section 1.2.1.3.

3.2.3.2 *Partial correctness.* For the proof of the partial correctness of protocol skeleton C we begin with some technical lemmas.

Lemma 3.2.2 *Using protocol skeleton C, the following assertions hold invariantly for all i and j with $i \neq j$:*

 (1) $linkstate(i,j) = up \ \Leftrightarrow \ j \in nbrs_i \vee <up> \in Q\,[j,i]$ *as last control message,*

 (2) $linkstate(i,j) = down \ \Leftrightarrow$

    $j \notin nbrs_i \vee <down> \in Q\,[j,i]$ *as last control message.*

Proof. Obvious from operations U_{ij} , D_{ij} , RU_i^C , and RD_i^C . $\qquad\qquad\square$

Lemma 3.2.3 *Using protocol skeleton C, the following assertions hold invariantly for all i, j, and x with $j \neq i$ and $x \neq i$:*

(1) $T_i[x, j] = d \ \lor \ T_i[x, j] = u \ \Rightarrow \ j \in nbrs_i$,

(2) $\exists! j$ with $T_i[x, j] = u \ \Leftrightarrow \ nbrs_i \neq \emptyset$,

(3) $j \in nbrs_i \ \Leftrightarrow \ Dtab_i[j, j] = 0$,

(4) $T_i[x, j] = d \ \Rightarrow \ D_i[x] = \min \{N, 1 + Dtab_i[x, j]\} \ \land$
$$Dtab_i[x, j] = \min_{a \in nbrs_i}\{Dtab_i[x, a] \mid T_i[x, a] \neq u\},$$

(5) $D_i[i] = 0 \ \land \ D_i[x] > 0$,

(6) $<x, l, t> \in Q[j, i] \ \Rightarrow \ l > 0 \ \land \ x \neq j$,

(7) $x \neq j \ \Rightarrow \ Dtab_i[x, j] > 0$.

Proof. (1) and (2) are obvious from operations RU_i^C, RD_i^C, and R_i^C.
(3). Use assertion (6) with operation R_i^C.
(4). Obvious from operations RU_i^C, RD_i^C, and R_i^C.
(5). The variable $D_i[i] = 0$ initially and is never changed. If $nbrs_i = \emptyset$ we have $D_i[x] = N$, otherwise assertion (4) can be used together with assertion (7) to prove that $D_i[x] > 0$.
(6). As $<x, l, t> \in Q[j, i]$ is only rendered true when j sends a message to i, and j only sends messages with $x \neq j$ and $l = D_j[x]$, we have $l > 0$ by assertion (5).
(7). For $x \neq j$, $Dtab_i[x, j]$ entries are only set to ∞, N, or to some value l from a received message $<x, l, t>$. By assertion (6) we always have $l > 0$. $\square$

Lemma 3.2.4 *Using protocol skeleton C, the following assertion holds invariantly for all i, j, and x with $i \neq j$:*

$linkstate(i, j) = down \ \lor$ *(1)*

$<up> \in Q[i, j]$ *as last control message* $\lor$ *(2)*

$(<x, l, t> \in Q[j, i] \ \Rightarrow$ *(3)*

     the last message $<a, b, c> \in Q[j, i]$ *with* $a = x$ *has* $(b = D_j[x] \ \land$
     $(c = 1 \ \Leftrightarrow \ T_j[x, i] = d) \land \ <a, b, c> \in Q[j, i]$ *after any control message* $))$.   *(4)*

Proof. Initially (1) holds. If (1) holds, it can be falsified by operation U_{ij}, but then (2) will hold. If (2) holds, it can be falsified by D_{ij}, but then (1) will hold. (2) can also be falsified by operation RU_j^C, but then for those x for which (3) is rendered true, (4) is rendered true for the same message. If (4) holds and is falsified by operation R_i^C, then (3) is also falsified. If (4) holds and is falsified because j changes $D_j[x]$ or $T_j[x, i]$, we have the following cases.
Case 1: $i \notin nbrs_j$. Then (1) or (2) holds (lemma 3.2.2).
Case 2: $i \in nbrs_j$. Then a message is sent such that (4) holds. If (4) is falsified because a control message is placed in $Q[j, i]$, then (1) or (2) now holds. If neither (1), (2) nor (3) holds for some x and a message is sent such that (3) is rendered true, this message is such that (4) holds for this message.
Thus the assertion holds invariantly. $\square$

Lemma 3.2.5 *Using protocol skeleton C, the following assertion holds invariantly for all i, j, and x with $i \neq j$ and $i \neq x$:*

$linkstate(i,j) = down \Rightarrow (Dtab_i[x,j] = \infty \wedge$ *no control message in $Q[j,i]$)* $\vee$
$< down > \in Q[j,i]$ *as last control message.*

Proof. We consider the effect of the relevant operations on the assertion.
– Operation D_{ij} validates the premise and places a $< down >$ in $Q[j,i]$ as the last control message.
– Operation U_{ij} falsifies the premise.
– Operation RU_i^C can only occur if $< down >$ is in $Q[j,i]$ as the last control message, if the premise is true.
– If RD_i^C receives the last $< down >$ left in $Q[j,i]$, there will be no control message left and $Dtab_i[x,j]$ is set to ∞.
Other operations do not influence the variables involved. $\square$

Lemma 3.2.6 *Using protocol skeleton C, the following assertion holds invariantly for all i, j, and x with $i \neq j$, $i \neq x$ and $j \neq x$:*

$linkstate(i,j) = up \Rightarrow$
$\qquad < up > \in Q[i,j]$ as last control message $\vee$ $\qquad\qquad\qquad$ (1)
$\qquad < x, D_j[x], t > \in Q[j,i]$ after any control message with
$\qquad\qquad (t = 1 \Leftrightarrow T_j[x,i] = d) \vee$ $\qquad\qquad\qquad\qquad\qquad\qquad$ (2)
$\qquad (Dtab_i[x,j] = N \wedge T_j[x,i] = d \wedge$ no control message in $Q[j,i] \wedge$
$\qquad\qquad < x, N, t > \in Q[i,j]$ after any control message $) \vee$ $\qquad$ (3)
$\qquad (Dtab_i[x,j] = D_j[x] \wedge$ no control message in $Q[j,i] \wedge$
$\qquad\qquad (T_i[x,j] = u \Rightarrow T_j[x,i] = d)).$ $\qquad\qquad\qquad\qquad\qquad$ (4)

Proof. We consider the effect of the relevant operations on the assertion.
– Operation D_{ij} falsifies the premise.
– Operation U_{ij} validates both the premise and (1).
– Operation RU_j^C can only be performed if (1) held. Afterwards (1) can still hold, or otherwise i is added to $nbrs_j$ and $< x, D_j[x], t >$ is sent to i. As $Q[j,i]$ is a queue, the message is placed after any control message. Hence (2) holds now.
– Operation RU_i^C. If (1) holds, it will still hold afterwards. If (2) holds, it will still hold afterwards, since the $< up >$ received occurred before the message under consideration. Neither (3) nor (4) could hold beforehand.
– Operation RD_j^C. Either the premise is not true or (1) continues to hold.
– Operation RD_i^C. Neither (3) nor (4) could hold beforehand. (1) and (2) continue to hold.
– Operation R_i^C with a message from j. If (1) held, it still holds. If (2) held, either

it still holds, or the message received is $<x, D_j[x], t>$ with $t = 1 \Leftrightarrow T_j[x, i] = d$. In the latter case we know that there can be no control message in $Q[j, i]$. R_i^C sets $Dtab_i[x, j] = D_j[x]$ and $T_i[x, j] = u \Leftrightarrow T_j[x, i] = d$, so (4) holds now, except in the very special case that $t = 1$ (hence $T_j[x, i] = d$), $olddist < N$, $odsn = j$, and $\forall a \in nbrs_i$ it is the case that $T_i[x, a] = u$, in which case $Dtab_i[x, j]$ is set to N, $T_i[x, j]$ to n or d, and $D_i[x]$ to N, and $<x, N, t>$ is sent to j. Hence (3) holds now. The other exception is the case that $D_j[x] < N$, $t = 1$, $olddist = N$, and $odsn = j$, where no messages are sent but $Dtab_i[x, j]$ is reset to N and $T_i[x, j]$ to d. (Otherwise there would be no downstream neighbor left for x.) For this case, we assume not only that lemma 3.2.6 held before operation R_i^C, but also that lemma 3.2.6 held with i and j interchanged. Let the assertions (1) to (4) with i and j interchanged be assertions (1') to (4'), respectively. We then know that (1') cannot hold, as $Q[j, i]$ contains no control messages. As $olddist = N$, $D_i[x] = N$, and $odsn = j$, we have $T_i[x, j] = d$. The message received was $< x, D_j[x], 1 >$ with $D_j[x] < N$ and $T_j[x, i] = d$, hence $Dtab_j[x, i] < N$. Thus neither (3') nor (4') can hold, and (2') must hold. Thus $<x, N, t> \in Q[i, j]$. Since operation R_i^C cannot falsify this, (3) holds now. If (3) or (4) held, we know by lemma 3.2.4 that (2) holds also.

– Operation R_i^C with a message from $k \neq j$. (1), (2), and (3) continue to hold. If (4) held, it either continues to hold or $Dtab_i[x, j]$ can be set to N and $T_i[x, j]$ to n or d in the case that $T_i[x, a] = u$ $\forall a \in nbrs_i$, $olddist < N$ and $odsn = k$. Hence we can conclude $T_j[x, i] = d$ and $<x, N, t>$ is sent to j. Thus (3) holds now.

– Operation R_j^C with a message from i. (1) continues to hold. If (2) holds, and $D_j[x]$ and/or $T_j[x, i]$ change, a new message is sent which reflects these changes. Thus (2) now holds for this new message. If (3) holds, we have the following two cases.

Case 1: only $T_j[x, i]$ changes, then a message to reflect this change is sent to i and (2) holds now.

Case 2: the message $<x, N, t>$ is received. If (4) did not hold, we had $D_j[x] < N$ and $T_j[x, i] = d$. $Dtab_i[x, j]$ is set to N. Thus either $D_j[x]$ or $T_j[x, i]$ changes so a message is sent to i to this effect and (2) now holds.

If (4) holds, it continues to hold unless $D_j[x]$ or $T_j[x, i]$ is changed. In this case a message is sent to i so (2) holds.

– Operation R_j^C with a message from $k \neq i$. (1) continues to hold. (2) continues to hold unless $D_j[x]$ or $T_j[x, i]$ is changed, in which case (2) will hold for the new message sent. In case (3) holds, only $T_j[x, i]$ could be changed, but then a message will be sent such that (2) holds. If (4) holds, it will continue to hold unless (2) holds with changed $D_j[x]$ or $T_j[x, i]$. $\square$

Lemma 3.2.7 *Using protocol skeleton C, the following assertion holds invariantly for all i and j with $i \neq j$:*

$linkstate(i,j) = up \Rightarrow \ <up> \in Q[j,i]$ as last control message $\vee$
$\qquad (Dtab_i[j,j] = 0 \wedge T_i[j,j] = d \wedge D_i[j] = 1 \wedge$ no control message in $Q[j,i]$).

Proof. If the last $<up>$ is received in RU_i^C, the variables specified are set to the right values. By lemma 3.2.3(7) we have that $Dtab_i[j,k] > 0$ for $k \neq j$, hence $T_i[j,j]$ does not change. Node j does not send any message about destination j (lemma 3.2.3(6)), hence $Dtab_i[j,j]$ is not changed. As $T_i[j,j] \neq u$, $Dtab_i[j,j]$ cannot be set to N either. $\qquad\square$

Lemma 3.2.8 *Using protocol skeleton C, the following assertion holds for all i, j, and x with $i \neq j$ and $i \neq x$:*

$\qquad T_i[x,j] = u \ \wedge \ Q[i,j] = \emptyset \ \wedge \ Q[j,i] = \emptyset \ \Rightarrow \ Dtab_i[x,j] = \min\{N, D_i[x]+1\}.$

Proof. Use lemma 3.2.3(1), lemma 3.2.2, lemma 3.2.6 and lemma 3.2.3(4). $\qquad\square$

Lemma 3.2.9 *Using protocol skeleton C, TERM implies*
$\forall i,j$ with $i \neq j : (\ linkstate(i,j) = up \ \Leftrightarrow \ j \in nbrs_i) \ \wedge$
$\qquad\qquad (j \in nbrs_i \ \Rightarrow \ \forall x \neq i : Dtab_i[x,j] = D_j[x]) \ \wedge$
$\qquad\qquad (j \notin nbrs_i \ \Rightarrow \ \forall x \neq i : Dtab_i[x,j] = \infty) \ \wedge$
$\qquad\qquad \forall x \neq i : \ D_i[x] = \min\{N, 1 + \min_{\forall j \neq i}\{Dtab_i[x,j]\}\}.$

Proof. TERM is equivalent to all queues being empty. Use lemmas 3.2.2, 3.2.3(4), 3.2.5, 3.2.6, 3.2.7, and 3.2.8. $\qquad\square$

Theorem 3.2.10 *Using protocol skeleton C, we have*
$TERM \ \Rightarrow \ \forall i,\ x : \ D_i[x] = \min\{N, d(i,x)\}.$

Proof. We prove this by showing that $D_i[x] \leq d(i,x)$ (property (1)) and $D_i[x] \geq \min\{N, d(i,x)\}$ (property (2)).

(1). Let $d(i,x) = \infty$. Then for all possible values of $D_i[x]$ we have $D_i[x] \leq d(i,x)$. Let $d(i,x)$ have some finite value k. Then $k = 0$ implies $i = x$ and $D_i[x] = 0$. For $k > 0$ there is some path $x = x_0, x_1, ..., x_k = i$ from x to i of length k. Thus all links (x_j, x_{j-1}) for $1 \leq j \leq k$ are up and $x_{j-1} \in nbrs_{x_j}$. Thus $Dtab_{x_j}[x,x_{j-1}] = D_{x_{j-1}}[x]$ and $D_{x_j}[x] \leq \min\{N, 1+D_{x_{j-1}}[x]\}$. Hence $D_i[x] = D_{x_k}[x] \leq D_{x_0}[x]+k = D_x[x] + k = k$. Note that this is not necessarily the path designated by the downstream neighbors.

(2). We use induction over the possible minimum-hop distances k to show that $d(i,j) \geq k \Rightarrow D_i[j] \geq \min\{N,k\}$. For $k = 0$ we have $d(i,j) \geq 0$ and $D_i[j] \geq 0$.

Assume $d(u, v) \geq k + 1$. For all neighbors $a \in nbrs_u$ we have $d(u, a) = 1$ and thus $d(v, a) \geq k$ (by the triangle inequality). Hence $D_a[v] \geq \min\{N, k\}$ by the induction hypothesis. So we have $D_u[v] = \min\{N, 1 + \min_{a \in nbrs_u}\{Dtab_u[v, a]\}\}$ $= \min\{N, 1 + \min_{a \in nbrs_u}\{D_a[v]\}\} \geq \min\{N, k + 1\}$. □

Corollary 3.2.11 *Interpreting N as ∞ in protocol skeleton C, TERM implies $D_i[x] = d(i, x)$ for all i and x.*

Proof. The maximum finite distance between two nodes in the network is bounded by $N - 1$. Hence $d(i, x) \geq N$ implies $d(i, x) = \infty$. □

This completes the proof of the partial correctness of the algorithm of Chu.

3.2.3.3   *Total correctness.* For a proof of the total correctness of protocol skeleton C, we still have to show that if there are no more topological changes, the algorithm can indeed terminate in finite time. However, the notion "time" is not defined in relation with this protocol skeleton. What we prove is that, after all topological changes have ceased, only a finite number of operations can be executed.

Theorem 3.2.12 *Protocol skeleton C cannot deadlock.*

Proof.   If there is a queue which contains a message, then there is always an operation which can receive that message: either RU_i^C, RD_i^C, or R_i^C for $Q[j, i]$, depending on the nature of the message. If all queues are empty, there is termination by definition. □

Thus it remains to show that the algorithm cannot go on generating messages forever, in the case that there are no more topological changes after a certain time. For this purpose we define a function F from the set of system states to the set W of $(N + 1)$-tuples of non-negative integers. The total ordering $<_W$ on W is defined as in section 1.2.2.3, ensuring that the relation is well founded. In order to prove the total correctness, it is sufficient to find a function F which is decreased by every operation of the protocol skeleton if there are no more topological changes, i.e., by all operations except U_{ij} and D_{ij}. We define F for a given system state as follows:

$$F = (cm,\ m(1) + 2d(1),\ \ldots,\ m(N - 1) + 2d(N - 1),\ 2m(N) + d(N)),$$

where

cm = the total number of control messages ($<up>$ or $<down>$) present in all message queues,

and where for each position k, $1 \leq k \leq N$, in the $(N + 1)$-tuple of F, we count messages and entries in distance tables pertaining to a distance of k:

$$m(k) = \sum_x m_x(k),$$

$$d(k) \;=\; \sum_x d_x(k),$$

$m_x(k) \;=\;$ the total number of messages $<y, l, t>$ with $x = y$ and $l = k$
present in all message queues,

$$d_x(k) \;=\; \sum_i \left(1 + |\{j | j \in nbrs_i \wedge D_i[x] = k \wedge Dtab_i[x, j] = Dtab_i[x, dsn_i[x]]\}| \right),$$

$dsn_i[x] \;=\;$ downstream neighbor of i for x : the node dsn with $T_i[x, dsn] = d$.

Lemma 3.2.13 *Using protocol skeleton C, F is strictly decreased by the operations* RU_i^C, RD_i^C, *and* R_i^C *for all i.*

Proof. RU_i^C decreases cm by 1, as does RD_i^C.

Consider operation R_i^C. Let the received message be $<x, l, t>$. cm cannot be changed, nor $m_y(k)$ or $d_y(k)$ with $y \neq x$. Note that R_i^C cannot change the set $nbrs_i$. As it depends on the old and new values of $D_i[x]$ and the old and new downstream neighbor of i for x how F changes, let us define *olddist* as the value of $D_i[x]$ before operation R_i^C, *newdist* as the value of $D_i[x]$ after operation R_i^C, and *odsn* and *ndsn* as the neighbor j of i with $T_i[x, j] = d$ before and after operation R_i^C, respectively. We distinguish the following cases.

Case 1: olddist < newdist. Then $d(olddist)$ decreases, and $d(newdist)$ and $m(newdist)$ increase. Hence F decreases.

Case 2: olddist > newdist. This is only possible if in the received message $<x, l, t>$ $t = 0$ and $l = newdist - 1$. Thus $m(newdist - 1)$ decreases, while $m(newdist)$ and $d(newdist)$ increase.

Case 3: olddist = newdist.

Case 3.1: olddist = newdist < N.

Case 3.1.1: odsn = ndsn. Then $m(newdist)$ is not increased because no new messages are sent. However, $d(newdist)$ could increase, if there is now one more neighbor with minimal distance to x. This can only happen if the received message had $l = newdist - 1$. Hence $m(newdist - 1)$ is decreased and F decreases. If $d(newdist)$ does not change, F decreases because $m(l)$ decreases.

Case 3.1.2: odsn ≠ ndsn. Then $m(newdist)$ is increased by 2. If $d(newdist)$ increases, we have $l = newdist - 1$ as above, and $m(newdist - 1)$ decreases. If $d(newdist)$ does not change, we must have that $Dtab_i[x, ndsn] = Dtab_i[x, odsn]$, as R_i^C can only change one value of $Dtab_i$ (unless $newdist = N$) at the time, hence this case cannot occur. Thus $d(newdist)$ decreases by 1. Hence the value of $2d(newdist) + m(newdist)$ does not change, and as $m(l)$ decreases, so does F.

Case 3.2: olddist = newdist = N.

Case 3.2.1: odsn = ndsn. Thus no new messages are sent. However, $d(newdist)$

could change. If $t = 1$ in the received message, then $d(newdist)$ can only decrease. $d(newdist)$ can increase by 1 if the message received from j was $< x, N, 0 >$ and $T_i[x, j] = u$ before R_i^C. Then $m(newdist)$ decreases by 1 and F is decreased because $2m_x(N) + d_x(N)$ is decreased.

Case 3.2.2: odsn $\neq$ ndsn. If $olddist = N$ and $t = 1$, nothing happens in R_i^C, so $odsn = ndsn$. Hence $t = 0$. If $l < N$, then we would have $newdist < N$, thus $l = N$. So $d(newdist)$ cannot decrease, which implies $Dtab_i[x, odsn]$ remains N. Hence the downstream neighbor is not changed, and we conclude that this case cannot occur.

Thus in all cases, F is strictly decreased. □

Theorem 3.2.14 *If the topological changes cease, then the algorithm of Chu can terminate in finite time.*

This completes the correctness proof of the algorithm of Chu.

4

Connection-management Protocols

Consider a communication network in which processors want to transmit many short messages to each other. The processors are not necessarily connected by a communication channel. Usually this service is provided for by protocols in the transport layer. A protocol can incorporate such a message in a packet and send the packet to the destination processor. As discussed in chapter 1, in the transport layer it is again necessary that communication errors are considered, even though we can assume that the communication over channels is handled correctly by the lower layers. Thus we have to assume that the communication network can lose packets, copy packets (due to necessary retransmissions), delay packets arbitrarily long, and deliver packets in a different order than the order in which they were sent.

We consider the design of some protocols that handle the communication of messages correctly, in the sense that there is no loss or duplication of messages (cf. Belsnes [Bel76]). To specify this more precisely, suppose processor i wants to transmit a message m to processor j. The message m is said to be *lost* if i thinks that j received m while this is not the case, and m is said to be *duplicated* if j receives two or more copies of m from i and thinks that they are different messages.

If a processor i has a message or a sequence of messages to send to j, it sets up a temporary *connection* with j, which is closed as soon as i knows that j received the message(s) (or that j is not in a position to receive them). If only a single message is transmitted during every connection, we talk about *single-message communication*. Note that this does not mean that only a single packet is sent over, as we might very well use a so-called *k-way handshake*, i.e., an exchange of k different packets between two processors. If a sequence of messages is to be sent over during one connection, we talk about *multiple-message communication*. It is assumed that it is not feasible to maintain any information about previous connections. As a consequence, it is easier to prevent loss and duplication within one and the same connection, than to do so between connections. We restrict ourselves first to single-message communication and consider the problem of *connection management*. It is then straightforward to give extensions for multiple-message communication.

Belsnes [Bel76] investigated k-way *handshake protocols* for connection management in a systematic manner. He showed that it is impossible to have a protocol which ensures correct communication under the assumptions stated above, when processors can lose their information about current connections, e.g. because of a crash. He showed also that in the absence of processor failures, there can be circumstances in which reasonable 1-way, 2-way, and 3-way handshakes can lead to loss or duplication. Belsnes [Bel76] proceeded to give (informally specified) 4-way and 5-way handshakes for which he showed informally that they communicate messages correctly.

In this chapter we give a rigorous proof that *any* 1-way, 2-way, or 3-way handshake must be liable to incorrect communication, even in the absence of processor failures. To this end, we introduce a protocol skeleton which abstracts the protocol features that are concerned with connection management. From this protocol skeleton we obtain all protocols which Belsnes considered in his paper [Bel76] by setting certain parameters and prescribing a certain order of operations. The protocol skeleton is a special instance of the class of protocols defined in chapter 2. However, we did not deal with issues of starting and terminating there. In section 4.1 we give a class of k-way handshakes (for any $k \geq 4$) which ensure correct communication in the absence of processor failures. As a result we obtain formal correctness proofs of Belsnes' 4-way and 5-way handshakes. In section 4.2 the connection-management protocols are extended to ensure correct multiple-message communication. Furthermore, we analyze the necessary changes in the model of communication to achieve reliable communication with shorter handshakes.

4.1 k-way Handshakes

We recall from chapter 1 that we use slightly different assumptions about the communication network when we are concerned with the transport layer. As two processors i and j which communicate are not necessarily connected by a direct communication channel, we model the set of routes between i and j as two communication links, but drop the assumption that they behave as FIFO queues. Thus we add the reorder operations E^r_{ij} and E^r_{ji} from section 1.2.1.2 to the protocol skeletons. We assume packets can get lost and that garbled packets are thrown away or "lost" by lower layers. We assume that a packet can be copied, due to a retransmission over a possibly different route. Thus we add the loss and duplication operations E_{ij}^l, E_{ji}^l, E_{ij}^d, and E_{ji}^d (section 1.2.1.2) to all protocol skeletons in this chapter. Hence the message queues $Q[i,j]$ and $Q[j,i]$ in fact have become multisets of packets in the context of this chapter.

The basic k-way protocol skeleton and its invariants will be presented in section 4.1.1. Loss and duplication of messages, as opposed to packets, will be formally defined in section 4.1.2. Since Belsnes' protocols depend critically on the use of error packets, we will deal with them in section 4.1.3. The selection of certain parameters will be discussed in section 4.1.4, resulting in a proof that 4-way handshakes are required to achieve a reliable communication of messages.

4.1.1 The basic protocol skeleton

Careful consideration of the k-way handshakes Belsnes [Bel76] gives for reliable single-message communication leads to the insight that the short packet exchanges basically follow a sliding-window protocol with a window size equal to 1 (see chapter 2, protocol skeleton SW). That is, inside one connection, a processor sends a packet of a certain type (number), and after receipt of a packet of the expected type (number), it sends a packet of the next type (number). Note that the results of chapter 2 for protocol skeleton SW do not carry over directly. Although lemma 2.1.1 and theorems 2.1.2 and 2.1.3 were proved without using the FIFO property of the message queues, it is not known whether the variables ever hold the initial values as specified in chapter 2 simultaneously – and this need not be the case. On the other hand, we need not be concerned now about sequence numbers wrapping around inside one connection, since we only consider k-way handshakes with k small. Our main concern is the identification of connections, to prevent confusion with earlier connections and their packets.

4.1.1.1 The protocol skeleton. A connection between two processors i and j is identified (in accordance with Belsnes) by means of two values which are provided by i and j, respectively. For this purpose, each processor has a function *new value* which produces a new, unique value each time it is called. The value produced by a call to *new value* is different from all previous values and cannot be guessed by any other processor. The connection-management protocols we consider rely heavily on the availability of such a function. (We do not go into the problem of finding such a function here. See e.g. Tomlinson [Tom75].)

We restrict attention to one pair of processors which repeatedly want to communicate. Hence we ignore the control information in the packets pertaining to the processor identities and assume that the packets concerning this one pair of processors are filtered out correctly. For the moment we are not interested in which packet contains the actual message either, and thus restrict our attention to the three control fields used for the connection management per se. For our purpose packets have the following form: $< mci, yci, seq >$, where mci is "my connection identifier" (i.e., the connection identifier used by the sender of the packet), yci is "your connection identifier" (the connection identifier used by the receiver in case of a reply), and seq is the sequence number of the packet within the connection.

Since we restrict our attention to the connections between one pair of processors i and j, we will only add i or j as a subscript to denote the processor to which a variable or operation pertains. The variable mci_i contains the connection identifier of processor i: it contains a value which was provided by the function *new value* when i opened the current connection with j. To represent the special case that i has no current connection with j, we need a special value which we denote by *nil*. We assume that the function *new value* cannot yield this value *nil*. We say that i's connection with j is *open* if $mci_i \neq nil$. We say that i's connection with j is *closed* if $mci_i = nil$. Thus from the viewpoint of i, a connection is the time during which mci_i contains one and the same unique value unequal to *nil*. The function *new value* produces a new unique value ($\neq nil$) each time it is called, to serve as an identifier of the new connection. The variable yci_i contains the connection identifier which i has copied from the packet it received from j. In case i has received no packet yet, $yci_i = nil$. The values in mci_i and yci_i are used to distinguish "old" and "new" packets.

Aside from the fact that a processor needs to remember the mci and yci during a connection, it needs a parameter w and a variable *stored* (local to the connection); see also chapter 2, protocol skeleton SW. As the window size is 1, the parameter w is either 0 or 1. It is constant during one connection and it encodes the direction of data transfer: $w_i = 1$ if i decided to send j some information, and $w_i = 0$ if i opened the connection on receipt of a packet from j. The variable $stored_i$ records the number of packets that i has received from j during the current connection and accepted as "valid". Thus $stored_i \geq 0$. Protocol skeleton SW also contains a variable $acked_i$, but as was shown in lemma 2.1.7, this is not necessary for a window size of 1. Likewise, i does not need the parameter w_j, as it is equal to $1 - w_i$. (In chapter 2 w_i and w_j are denoted by w_{ji} and w_{ij}, respectively, as both processors need both parameters.)

The parameters cf_i and cs_i depend only on w_i, and are used to decide whether the connection being closed was a failure (no message came across because the number of different packets received in this connection is less than or equal to cf_i), or a success (the message came across because the number of different packets received in this connection is greater than or equal to cs_i). Necessarily $cs_i > cf_i$. Thus connection management aims at a one-to-one correspondence between connections closed as a success in one processor and those closed as a success in the other processor. The number k in the k-way handshake pertains to the total number of (different) packets that need to be exchanged in both directions for a successful connection. Thus $k \geq cs_i + cs_j$.

The procedure *error* could for example be "ignore" or "send an error packet". We will first prove assertions that hold irrespective of the precise contents of the procedure *error*, under the assumption that it does not change any of the protocol variables. We discuss what the procedure *error* should do in section 4.1.3.

As all connection-management protocols that we consider can be formulated in a symmetric way, we only specify the skeletons for processor i and link (i, j), with the understanding that the remaining part of the skeletons can be obtained by replacing all i's by j's and vice versa. Protocol skeleton $CM0$ gives i the possibility to perform the operations S_i^{CM0} (send), R_i^{CM0} (receive), and C_i^{CM0} (close) in any order and as often as desired, as long as their guards are true. Both the send and receive operation provide for the opening of a (new) connection as required. The basic protocol skeleton for k-way handshakes for connection management can be formulated as follows.

Protocol skeleton $CM0$:

Initially $mci_i = nil$, $yci_i = nil$, $stored_i = 0$, $w_i = 0$, $Q[i, j] = \emptyset$.

S_i^{CM0} :   **begin if** $mci_i = nil$ **then** $mci_i := new\ value$; $w_i := 1$ **fi**;
                    send $<mci_i, yci_i, stored_i + w_i - 1>$ to j
            end

R_i^{CM0} : $\{\, Q[j, i] \neq \emptyset \,\}$
        begin receive $<x, y, z>$ from j;
                if $mci_i = nil \wedge z = 0$
                then $mci_i := new\ value$; $yci_i := x$; $stored_i := 1$
                elif $(x = yci_i \vee stored_i = 0) \wedge y = mci_i \wedge z = stored_i$
                then $stored_i := stored_i + 1$; **if** $z = 0$ **then** $yci_i := x$ **fi**
                else $error(<x, y, z>)$
                fi
        end

C_i^{CM0} : $\{\, mci_i \neq nil \,\}$
        begin if $stored_i \leq cf_i$ **then** report failure
                elif $stored_i \geq cs_i$ **then** report success
                fi; $mci_i := nil$; $yci_i := nil$; $stored_i := 0$; $w_i := 0$
        end

E_{ij}^l, E_{ij}^d, and E_{ij}^r as in section 1.2.1.2.

Note that we consider only meaningful closes, as $mci_i \neq nil$ is a guard for operation C_i^{CM0}.

4.1.1.2 Invariants. Since i and j use the same operations S^{CM0}, R^{CM0}, and C^{CM0}, assertions that hold for i hold for j also, with i and j interchanged. We will only state and prove them for one processor. In order to formulate the assertions, we need some predicates to express events like "a connection (with a certain setting of the local protocol variables) was closed", "a packet (with certain values in its fields) would be accepted as valid", and "a packet (with certain values in its fields) has been accepted as valid".

Definition 4.1.1

(1) *An (m, y, w, s)-close for i is an operation C_i^{CM0}, invoked at some time by i, where the parameters reflect the values of the protocol variables at the time of the operation C_i^{CM0}: $mci_i = m$, $yci_i = y$, $w_i = w$ and $stored_i = s$.*

(2) *The predicate $closed_i(m, y, w, s)$ is rendered true when i does an (m, y, w, s)-close, i.e., it is false before the (m, y, w, s)-close and remains true ever after.*

(3) *For a packet $<x, y, z> \in Q[j, i]$ we say*
   - (i) *x is valid if $x = yci_i \lor stored_i = 0$, notation: $valid_i(x)$,*
   - (ii) *y is valid if $y = mci_i \lor mci_i = nil$, notation: $valid_i(y)$,*
   - (iii) *z is valid if $z = stored_i$, notation: $valid_i(z)$,*
   - (iv) *$<x, y, z>$ is valid if x, y, and z are valid, notation: $valid_i(<x, y, z>)$,*
   - (v) *$<x, y, z>$ is invalid if it is not valid, notation: $\neg valid_i(<x, y, z>)$.*

(4) *The predicate $accepted_i(<x, y, z>)$ is rendered true when i does an operation R_i^{CM0} in which the received packet $<x, y, z>$ is accepted as valid, i.e., the predicate is false before the operation, and remains true ever after.*

Note that it depends on the state of the future receiver of the packet whether the packet is valid or not: the predicate reflects what would happen (acceptance or not) if the packet were received now. Thus, while the values in the packet cannot change, the validity of the values can be changed if the state of the future receiver is changed.

We first establish relations between the local variables of a processor (in lemma 4.1.1). In lemma 4.1.2 we state the implications of the (past) existence of a packet in the network. In which way the variables in both processors are or have been related if at least one packet is received and accepted as valid, is stated in lemma 4.1.3. In which cases processors have reached complete agreement is stated in lemmas 4.1.4 and 4.1.5. Closes of i are related to closes of j in lemma 4.1.6.

Lemma 4.1.1 *Using protocol skeleton $CM0$, the following assertions hold invariantly.*

    (1) $mci_i = nil \Rightarrow yci_i = nil \wedge w_i = 0 \wedge stored_i = 0$,

    (2) $mci_i \neq nil \Rightarrow (w_i = 0 \vee w_i = 1) \wedge stored_i \geq 0$,

    (3) $mci_i \neq nil \wedge yci_i = nil \Leftrightarrow w_i = 1 \wedge stored_i = 0$,

    (4) $closed_i(m, y, w, s) \Rightarrow m \neq mci_i \wedge m \neq nil \wedge (w = 0 \vee w = 1) \wedge s \geq 0 \wedge$
$$(y = nil \Leftrightarrow w = 1 \wedge s = 0).$$

Proof. (1), (2), and (3) are obvious from the protocol skeleton. (4) follows because (2) and (3) hold before the operation C_i^{CM0} which rendered the premise true. $\quad\square$

Lemma 4.1.2 *Using protocol skeleton $CM0$, the following assertions hold invariantly:*

    (1) $<x, y, z> \in Q[i, j] \Rightarrow (x = mci_i \wedge z < stored_i + w_i \wedge$
$$(y = yci_i \vee (y = nil \wedge z = 0 \wedge w_i = 1))) \vee$$
$$\exists\, y', w', s' : closed_i(x, y', w', s') \wedge$$
$$(y = y' \vee (y = nil \wedge z = 0 \wedge w' = 1)) \wedge z < s' + w',$$

    (2) $accepted_j(<x, y, z>) \Rightarrow (x = mci_i \wedge z < stored_i + w_i \wedge$
$$(y = yci_i \vee (y = nil \wedge z = 0 \wedge w_i = 1))) \vee$$
$$\exists\, y', w', s' : closed_i(x, y', w', s') \wedge$$
$$(y = y' \vee (y = nil \wedge z = 0 \wedge w' = 1)) \wedge z < s' + w',$$

    (3) $accepted_i(<x, y, z>) \Rightarrow$
$$(x = yci_i \wedge (y = mci_i \vee z = w_i = 0) \wedge z < stored_i) \vee$$
$$\exists\, y', w', s' : closed_i(m', x, w', s') \wedge (y = m' \vee z = w' = 0) \wedge z < s'.$$

Proof. (1). The premise becomes true when i does an operation S_i^{CM0} and sends $<x, y, z>$. Hence at that moment $x = mci_i$, $y = yci_i$, and $z < stored_i + w_i$. If $y = nil$, then $w_i = 1$ and $stored_i = 0$, hence $z = 0$. Operation R_i^{CM0} can increase $stored_i$, which leaves $z < stored_i + w_i$ true, and can change yci_i, but only in case $stored_i$ was 0 before, thus $y = nil \wedge z = 0 \wedge w_i = 1$ holds now. Operation C_i^{CM0} falsifies $x = mci_i$ but then $closed_i(x, y', w', s')$ holds for some y', w', and s', such that $y' = y \vee (y = nil \wedge z = 0 \wedge w' = 1)$ and $z < s' + w'$ holds.

(2). Follows from (1) because $<x, y, z> \in Q[i, j]$ before the operation R_j^{CM0} which rendered the premise true.

(3). The premise becomes true when i does an operation R_i^{CM0} in which $<x, y, z>$ from $Q[j, i]$ is valid and is accepted. There are two cases.

Case 1: i was closed. Thus $z = 0$ and after the opening of the connection by i we have $yci_i = x$, $w_i = 0$, and $stored_i = 1$. Hence the assertion holds.

Case 2: i was open. Thus $y = mci_i$, $z = stored_i - 1$, $x = yci_i$ at the completion of R_i^{CM0}. Hence the assertion holds.

Another operation R_i^{CM0} during the same connection can only increase $stored_i$, which keeps the assertion true. Operations S_i^{CM0}, S_j^{CM0}, C_j^{CM0} and R_j^{CM0} do not change any of the variables involved. Finally, when i does an operation C_i^{CM0} to close this particular connection, we have that for some m', w', and s', $closed_i(m', x, w', s')$ and $y = m' \vee (z = w' = 0)$ and $z < s'$ become true. This cannot be falsified in future by any of the operations. □

Lemma 4.1.3 *Using protocol skeleton CM0, the following assertions hold:*
- (1) $stored_i \geq 1 \Rightarrow \exists\, y :\ accepted_i(yci_i, y, stored_i - 1) \wedge$
  $(y = mci_i \vee stored_i - 1 = w_i = 0)$,
- (2) $stored_i \geq 1 \Rightarrow (mci_j = yci_i \wedge w_j + w_i \leq 1 \wedge stored_i \leq stored_j + w_j) \vee$
  $\exists\, y, w, s :\ closed_j(yci_i, y, w, s) \wedge w + w_i \leq 1 \wedge stored_i \leq s + w,$
- (3) $closed_i(m', y', w', s') \wedge s' \geq 1 \Rightarrow$
  $(mci_j = y' \wedge w_j + w' \leq 1 \wedge s' \leq stored_j + w_j) \vee$
  $\exists\, y, w, s :\ closed_j(y', y, w, s) \wedge w + w' \leq 1 \wedge s' \leq s + w.$

Proof. (1). Obvious from the protocol skeleton.

(2). Consider the operation R_i^{CM0} in which the premise is first rendered true: thus now $stored_i = 1$. Combining assertion (1) and lemma 4.1.2(2) with i and j interchanged directly leads to the desired result after observing that the cases $w_i + w_j = 2$ and $w + w_i = 2$, respectively, lead to $stored_i - 1 = 1$, and hence to a contradiction. Thus after successive R_i^{CM0} operations where $stored_i$ is increased to a larger value, $w_i + w_j \leq 1$ and $w + w_i \leq 1$, respectively, still hold.

(3). The operation C_i^{CM0} which falsifies $stored_i \geq 1$ leads to assertion (3). All other operations leave the assertion invariant for the same reasons as in (2). □

Note that the premise $stored_i \geq 1$ is not sufficient for a complete agreement between processors i and j with regard to connection identifiers and the parameters w_i and w_j. According to chapter 2, only values such that $w_i + w_j \geq 1$ pertain to a valid protocol.

Lemma 4.1.4 *Using protocol skeleton CM0, the following assertions hold:*
- (1) $mci_i = yci_j \neq nil \wedge mci_j = yci_i \neq nil \Rightarrow w_i + w_j = 1,$
- (2) $closed_i(yci_j, mci_j, w, s) \Rightarrow w + w_j = 1.$

Proof. (1). Initially assertion (1) is vacuously true because i and j are closed. We consider the effect of the relevant operations upon the assertion.

– Operation S_i^{CM0} keeps the assertion invariant, because if i already had an open connection with j, S_i^{CM0} does not change any variables, and if i was closed, S_i^{CM0} puts $mci_i := new\ value$, hence $mci_i = yci_j$ cannot hold yet. Thus S_i^{CM0} keeps (1) invariant, as does S_j^{CM0}.

– Operations C_i^{CM0} and C_j^{CM0} keep (1) invariant because mci_i and mci_j, respectively, are set to *nil*.

– Operation R_i^{CM0} keeps (1) invariant: if i had an open connection with j already, neither w_i nor w_j is changed, hence the sum stays the same. However, yci_i might change to some value x, such that $mci_i = yci_j \wedge yci_i = mci_j$ now holds. If it does, the packet received was $<x, y, z>$ with $y = mci_i$, $z = stored_i = 0$, after which $stored_i$ was set to 1. Hence $w_i = 1$. Thus, if $mci_j = yci_i$, $w_i + w_j \leq 1$ (lemma 4.1.3). Hence $w_j = 0$ and $w_i + w_j = 1$. If i opens the connection with j, R_i^{CM0} puts $mci_i := new\ value$, thus $mci_i = yci_j$ cannot hold yet.

– Operation R_j^{CM0} keeps the assertion invariant, like R_i^{CM0}.

(2). If operation C_i^{CM0} renders $closed_i(yci_j, mci_j, w, s)$ true, we know with (1) that the assertion holds. S_i^{CM0} and R_i^{CM0} do not change any relevant variables, nor do S_j^{CM0} and R_j^{CM0}. Operation C_j^{CM0} falsifies $closed_i(yci_j, mci_j, w, s)$ by setting yci_j and mci_j to *nil*.　　　　　□

Lemma 4.1.5 *Using protocol skeleton CM0, the following assertions hold:*

(1) $stored_i + w_i \geq 2 \Rightarrow (mci_j = yci_i \wedge yci_j = mci_i \wedge w_i + w_j = 1 \wedge$
$\qquad stored_i \leq stored_j + w_j \wedge stored_j \leq stored_i + w_i) \vee$
$\qquad \exists\ s:\ closed_j(yci_i, mci_i, 1 - w_i, s) \wedge stored_i \leq s + 1 - w_i \wedge$
$\qquad s \leq stored_i + w_i,$

(2) $closed_i(m, y, w, s) \wedge s + w \geq 2 \Rightarrow (mci_j = y \wedge yci_j = m \wedge w + w_j = 1 \wedge$
$\qquad s \leq stored_j + w_j \wedge stored_j \leq s + w) \vee$
$\qquad \exists\ s':\ closed_j(y, m, 1 - w, s') \wedge s \leq s' + 1 - w \wedge s' \leq s + w,$

(3) $closed_i(yci_j, mci_j, w, s) \Rightarrow \neg(stored_i + w_i \geq 2) \wedge$
$\qquad (mci_i \neq nil \Rightarrow \neg\exists\ m',\ w',\ s':\ closed_j(m', mci_i, w', s')),$

(4) $stored_i + w_i \geq 2 \wedge stored_j + w_j \geq 2 \Rightarrow mci_i = yci_j \wedge yci_i = mci_j.$

Proof. (1). Follows from the previous lemmas if we note that for example in the case that j is still open with $mci_j = yci_i$, $stored_j \geq 1$, and thus lemma 4.1.3 can be used for j. Then $w_i + w_j = 1$ follows from lemma 4.1.4(1).

(2). Follows from assertion (1).

(3). $closed_i(yci_j, mci_j, w, s)$ implies $yci_j \neq nil$ and hence $mci_j \neq nil$, so j is open, $stored_j \geq 1$, $w + w_j = 1$, and $s \geq 1$. Initially assertion (3) holds. If R_j^{CM0} or S_j^{CM0} opens a connection and sets mci_j, $closed_i(yci_j, mci_j, w, s)$ cannot hold yet. It can become true in two ways: first, by an operation C_i^{CM0} if $mci_i = yci_j$ and $yci_i = mci_j$. Hereafter $stored_i$ and w_i are 0, hence $stored_i + w_i \geq 2$ does not hold. Secondly, if $closed_i(m, mci_j, w, s)$ holds already for some m, by an operation R_j^{CM0} which sets yci_j to that value m. Hence $w_j = 1$. However, after the C_i^{CM0} operation which led to $closed_i(m, mci_j, w, s)$, $\neg(stored_i + w_i \geq 2)$ did hold. The only way

$stored_i + w_i \geq 2$ can become true is by an R_i^{CM0} operation in which the packet $<yci_i, mci_i, 1 - w_i>$ is accepted. However, since $\neg closed_j(m', mci_i, w', s')$ held for all m', w', and s' when the connection was opened by i (as mci_i was set to a new value), and processor j either has $yci_j = nil$ or $yci_j = m \neq mci_i$, there can be no m' such that $<m', mci_i, z> \in Q[j, i]$ holds. Thus $\neg(stored_i + w_i \geq 2)$ holds as long as j is open with the current connection. The only way $closed_j(m', mci_i, w', s')$ can become true is by an operation C_j^{CM0}, but C_j^{CM0} falsifies $closed_i(yci_j, mci_j, w, s)$.
(4). Use assertions (1) and (3). $\qquad\square$

Lemma 4.1.6 *Using protocol skeleton* $CM0$, *the following assertions hold:*
Let $closed_i(m, y, w, s)$ *be true. Then*

   (1) $\exists\, w', s' :\ closed_j(y, m, w', s') \Rightarrow w + w' = 1 \wedge (s' = s + w \vee s' = s + w - 1)$,
   (2) $\exists\, w', s', m' \neq y :\ closed_j(m', m, w', s') \Rightarrow\ w' = 0 \wedge s' = 1$,
   (3) $\exists\, w'', s'', m'' \neq m :\ closed_i(m'', y, w'', s'') \Rightarrow (s = 1 \wedge w = 0) \vee$
       $(s'' = 1 \wedge w'' = 0) \vee (w = s = s'' = 0 \wedge w = w'' = 1)$,
   (4) *if* j *never does an* (m', m, w', s')-*close for some* m', w', *and* s' *and if connections are always closed eventually, then* $s + w = 1$,
   (5) *if* j *never does a* (y, y', w', s')-*close for some* y', w', *and* s' *and if connections are always closed eventually, then* $s = 0$, $w = 1$, *and* $y = nil$.

Proof. (1). $m \neq nil$ and $y \neq nil$ imply $s \geq 1$ and $s' \geq 1$. From lemma 4.1.4 it follows that $w + w' = 1$. Hence $s + w \geq 2$ or $s' + w' \geq 2$. Thus we can use lemma 4.1.5 for either i or j to obtain the desired result.
(2). Since $m \neq nil$, $s' \geq 1$. We know $s' + w' \geq 2$ would imply $m' = y$, thus $s' = 1$ and $w' = 0$.
(3). Assume $s + w \geq 2$ and $s'' + w'' \geq 2$. Then by lemma 4.1.5 we have $mci_j = y \wedge yci_j = m \vee closed_j(y, m, 1 - w', s')$ but also the contradicting $mci_j = y \wedge yci_j = m'' \vee closed_j(y, m'', 1 - w', s')$. Hence $s + w = 1$ or $s'' + w'' = 1$. Now if $y = nil$ then $s = s'' = 0$ and $w = w'' = 1$. If $y \neq nil$, $s \geq 1$ and $s'' \geq 1$. Thus either $w = 0 \wedge s = 1$ or $w'' = 0 \wedge s'' = 1$ holds.
(4). For $s + w \geq 2$, lemma 4.1.5 tells us that j must have been open with $yci_j = m$, hence we have a contradiction and $s + w = 1$.
(5). For $s \geq 1$, lemma 4.1.3 tells us that j must have been open with $mci_j = y$, hence we have a contradiction and $s = 0$. Hence $w = 1$ and $y = nil$. $\qquad\square$

4.1.2 Correct communication

So far we have not even said what we mean by correct communication. We will define this concept below and establish bounds for the closing parameters cs_i and cf_i in order that the protocol skeleton achieves correct communication.

4.1.2.1 Loss and duplication. In order to derive results on the problem of loss and duplication of messages in the protocol skeleton, we need a formal definition of this problem in terms of the parameters of the protocol skeleton. Informally we talk about *loss* if i sent j a message and thinks it has arrived, while j has not received it. We talk about *duplication* if j receives a message from i and treats it as a new message while it really was an old message from i which occurred in a retransmission of a packet received by j previously.

Definition 4.1.2

(1) A failure (m, y, w)-close for i is an (m, y, w, s)-close for i where i reports failure, thus with $s \leq cf_i$. In short we will talk about a failure close *for i.*

(2) A successful (m, y, w)-close for i is an (m, y, w, s)-close for i where i reports success, thus with $s \geq cs_i$. In short we will talk about a successful close *for i.*

(3) The predicate $sclosed_i(m, y, w)$ is rendered true when i does a successful (m, y, w)-close, i.e., it is false before the close and remains true ever after.

(4) Loss is the situation in which i does a successful $(m, y, 1)$-close while j never does a successful (m', m, w)-close for some m' and w.

(5) Duplication is the situation in which i does a successful $(m, y, 0)$-close while j never does a successful (m', m, w)-close for some m' and w.

(6) Correct communication is the situation in which for all closes there exist m, y, w, and w' such that the following holds:

   i does a successful (m, y, w)-close eventually if and only if
   j does a successful (y, m, w')-close eventually.

The definition of loss is clearly reasonable. Consider the situation in which duplication can arise. Typically j sends an opening packet, say, $< x, nil, 0 >$ twice. Processor i, upon receipt of the first one, opens with $w_i = 0$, $mci_i := new\ value$ and $yci_i = x$. Let the value of mci_i be m now. If i closes successfully (possibly after more packet exchanges), it does a successful $(m, x, 0)$-close. If i receives j's retransmission of the original opening packet after this close, it will open with $w_i = 0$, $mci_i := new\ value$, and $yci_i = x$. Hence $mci_i \neq m$, and let $mci_i = m'$. If i closes successfully again with a successful $(m', x, 0)$-close, we have the duplication problem: consider processor j. Processor j can only do a successful (x, y, w)-close for some y and w once since, if it closes and opens again, $mci_j := new\ value$. Thus either i's successful $(m, x, 0)$-close does not correspond to a successful (x, m, w)-close or i's successful $(m', x, 0)$-close does not correspond to a successful (x, m', w)-close, for some w. Note that correct communication does not mean that the assertion $sclosed_i(m, y, w) \Leftrightarrow sclosed_j(y, m, w')$ is always true, e.g. i may close first while j is still open; thus the assertion does not hold without referring to (possibly different) time moments. However, correct communication does mean that eventually the assertion will hold.

Theorem 4.1.7

(1) *Correct communication implies no loss and no duplication,*

(2) *if no loss and no duplication occurs during a finite number of successful closes, then we have correct communication,*

(3) *correct communication preserves the order of successful closes, i.e., the order of the successful closes in one processor is the same as the order of the (corresponding) successful closes in the other processor.*

Proof. (1). Obvious.

(2). Let i do a successful (m_0, y_0, w_0)-close C_0. No loss or duplication implies j does a successful (m_1, y_1, w_1)-close C_1 with $y_1 = m_0$. Assume $y_0 \neq m_1$. Then (lemma 4.1.6(2)) $w_1 = 0$. In general, for $k \geq 1$, let one processor do a successful $(m_{k-1}, y_{k-1}, w_{k-1})$-close C_{k-1}, while the other processor does a successful (m_k, y_k, w_k)-close C_k with $m_k \neq y_{k-1}$. Then $w_k = 0$, and because of no loss and no duplication, the first processor does a successful $(m_{k+1}, y_{k+1}, w_{k+1})$-close C_{k+1} with $y_{k+1} = m_k$. Since $y_{k+1} \neq y_{k-1}$, we have $m_{k+1} \neq m_{k-1}$ and $w_{k+1} = 0$. Let t_k be the time that the connection with $mci = m_k$ is opened. Since $w_k = 0$, *stored* is set to 1 and there exists a time t, $t < t_k$, that the other processor is open with $mci = y_k$. Because $y_k = m_{k-1}$, $t < t_k$ and $t_{k-1} \leq t$, we have $t_{k-1} < t_k$. Since also $t_k < t_{k+1}$, $C_{k-1} \neq C_{k+1}$. Consider the sequence of closes $C_0, C_1, \ldots$ defined by the condition that there are no losses and no duplication. Then we have that for each C_k, $k \geq 1$, there is a C_{k+1} with $y_{k+1} = m_k$, $w_{k+1} = 0$, $t_{k+1} > t_l$ for all l, $0 \leq l \leq k$ and thus $C_{k+1} \neq C_l$ for all l, $0 \leq l \leq k$. Hence this sequence is infinite. Contradiction. Thus $y_0 = m_1$ and i's successful (m_0, y_0, w_0)-close implies a successful (y_0, m_0, w_1)-close by j. The same argument holds for the reverse implication.

(3). Let i do a successful (m_0, y_0, w_0)-close at time t_0, and a successful (m_1, y_1, w_1)-close at time t_1. Correct communication implies that j does a successful (y_0, m_0, w)-close for some w, and a successful (y_1, m_1, w')-close for some w', say at times t_2 and t_3, respectively. Assume without loss of generality that t_0 is the smallest value. From lemmas 4.1.3 and 4.1.5 it follows that between t_0 and t_2 the predicates $closed_i(yci_j, mci_j, w, s)$ and $\neg closed_j(m'', mci_i, w'', s'')$ hold. Thus also $\neg closed_j(y_1, m_1, w', s')$ holds. So $t_3 > t_2$, and as $t_1 > t_0$, the order is preserved. $\square$

We note that the condition of a finite number of closes in theorem 4.1.7(2) is only necessary in the general case where no assumption is made yet on the value of the parameter cs. It is clear from the proof that this condition can be dropped if it is known that $cs > 1 - w$.

4.1.2.2 Parameters for closing.
It is clear that the values for the parameters cs and cf cannot be chosen arbitrarily, if we want to avoid loss and duplication.

Lemma 4.1.8 *To avoid loss and duplication, without further assumptions about the order of operations in protocol skeleton $CM0$, it is necessary that*

(1) $cf_i \geq 1 - w_i$,

(2) $cs_i > cf_j + 1 - w_i$,

(3) $cs_i \geq 2$.

Proof. (1). It is clear from lemma 4.1.6 that if i wants to close while $stored_i + w_i = 1$, i had better decide the connection was a failure, since j might not have opened the corresponding connection at all. (If i were not able to close, deadlock would arise.) Hence $cf_i + w_i \geq 1$ and $cf_i \geq 1 - w_i$.

(2). If i does an (m, y, w, cs_i)-close, and j does a (y, m, w', s')-close for some w' and s', we know by lemma 4.1.6 that it might be the case that $s' = cs_i + w_i - 1$. Hence we need $cf_j < s' = cs_i + w_i - 1$ to avoid loss and duplication, and thus we have $cs_i > cf_j + 1 - w_i$.

(3). Substituting the minimum value for cf_j gives $cs_i > cf_j + 1 - w_i \geq 1 - w_j + 1 - w_i \geq 1$ since $w_i + w_j \leq 1$. Hence $cs_i \geq 2$. $\qquad\square$

Consider the minimum values we can choose for cf_i and cs_i: namely $cf_i = 1 - w_i$ and $cs_i = 2$. Now if $w_i = 0$, $cs_i = cf_i + 1$ and for each value of $stored_i$ processor i knows how to close, as a failure or a success. But what if $w_i = 1$, $cf_i = 0$ and $cs_i = 2$. What should i report: success or failure, if it closes with $stored_i = 1$? If i reports success we have the possibility of loss. If i reports failure, we have the possibility of duplication. So i had better not close at all if $stored_i = w_i = 1$. But this leaves us with the following problem: assume $stored_i = w_i = 1$ and i sends a packet with sequence number 1 to j. Upon receipt of this, j puts $stored_j$ to 2 and closes successfully. Now i will never get a packet with the right mci and yci fields and sequence number 1, hence $stored_i$ cannot rise to 2, and i cannot close. The first idea which comes to mind to repair this livelock problem is to forbid j to close with $stored_j = 2$ and defer closing until $stored_j = 3$. Now i is o.k. but j might have a problem if it does not receive the valid packet from i to enable it to set $stored_j$ to 3. But there is one difference: if j is forced to close with $stored_j = 2$, it does know how, namely successfully. Processor j can use this in the following way: it keeps on retransmitting its packet with sequence number 1 (this cannot cause confusion later because it contains a $yci_j \neq nil$). Now if i is still open i

can eventually respond with a valid packet with sequence number 2, so j can set $stored_j$ to 3 and close. Note that this packet exchange is a 5-way handshake. On the other hand, if i had already closed, this will result in a call to the procedure *error*. This procedure might send a special packet to j to indicate that it is not open any more with the value $mci_i = yci_j$ (even if i opened again in the meantime). We will call such a packet an *error packet*. But if j receives this error packet, it knows that $stored_i$ has been 2 and that i closed successfully because i would not have closed when $stored_i = 1$. Hence j can safely close successfully.

As error packets can be used to an advantage in connection management (as Belsnes already noted), we will introduce and discuss them in more detail in the next section.

The strategy which makes use of error packets works if processors stay up and if we assume that some packet will eventually get through if we keep on trying. That it does not work when processors go down should not bother us too much, since it is not possible to design a protocol that always works correctly in the presence of processor breakdowns anyway (cf. [Bel76]). The reason we need a 5-way handshake is that i (as processor with $w_i = 1$) cannot use the same trick as j does: waiting for an error packet. If i, while $stored_i = 1$, receives an error packet indicating that j had already closed, it cannot decide whether j closed as a failure (with $stored_j = 1$) or as a success (with $stored_j = 2$), as j is not allowed to remember this information after the close (and hence cannot communicate it to i).

We remark that the informal argument given above that a 5-way handshake works in the absence of processor failures, if i and j know that they will not do arbitrary closes, is not watertight and in fact contains a flaw, as we will see in the sequel. Unfortunately, the same flaw is present in the analysis of the 4-way handshake proposed by Belsnes [Bel76]. The problem is the following: j, being in a state with $stored_j = 2$ and receiving an error packet from i stating that i is not open with the corresponding mci, concludes that i has closed. But it might be the case that this error packet was sent *before* the packet exchange which led to $stored_j = 2$ took place. In that case, i might be open still, even with $stored_i = 1$, and j's conclusion that i closed successfully is not warranted.

Note that the extra information that is used by the processors in a 5-way handshake as discussed above, except the information deriving from the protocol skeleton, is information about the circumstances in which a connection is closed and when it is not. But if we want to use this kind of information, there is no need to restrict it to "i does not close with $stored_i = 1$ if $w_i = 1$". It is more fruitful to demand that no processor closes "arbitrarily". In order to be able to define the notion of a *non-arbitrary close* precisely, we need an analysis of possible error packets and their consequences.

4.1.3 Error handling

In order to analyze the effect of sending error packets, we begin by assuming that error packets are sent whenever the procedure *error* is called, and that the error packet contains all information available in the sender of the error packet, for use by the receiver. We recall that the procedure *error* is called upon receipt of an invalid packet (definition 4.1.1(3)). In the first field of the error packet we write "error" to distinguish it from other packets, in the second field we write the values of *mci* and the y-field of the invalid packet (separated by a slash (/)). In the third field we write the values of *yci* and the x-field of the invalid packet (separated by a slash (/)), and in the third field the value of *stored* and the z-field of the invalid packet (separated by a slash (/)). Since we will see that neither all information is used nor all error packets sent are meaningful, we will decide later in what circumstances an error packet should be sent and what fields the actual error packet should contain. The next step is to decide what the receiver of an error packet should do. As we saw above, it might be the case that the receiver had better close the current connection. Thus we will provide the possibility of closing upon receipt of an error packet.

For the time being, we define the procedure error and a corresponding receive operation as follows.

proc $error(<x, y, z>) = $ send $<$error$, mci/y, yci/x, stored/z>$ to j

RE_i^{CM0} : { $Q[j, i]$ contains an error packet }
      begin receive the error packet;
              if the values in the packet compared with the current local values
                  make a close desirable
              then do C_i^{CM0}
              fi
     end

Note that lemmas 4.1.1 up till 4.1.8(1) hold irrespective of the closing strategy and error procedure used, but that lemmas 4.1.8(2) and 4.1.8(3) might not hold any more, since refining the protocol skeleton might give the processors extra information (such as: they agreed not to close in certain circumstances, see section 4.1.3.3).

4.1.3.1 Invalid packets.
We first investigate what values the fields of an invalid packet can contain.

Lemma 4.1.9 *Using protocol skeleton $CM0$, the following assertions hold:*
Let a packet $<x, y, z> \in Q[j, i]$ be invalid. Then

(1) $y \neq nil \Rightarrow mci_i = y \vee \exists\, y', w', s' : closed_i(y, y', w', s')$,

(2) $z \geq 1 \Rightarrow (mci_i = y \wedge yci_i = x) \vee \exists\, w', s' : closed_i(y, x, w', s')$,

(3) $mci_i = nil \Rightarrow z \geq 1$,

(4) $mci_i \neq nil \wedge valid_i(y) \Rightarrow$
$$y = mci_i \wedge z < stored_i \wedge ((valid_i(x) \wedge accepted_i(x, y, z)) \vee z = 0),$$

(5) $mci_i \neq nil \wedge valid_i(x) \wedge y = nil \wedge w_i = 0 \Rightarrow accepted_i(<x, y, z>)$.

Proof. By assumption $<x, y, z> \in Q[j, i]$ and $\neg valid_i(<x, y, z>)$ hold.
(1). Use lemmas 4.1.2 and 4.1.3.
(2). Use lemmas 4.1.2 and 4.1.5.
(3). If i is closed, every packet with $z = 0$ is accepted as valid, hence $z \geq 1$.
(4). Thus $y = mci_i$. There are two cases.
Case 1: $z = 0$. Let $stored_i = 0$. Then x is valid and z is valid which leads to a contradiction with $\neg valid_i(<x, y, z>)$. Thus $stored_i \geq 1$ and hence $stored_i < z$.
Case 2: $z \geq 1$. By assertion (2) we have that $y = mci_i$ and $x = yci_i$. Thus x is valid and, necessarily, z is not. Using lemmas 4.1.2 and 4.1.5 we conclude that $z \leq stored_i$. Hence $z < stored_i$. Since $stored_i$ increases by 1 at a time and $z < stored_i$, we have $accepted_i(x, y, z)$ by lemma 4.1.3.
(5). Since $w_i = 0$ we have $stored_i \geq 1$, and $valid_i(x)$ implies $x = yci_i$. As $y = nil$, $z = 0$. Use lemma 4.1.3. $\qquad\square$

Note that in assertions (4) and (5), where we have $accepted_i(<x, y, z>)$, the packet $<x, y, z>$ must have been sent twice or else it has been duplicated, as it is accepted and thus received, as well as still in the queue. Thus it does not make much sense to send an error packet: the connection was progressing satisfactorily, as the packet $<x, y, z>$ was accepted, and the receipt of a copy of the packet does not indicate that the current connection should not have been made. It might indicate that the last packet of the current connection sent by the receiver of the copy has been lost. In that case the other processor would have retransmitted packet $<x, y, z>$ after a timeout, as that lost packet also serves as an acknowledgement (see chapter 2).

Furthermore, in assertion (4), for the case that $mci_i \neq nil$, $valid_i(y)$, $\neg valid_i(x)$ and $z = 0$, it might be the case that j opened twice with $yci_j = mci_i = y$. Since $stored_i > z$, $stored_i \geq 1$ and $mci_i = yci_i$ or $closed_j(yci_i, y', w', s')$ for some y', w', and s'. By lemma 4.1.2 $<x, y, z> \in Q[j, i]$ implies $mci_j = x \wedge yci_j = y$ or for some w' and s' $closed_j(x, y, w', s')$. If $y' = y$, j has opened twice with $yci_j = y$, since $x \neq yci_i$. That a processor opens two connections with the same value of $yci_i \neq nil$

is a situation to beware of, as closing them both successfully implies duplication (see section 4.1.2.1).

4.1.3.2   *Error packets.* Because of lemma 4.1.9, we now require that error packets are only sent upon receipt of an invalid packet in case a copy of this packet was *not* accepted before during the current connection. For the other case that i had already accepted a packet containing the same values in the current connection, i had better retransmit its last packet, because it probably got lost.

Since i does not know, nor can do anything, about previous connections, it is clearly reasonable that i only considers error packets pertaining to its current connection, that is, an error packet sent by j upon receipt of a packet $<x, y, z>$ from i with $x = mci_i$.

The following lemma summarizes what i can conclude from the receipt of an error packet pertaining to i's current connection.

Lemma 4.1.10 *Using protocol skeleton CM0, the following assertions hold:*
Let $<error, m'/y, y'/x, s'/z> \in Q[j, i]$ *with* $x = mci_i$. *Then*

(1) $m' = y \Rightarrow z = w_i = 0 \wedge y = yci_i \wedge stored_i = 1 \wedge$
$$(mci_j \neq yci_i \vee yci_j \neq mci_i) \wedge \neg \exists\ w, s : closed_j(yci_i, mci_i, w, s),$$

(2) $m' \neq y \wedge y \neq nil \Rightarrow y = yci_i \wedge \exists\ y'', w, s : closed_j(y, y'', w, s),$

(3) $y = nil \wedge yci_i \neq nil \Rightarrow m' \neq yci_i \wedge m' \neq nil \wedge$
$$((mci_j = yci_i \wedge \exists\ y'', w, s : closed_j(m', y'', w, s)) \vee$$
$$(mci_j = m' \wedge \exists\ y''', w'', s'' : closed_j(yci_i, y''', w'', s'')) \vee$$
$$(\exists\ y'', w, s : closed_j(m', y'', w, s) \wedge$$
$$\exists\ y''', w'', s'' : closed_j(yci_i, y''', w'', s''))).$$

Proof.   (1). Since $m' = y$, we had $valid_j(y)$, $y \neq nil$ and $m' \neq nil$, when j received $<x, y, z>$. Since $x = mci_i$ and $y \neq nil$, $y = yci_i = m'$. Since error packets are not sent if a copy of the invalid packet was already accepted during the current connection, we know by lemma 4.1.9(4) that $\neg valid_j(x) \wedge z = 0$. Moreover, when j sent the error packet, $stored_j \geq 1$. Thus $mci_j = m' \wedge yci_j \neq nil \wedge yci_j \neq x$ or $closed_j(m', y', w, s) \wedge y' \neq x$. If $stored_i + w_i \geq 2$, then by lemma 4.1.5 $mci_j = yci_i \wedge yci_j = mci_i$ or there exists an s such that $closed_j(yci_i, mci_i, 1 - w_i, s)$ holds, which is a contradiction. Thus $stored_i + w_i = 1$, and since $y = yci_i = mci_j$, $stored_i = 1$ and $w_i = 0$.

(2). Since $x = mci_i$ and $y \neq nil$, $yci_i = y$ and $stored_i \geq 1$. At the time $<x, y, z>$ was sent, $y \neq nil$ already, thus $mci_j = yci_i \vee closed_j(yci_i, y'', w, s)$ for some y'', w, and s. Since $m' \neq y$ at the time $<x, y, z>$ was received by j, $closed_j(yci_i, y'', w, s)$ was true already. Hence it still is.

(3). Because $y = nil$, we have $w_i = 1$, $m' \neq y$ and $m' \neq nil$. Since j sent an error packet, at that time $\neg(w_j = 0 \wedge x = yci_j)$. Assume $w_j = 1$. Then $m' \neq yci_i$ (otherwise $w_i + w_j \leq 1$). Assume $x \neq yci_j$. Assume also $m' = yci_i$. Then $stored_i \geq 1$ and $stored_i + w_i \geq 2$ and lemma 4.1.5 leads to a contradiction. Thus $m' \neq yci_i$ in both cases. Hence assertion (3) holds. $\quad\square$

Thus, in case (3) of lemma 4.1.10, i cannot draw the conclusion that j already closed the connection with $mci_j = yci_i$.

Definition 4.1.3

(1) *An error (m, y, w, s)-close for i is an (m, y, w, s)-close for i upon receipt of an error packet $<error, m'/y, y'/m, s'/z>$ for some m', y', s', and z, i.e., an operation C_i^{CM0} called from the operation RE_i^{CM0}. In short we will talk about an error close for i.*

(2) *The predicate $eclosed_i(m, y, w, s)$ is rendered true when i does an error (m, y, w, s)-close, i.e., it is false before the (m, y, w, s)-close and remains true ever after.*

The reason that we require not only $mci_i = m$ but also $yci_i = y$ for a close is that in the case where $s + w \geq 2$ (and i knows that j has been open with $mci_j = yci_i$ and $mci_i = yci_j$), i would like to conclude that j has already closed this connection, so it can close too. We know from lemma 4.1.10 that this conclusion is only warranted if $y = yci_i$.

Lemma 4.1.11 *Using protocol skeleton $CM0$, the following assertion holds:*
$$stored_i + w_i \geq 2 \Rightarrow \neg\exists\, y', w', s' : eclosed_j(yci_i, y', w', s').$$

Proof. Assume $stored_i + w_i \geq 2$ and $eclosed_j(yci_i, y', w', s')$. Then we have that $closed_j(yci_i, y', w', s')$ and by lemma 4.1.5 we have $y' = mci_i$ and $s' \geq 1$. Thus j received the error packet $<error, m''/y', y''/yci_i, s''/z>$ for some m'', y'', s'', and z. Hence i sent the error packet upon receipt of $<yci_i, y', z>$ from j. Thus $m'' \neq y'$ otherwise i would not have sent the error packet. By lemma 4.1.10(2) we have $closed_i(y', y'', w'', s'')$ for some w''. Since i is open still with $y' = mci_i$, we have a contradiction. $\quad\square$

4.1.3.3 Arbitrary closes. As discussed in section 4.1.2.2, processors would like to know in what circumstances the other processor would close, and in what circumstances it would not. Thus we will define the allowed circumstances for closes, leading to the *non-arbitrary closes*, while we will call all other closes *arbitrary*. In order to be able to define an arbitrary close we introduce a new parameter *last* which contains the number of different packets which should be (at least) received by a processor during one connection before that may be closed.

Definition 4.1.4 *Let i do an (m, y, w, s)-close. The close is called* arbitrary *if none of the following hold:*
 *(i) i goes down (*break-down close*),*
 (ii) $eclosed_i(m, y, w, s)$,
 (iii) $s \geq last_i$.

Case (iii) corresponds to the requirement of a "complete" packet exchange in this connection. For example, a 4-way handshake would correspond to $last = 2$ for both sender and receiver. The parameter $last_i$ possibly depends on w_i, or else it is a constant. It is clear from lemma 4.1.10 that most of the information included in error packets is not used at all. Consider an error packet that i might receive: $<error, mci_j/y, yci_j/x, stored_j/z>$. Processor i needs x and y to test against mci_i and yci_i to ensure that it would be an error close and to avoid a non-arbitrary close. The variables $stored_j$ and z were never used throughout the analysis, hence we can discard them. Although the values of mci_j and yci_j give some information about the state in which j was when it received the invalid packet $<x, y, z>$, the decision of i which action to take should not depend on that information, but on the value of $stored_i$ and w_i. The following cases arise.
Case 1: $stored_i + w_i \geq 2$. Then j has closed the corresponding connection and it is irrelevant for i's current connection whether j has opened again. Processor i should close successfully.
Case 2: $stored_i = 1$, $w_i = 0$. Processor i should do a failure close to avoid duplication.
Case 3: $stored_i = 0$, $w_i = 1$. Then j is open with another connection and is not ready to reply to this new opening packet. Processor i could wait and try again or do a failure close.

   Hence an error packet of the form $<error, y, x>$ is sufficient, always assuming error packets are only sent upon the receipt of invalid packets which were not already accepted during the same connection. Reconsidering the fields in normal packets $<x, y, z>$ and lemma 4.1.9(4)–(5), one might be tempted to include the field x only in packets with $z = 0$, since the receiver knows that it must be valid if y is valid and $z \geq 1$. But that does not work because, in case y happened to be invalid, the error packet must contain x. Thus we redefine the procedure *error* to send an error packet only in case the invalid packet received pertained to another connection, and to include only the x and y fields of the invalid packet as information. We also redefine operation R_i^{CM0} to incorporate the receipt of an error packet and a possible error close. Finally, we restrict operation C_i^{CM0} with the extra guard $stored_i \geq last_i$, to forbid arbitrary closes. Leaving the sending operations unchanged, we arrive at the following protocol skeleton.

Protocol skeleton CM:

Initially $mci_i = nil$, $yci_i = nil$, $stored_i = 0$, $w_i = 0$, $Q\,[i,j] = \emptyset$.

S_i^{CM} : **begin if** $mci_i = nil$ **then** $mci_i := new\ value$; $w_i := 1$ **fi**;
  send $<mci_i, yci_i, stored_i + w_i - 1>$ to j
 end

R_i^{CM} : $\{\ Q\,[j,i] \neq \emptyset\ \}$
  begin receive $<x, y, z>$ from j;
    if $x \neq$ error
    then if $mci_i = nil \wedge z = 0$
      then $mci_i := new\ value$; $yci_i := x$; $stored_i := 1$
      elif $(x = yci_i \vee stored_i = 0) \wedge y = mci_i \wedge z = stored_i$
      then $stored_i := stored_i + 1$; **if** $z = 0$ **then** $yci_i := x$ **fi**
      elif $mci_i = nil \vee y \neq mci_i \vee (x \neq yci_i \wedge stored_i \neq 0)$
      then send $<$error$, y, x>$ to j
      fi
    elif $y = yci_i \wedge z = mci_i$ **co** error close **co**
    then if $stored_i \leq cf_i$ **then** report failure
      elif $stored_i \geq cs_i$ **then** report success
      fi; $mci_i := nil$; $yci_i := nil$; $stored_i := 0$; $w_i := 0$
    fi
  end

C_i^{CM} : $\{\ mci_i \neq nil \wedge stored_i \geq last_i\ \}$
  begin if $stored_i \leq cf_i$ **then** report failure
    elif $stored_i \geq cs_i$ **then** report success
    fi; $mci_i := nil$; $yci_i := nil$; $stored_i := 0$; $w_i := 0$
  end

E_{ij}^l, E_{ij}^d, and E_{ij}^r from section 1.2.1.2.

Summarizing, we can state the implications of closing upon receipt of an error packet in operation R_i^{CM}.

Lemma 4.1.12 *Using protocol skeleton CM, the following assertions hold:*
(1) $eclosed_i(m, y, w, s) \wedge s + w \geq 2 \Rightarrow$
  $\exists\ w', s' : closed_j(y, m, w', s') \wedge s' + w' \geq s \wedge \neg eclosed_j(y, m, w', s')$,
(2) $eclosed_i(m, y, 0, 1) \wedge closed_j(y, m, w', s') \Rightarrow s' \leq 1$,
(3) $eclosed_i(m, nil, 1, 0) \wedge closed_j(m', m, w', s') \Rightarrow s' \leq 1$.

Proof. (1). Apply lemmas 4.1.5, 4.1.10 and 4.1.11.

(2). Apply lemmas 4.1.10 and 4.1.6. (3). Apply lemma 4.1.6.   □

4.1.4 The selection of parameters

4.1.4.1 The 4-way handshake.
The crucial theorem for k-way handshakes for connection management can now be formulated as follows:

Theorem 4.1.13 *Using protocol skeleton CM, let the following three conditions hold:*

(i)   connections do not stay open indefinitely,

(ii) there are no processor breakdowns,

(iii) $last_i \geq 2$, and $last_j \geq 2$.

Then for all closes there exist m, y, w, w', s, and s' such that the following holds:

i *does an* (m, y, w, s)-*close with* $s + w \geq 2$ *eventually if and only if*
j *does a* (y, m, w', s')-*close with* $s' + w' \geq 2$ *eventually.*

Proof. Note that the conditions ensure that the following assertion holds:
$$closed_i(m, y, w, s) \Rightarrow eclosed_i(m, y, w, s) \lor s \geq last_i.$$
We first show the "only if" part of the theorem. Suppose i does an (m, y, w, s)-close with $s + w \geq 2$. We have two cases.

Case 1: Processor i closed because $stored_i \geq last_i$. Hence $s \geq 2$ and by lemma 4.1.5, $mci_j = y \land yci_j = m \land 2 \leq stored_j + w_j$ or $closed_j(y, m, w', s') \land 2 \leq s' + w'$ for some w' and s'. Since j will not stay open indefinitely, j will eventually do a (y, m, w', s')-close with $s' + w' \geq 2$.

Case 2: $eclosed_i(m, y, w, s)$ holds. Hence (lemma 4.1.12) there exist w' and s' such that $closed_j(y, m, w', s') \land \neg eclosed_j(y, m, w', s')$ hold. Thus $s' \geq last_j$. Hence we have $s' \geq 2$, and thus $s' + w' \geq 2$.

Next suppose j does a (y, m, w', s')-close with $s' + w' \geq 2$. Then we can use the same argument with i and j interchanged.   □

Corollary 4.1.14 *Under the assumptions from theorem 4.1.13, we can achieve correct communication by taking $cs = 2 - w$.*

Proof. Take $cf_i = 1 - w_i$, $cf_j = 1 - w_j$, $cs_i = 2 - w_i$ and $cs_j = 2 - w_j$. Then every (m, y, w, s)-close with $s + w \geq 2$ is successful and vice versa. Thus theorem 4.1.13 ensures correct communication.   □

Note that we did not exclude the case that i and j become disconnected in the requirements for theorem 4.1.13. This case is handled by just leaving connections open until i and j are connected again. Thus the assumption that connections do not stay open indefinitely implies the assumption that the network becomes disconnected only temporarily. If a processor cannot see whether the network is temporarily disconnected, there is no difference from the case that all packets sent in a certain time interval are lost.

Lemma 4.1.15 *Using protocol skeleton CM, let the following two conditions hold:*
(i)   *connections do not stay open indefinitely,*
(ii) *there are no processor breakdowns.*
Then it is not possible to avoid loss and duplication by taking $last = 2 - w$*, without further assumptions.*

Proof.   Let i open with $stored_i = 0$ and $w_i = 1$ and send an opening packet $< mci_i, nil, 0 >$ to j. Processor j opens with $stored_j = 1$ and $w_j = 0$, $mci_j :=$ *new value* and $yci_j := mci_i$. Processor j replies with $<mci_j, yci_j, 0>$ and retransmits after some time. Now j receives an error packet $<error, mci_j, yci_j>$ because i has closed in the meantime. What should j do? Processor j knows that i has been open with $mci_i = yci_j$ and that i has not closed arbitrarily.

There are three things which could have happened (see figure 4.1), and unfortunately j has no way to decide which one did.
Case 1: Processor i received j's packet, sent a reply packet, and closed with $stored_i + w_i = 2$, but i's reply packet got lost. Since i closed successfully, j should do a successful close, too (otherwise we have a loss).
Case 2: Processor i has closed with $stored_i + w_i = 2$, but on a different packet from j, since this was the second connection for j with $yci_j = mci_i$. Hence j should do a failure close, otherwise we have a duplication.
Case 3: Processor i has closed with $stored_i + w_i = 1$, on receipt of an error packet from j, sent during an earlier connection, e.g. when i and j tried to start up a connection simultaneously. Since i did a failure close, j should too, otherwise we have a duplication.
Thus there is no way to choose the parameters cf and cs such that correct communication is achieved in all three cases. $\square$

As the Tomlinson handshake [Tom75] can be viewed as a special instance of the 3-way handshake above (protocol skeleton CM with $last = 2 - w$), it does not ensure correct communication. Summarizing the previous results, we conclude that correct communication requires a 4-way handshake.

Theorem 4.1.16 *For correct communication using k-way handshakes in the absence of processor breakdowns, it is necessary as well as sufficient that* $k \geq 4$.

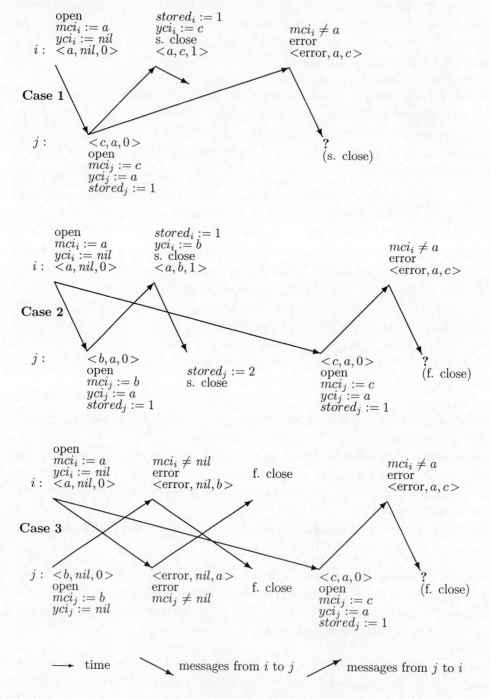

Figure 4.1 DILEMMA OF j ON RECEIPT OF ERROR PACKET WHEN $last = 2 - w$.

4.1.4.2 Discussion. The obvious way to choose *last* is either $last = k$, leading
to a $(2k)$-way handshake (an "even handshake"), or $last = k - w$, leading to a
$(2k - 1)$-way handshake (an "odd handshake"). However, the protocol skeleton
would work also with, for example, $last = k - 2w$. This choice would even lead
to correct communication under the conditions of theorem 4.1.13. It does however
have the drawback that a successful packet exchange now relies more on error
packets which might have to be sent even if no packets get lost. Let $k = 4$, $w_i = 1$
and $w_j = 0$. Then i can close when $stored_i = 2$, but j should only close with
$stored_j = 4$. However, j will never set $stored_j$ to 4, since for that it needs a packet
which i is only allowed to send when $stored_i = 3$. Hence j always needs an error
packet for closing, unless i does not close with $stored_i = 2$. (Although i is allowed
to close in that state, the protocol skeleton does not force i to close.)

There is a difference between even and odd handshakes, as Belsnes [Bel76] already
pointed out, which might be important in practical cases. Both work correctly in
the absence of processor breakdowns, if $last \geq 2$. If the last packet is lost, it is
substituted as it were, by an error packet. Now the receiver of the error packet
concludes that the other processor has closed successfully and closes successfully
too. If, however, the last packet was not lost, but the processor which had to send it
went down, we either have a loss or a duplication problem. For an even handshake,
the last packet sent goes from the processor with $w = 0$ to the one with $w = 1$,
hence we might have loss of packets. In the case of an odd handshake, the last
packet goes from the processor with $w = 1$ to the one with $w = 0$, hence we might
get duplication. Hence if, in a practical situation, a loss is more disastrous than
a duplication, one might consider whether the loss in efficiency caused by using a
5-way instead of a 4-way handshake is outweighed by the advantage of avoiding
loss instead of duplication.

Up till now we did not consider in which packet during the packet exchange the
actual message which had to be communicated is to be incorporated. As we can
see from the analysis, it really does not matter, as long as we do not use the very
last packet in the case of an odd handshake.

As we restricted ourselves to a protocol skeleton, it is clear that for an actual implementation there remains a lot to be specified before getting a working protocol.
For example, a timeout mechanism should be added to control the retransmissions
of packets, and some order of operations should be defined. Note that there is
some freedom in the specification of the protocol skeleton that does not contribute
to an efficient correct communication. For example, it does not help if closing is
postponed when $stored \geq last$. A restriction of the protocol skeleton which would
reduce the number of erroneous openings is the following. In the current formulation, a closed processor always opens if it receives a packet with $z = 0$, because

it considers it as an opening packet. However, it also could be a (former) reply to an opening packet. The latter case can be excluded by testing the y-field: real opening packets contain a y-field equal to *nil*. The reason we did not incorporate these restrictions in the protocol skeleton is that it is not necessary for the proof and leaves visible the basic structure which is responsible for the desired property of the protocol, namely reliable connection management.

The advantage of such a general setup is primarily that the proofs capture all protocols which can be viewed as instances of the protocol skeleton. The next section contains examples of extensions of this basic protocol skeleton for multiple message exchanges. Thus we know how far we can get towards a reliable connection management by a certain setting of parameters. Secondly, if we want more, e.g. reliable communication in the presence of processor breakdowns, we know that we should either devise a protocol skeleton based on a different principle, or else relax the assumptions. In section 4.2 we will investigate the effect of relaxing several assumptions. Thirdly, we have learned from this analysis that the problem with connection management under the stated assumptions, namely that any last packet in a finite packet exchange can be lost, is solved partly by allowing that certain error packets are substituted for the lost packet.

4.2 Other Connection-management Protocols

A 4-way handshake might be too high a price for correct communication, especially since correctness is only guaranteed if processors do not go down while they have an open connection. Therefore we investigate the question how the assumptions can be relaxed while keeping the communication as reliable as possible. There are basically five ways to relax the assumptions.

First, we can drop the requirement of a single message per connection. This reduces the overhead per message sent. Multiple-message communication can be obtained by a simple extension of the basic protocol skeleton. It is discussed in section 4.2.1.

Secondly, we could allow the processors to remember information about previous connections. This increases the memory requirements of the processors, and makes communication more sensitive to processor failures. This is because now at any moment a breakdown could cause loss of crucial information, while originally this was the case only for connections which happened to be open. However, depending on the communication environment, this might be worth the advantage of a 3-way handshake instead of a 4-way handshake. We will show in section 4.2.2 how one can achieve correct communication in the absence of processor breakdowns with a 3-way handshake.

Thirdly, we could be less strict about correctness. For example, we could let a failure close mean: *It is possible that no message came across* instead of *No message came across*, thus leaving it to the host of the processor to decide whether to send it once more. This could introduce duplication on a higher level. We will show in section 4.2.3 that a 2-way handshake suffices in those circumstances.

Fourthly, we could try to base the protocol on a different principle, using something that is more or less common to all processors, such as time. An example of this is the timer-based protocol described by Fletcher and Watson [FW78]. The correctness proof in [Tel91], however, shows that the communication is less reliable, in the sense described above. We relate timer-based protocols for connection management to the approach described here in section 4.2.4.

The fifth way out could be to restrict the type of errors that can occur in the communication network. For example, one can assume that packets can be lost, but it is assumed that communication over the network has the FIFO property. It depends entirely upon the actual network if this is at all possible. This almost amounts to defining the problem of connection management away.

4.2.1 Extensions to multiple-message communication

If we state theorem 4.1.13 in a slightly more general form, it is easily seen that protocol skeleton CM not only handles single-message communication correctly, but also multiple-message communication. Let n, $n \geq 1$, be the number of messages to be transmitted.

Lemma 4.2.1 *Using protocol skeleton CM, let the following three conditions hold:*
(i)   connections do not stay open indefinitely,
(ii) there are no processor breakdowns, and
(iii) $last_i \geq n + 1$, and $last_j \geq n + 1$.
Then for all closes there exist m, y, w, w', s, and s' such that the following holds:
   i does an (m, y, w, s)-close with $s + w \geq n + 1$ eventually if and only if
   j does a (y, m, w', s')-close with $s' + w' \geq n + 1$ eventually.

Proof.   Proof of theorem 4.1.13 with 2 replaced by $n + 1$. $\square$

4.2.1.1 One-sided multiple-message communication. It is usually not the case that n is a constant, and we would like to be able to choose n different for each connection. It is possible to incorporate this feature in the protocol skeleton, by including the value of n in the opening packet of the sender. Thus we formulate an extended protocol skeleton for multiple-message communication, consisting of the three basic operations S^{CM1}, R^{CM1} and C^{CM1}. We include the messages $D[1]$,

..., $D[n]$ to be sent and fill in values for cf and cs. We assume that the values of n and $D[1]$ up to $D[n]$ are supplied by a higher layer of the sender, and that $n \geq 1$ always. Note that, in contrast to e.g. a sliding-window protocol, we need that the message field and the seq field in a packet are large enough to contain the value $n + 1$, and that we cannot use sequence numbers modulo some value. This is due to the assumption that packets can arrive out of order, while the sliding-window protocol was designed for links which have the FIFO property.

Protocol skeleton $CM1$:

Initially $mci_i = nil$, $yci_i = nil$, $stored_i = 0$, $w_i = 0$, $last_i = 1$, $Q[i, j] = \emptyset$.

E^l_{ij}, E^d_{ij}, and E^r_{ij} from section 1.2.1.2,

S^{CM1}_i :   **begin if** $mci_i = nil$
             then $mci_i := new\ value$; $w_i := 1$; $last_i := n + 1$; $D[0] := n$
             fi; $seq := stored_i + w_i - 1$;
             if $w_i = 1$ **then** send $<mci_i, yci_i, seq, D[seq]>$ to j
             else send $<mci_i, yci_i, seq, \emptyset>$ to j
             fi
          end

R^{CM1}_i : { $Q[j, i] \neq \emptyset$ }
       begin receive $<x, y, z, d>$ from j;
          if $x \neq$ error
          then if $mci_i = nil \wedge z = 0$
             then $mci_i := new\ value$; $yci_i := x$; $stored_i := 1$; $last_i := d + 1$
             elif $(x = yci_i \vee stored_i = 0) \wedge y = mci_i \wedge z = stored_i$
             then if $z = 0$ **then** $yci_i := x$ **elif** $w_i = 0$ **then** $D[z] := d$ **fi**;
                $stored_i := stored_i + 1$
             elif $mci_i = nil \vee y \neq mci_i \vee (x \neq yci_i \wedge stored_i \neq 0)$
             then send $<$error$, y, x>$ to j
             fi
          elif $y = yci_i \wedge z = mci_i$ **co** error close **co**
          then if $stored_i \leq 1 - w_i$ **then** report failure
             elif $stored_i \geq 2 - w_i$ **then** report success
             fi; $last_i := 1$; $mci_i := nil$; $yci_i := nil$; $stored_i := 0$; $w_i := 0$
          fi
       end

C_i^{CM1} : { $mci_i \neq nil \wedge stored_i \geq last_i$ }
    begin report success; $mci_i := nil$; $yci_i := nil$;
         $stored_i := 0$; $w_i := 0$; $last_i := 1$
    end

All lemmas from section 4.1 except lemmas 4.1.8(2) and 4.1.8(3) still hold for protocol skeleton $CM1$. In addition we need the following notation and lemma about *last*, which now can be changed in the protocol skeleton.

Definition 4.2.1
  (1) An (m, y, w, s, l)-close *for i is an operation* C_i^{CM1} *or an operation* R_i^{CM1} *where mci_i is set to nil (i.e., an error close), invoked by i, where the parameters reflect the values of the protocol variables at the time of the operation:* $mci_i = m$, $yci_i = y$, $w_i = w$, $stored_i = s$ *and* $last_i = l$.
  (2) The predicate $closed_i(m, y, w, s, l)$ *becomes true when i does an (m, y, w, s, l)-close, i.e., it is false before the (m, y, w, s, l)-close and remains true ever after.*

Lemma 4.2.2 *Let i and j communicate using protocol skeleton $CM1$. Then*
  (1) *lemmas 4.1.1–4.1.6 and 4.1.9–4.1.12 hold,*
  (2) $stored_i \geq 1 \Rightarrow$
         $(mci_j = yci_i \wedge last_i = last_j) \vee \exists\, y', w', s' : closed_j(yci_i, y', w', s', last_i)$.

Proof. Obvious from protocol skeleton $CM1$.   □

Theorem 4.2.3 *Let i and j communicate using protocol skeleton $CM1$. Let the following conditions hold:*
  (i) *connections do not stay open indefinitely, and*
  (ii) *there are no processor breakdowns.*
Then for all closes there exist n, m, y, w, w', s, and s' such that the following holds:
    one processor does an $(m, y, w, s, n + 1)$-close with $s + w \geq 2$ implies that the other processor does a $(y, m, w', s', n + 1)$-close with $s' + w' \geq n + 1 \geq 2$ eventually.

Proof. Use lemmas 4.2.1 and 4.2.2, and note that the guard of operation C_i^{CM1} ensures that $s + w \geq n + 1$.   □

Theorem 4.2.4 *Under the assumptions of theorem 4.2.3, i and j can correctly communicate finite non-empty message sequences using protocol skeleton $CM1$.*

Proof. The only thing left to check is that inside one connection no loss or duplication of messages occurs. It is clear from operation R^{CM1} that message $D[m]$ is accepted when s is set to $m + 1$. Since s is increased one by one, all messages $D[1], ..., D[k]$ belonging to the current connection are accepted exactly once if the processor closes with $s = k + 1$. Since for the receiver $w = 0$, $s + w \geq n + 1$ implies that all n messages are accepted. □

Note that, although we need a 4-way handshake to send a single message, we only need a $2(n + 1)$-way handshake to send n messages, not a $4n$-way handshake.

4.2.1.2 Two-sided multiple-message communication.
Another immediate extension is to allow the message transfer in a connection to be two sided. In order to decide how many packets need to be exchanged in the case that the "receiver" has more messages to send than the "sender", we need the corresponding version of lemma 4.2.1 for odd handshakes in the basic protocol skeleton (lemma 4.2.1 corresponds to even handshakes).

Lemma 4.2.5 *Using protocol skeleton CM, let the following three conditions hold:*
(i)   connections do not stay open indefinitely,
(ii) there are no processor breakdowns, and
(iii) $last_i \geq n + 2 - w_i$, and $last_j \geq n + 2 - w_j$.
Then for all closes there exist m, y, w, w', s, and s' such that the following holds:
*   i does an (m, y, w, s)-close with $s \geq n + 1$ eventually if and only if*
*   j does a (y, m, w', s')-close with $s' \geq n + 1$ eventually.*

Proof. Analogous to the proof of lemma 4.2.1. □

Since an odd handshake is most efficient when the "sender" has fewer messages to send than the "receiver", and an even handshake is most efficient when the "sender" has more to send, we can let the protocol skeleton decide on the spot. Let n_i be the number of messages to be sent over by i. Note that, instead of $n \geq 1$ for the one-way case, we now have $n_i \geq w_i$, hence the "sender" transmits a non-empty sequence, while the "receiver" may transmit an empty sequence of messages. Again, $cf_i = 1 - w_i$ and $cs_i = 2 - w_i$. We assume $D[seq] = \emptyset$ for $seq > n_i$. Thus we extend the protocol skeleton as follows.

Protocol skeleton $CM2$:

Initially $mci_i = nil$, $yci_i = nil$, $stored_i = 0$, $w_i = 0$, $last_i = 1$, $Q[i, j] = \emptyset$.

E_{ij}^l, E_{ij}^d, and E_{ij}^r from section 1.2.1.2,

S_i^{CM2} :   **begin if** $mci_i = nil$
       then $mci_i := new\ value$; $w_i := 1$; $last_i := n_i + 1$; $D[0] := n_i$
       fi; $seq := stored_i + w_i - 1$; send $<mci_i, yci_i, seq, D[seq]>$ to j
    end

R_i^{CM2} : $\{\ Q[j,i] \neq \emptyset\ \}$
  begin receive $<x, y, z, d>$ from j;
    if $x \neq$ error
    then if $mci_i = nil \wedge z = 0$
      then $mci_i := new\ value$; $yci_i := x$; $stored_i := 1$;
         $D[0] := n_i$; $last_i := \max\{d + 1, n_i + 2\}$
      elif $(x = yci_i \vee stored_i = 0) \wedge y = mci_i \wedge z = stored_i$
      then if $z \neq 0$ **then** $D[z] := d$
         else $yci_i := x$; $last_i := \max\{d + 1, n_i + 2 - w_i\}$
         fi; $stored_i := stored_i + 1$
      elif $mci_i = nil \vee y \neq mci_i \vee (x \neq yci_i \wedge stored_i \neq 0)$
      then send $<error, y, x>$ to j
      fi
    elif $y = yci_i \wedge z = mci_i$ **co** error close **co**
    then if $stored_i \leq 1 - w_i$ **then** report failure
      elif $stored_i \geq 2 - w_i$ **then** report success
      fi; $last_i := 1$; $mci_i := nil$; $yci_i := nil$; $stored_i := 0$; $w_i := 0$
    fi
  end

C_i^{CM2} : $\{\ mci_i \neq nil \wedge stored_i \geq last_i\ \}$
  begin report success; $mci_i := nil$; $yci_i := nil$;
    $stored_i := 0$; $w_i := 0$; $last_i := 1$
  end

We have the following supplementing notation and lemma about *last*.

Definition 4.2.2

(1) *An* (m, y, w, s, l, n)-close *for* i *is an operation* C_i^{CM2}, *or an operation* R_i^{CM2} *where* mci_i *is set to nil (i.e., an error close), invoked by* i, *where the parameters reflect the values of the protocol variables at the time of the operation:* $mci_i = m$, $yci_i = y$, $w_i = w$, $stored_i = s$, $last_i = l$ *and* $n_i = n$.

(2) *The predicate* $closed_i(m, y, w, s, l, n)$ *is rendered true the moment when* i *does an* (m, y, w, s, l, n)-close, *i.e., it is false before the* (m, y, w, s, l, n)-close *and remains true ever after.*

Lemma 4.2.6 *Let i and j communicate using protocol skeleton CM2. Then*
- *(1)* *lemmas 4.1.1–4.1.6 and 4.1.9–4.1.12 hold,*
- *(2)* $mci_i \neq nil \Rightarrow last_i \geq n_i + 2 - w_i,$
- *(3)* $stored_i + w_i = 1 \Rightarrow last_i > stored_i,$
- *(4)* $stored_i + w_i \geq 2 \Rightarrow (mci_j = yci_i \wedge yci_j = mci_i \wedge last_i = last_j) \vee$
$$\exists \, w', s', n' : \; closed_j(yci_i, mci_i, w', s', last_i, n').$$

Proof. Obvious from the protocol skeleton.   □

Theorem 4.2.7 *Let i and j communicate using protocol skeleton CM2. Let the following conditions hold:*
- *(i)*   *connections do not stay open indefinitely, and*
- *(ii)* *there are no processor breakdowns.*

Then for all closes there exist m, y, w, w', s, s', n, n', and l such that the following holds:

> *one processor does an (m, y, w, s, l, n)-close with $s + w \geq 2$ implies that the other processor does a (y, m, w', s', l, n')-close eventually with $s' \geq n + 1$ and $s \geq n' + 1$.*

Proof. Use lemmas 4.2.5 and 4.2.6.   □

Corollary 4.2.8 *Under the assumptions of theorem 4.2.7 we can correctly communicate finite, non-empty message sequences in both directions at once with protocol skeleton CM2.*

4.2.2 Correct communication with a 3-way handshake

It is possible to achieve correct communication with a 3-way handshake if processors are allowed to maintain some information about previous connections, in contrast with the assumption in section 4.1. Let us reconsider the proof of lemma 4.1.15 to see what the problem was in the old model. A processor open with $w = 0$ and $stored = 1$ which receives an error packet does not have enough information to decide whether to do a successful close or a failure close. The processor does know that the other processor closed, but that could have been a successful close as well as a failure close. As the assumption in section 4.1 is that processors are not allowed to remember any information about previous connections, the other processor does not know either whether that particular close was successful or not. Thus if we drop the assumption that processors may not remember anything about previous connections, and include some information about previous connections in error packets, we might achieve that the receiver of an error packet has sufficient information to decide how to close.

In the sequel we will show that this is indeed possible. Since failure closes in no way contribute to correct communication, it is perhaps not surprising that we need information about past *successful* closes. It turns out that it is sufficient for a processor to remember the *yci*-value of its last successful close. The processor will maintain this value in the variable *lsc*. The extra information that is included in error packets is whether the *x*-field in the invalid packet $<x, y, z>$ is equal to the value in *lsc* or not, thus we need only one extra bit in the error packet. Whether a processor that receives an error packet closes as a success or as a failure will now depend on this bit too, not only on its value of *stored* and *w*. The protocol skeleton for the 3-way handshake is as follows.

Protocol skeleton $CM3$:

Initially $mci_i = nil$, $yci_i = nil$, $stored_i = 0$, $w_i = 0$, $lsc_i = nil$, $Q[i, j] = \emptyset$.

S_i^{CM3} :   **begin if** $mci_i = nil$ **then** $mci_i := new\ value$; $w_i := 1$ **fi**;
                send $<mci_i, yci_i, stored_i + w_i - 1>$ to j
     end

R_i^{CM3} : $\{\ Q[j, i] \neq \emptyset\ \}$
     begin receive $<x, y, z>$ from j;
          if $x \neq$ error
          then if $mci_i = nil \wedge z = 0$
             then $mci_i := new\ value$; $yci_i := x$; $stored_i := 1$
             elif $(x = yci_i \vee stored_i = 0) \wedge y = mci_i \wedge z = stored_i$
             then $stored_i := stored_i + 1$; **if** $z = 0$ **then** $yci_i := x$ **fi**
             elif $mci_i = nil \vee y \neq mci_i \vee (x \neq yci_i \wedge stored_i = 0)$
             then if $lsc_i = x$ **then** $b := true$ **else** $b := false$ **fi**;
                 send $<$error$, y, x, b>$ to j
             fi
          elif $y = yci_i \wedge z = mci_i$ **co** error close **co**
          then if $stored_i \leq 0$ **then** report failure
             elif $stored_i \geq 2 - w_i$ **then** report success; $lsc_i := yci_i$
             elif $b = true$ **then** report success; $lsc_i := yci_i$
             else report failure
             fi; $mci_i := nil$; $yci_i := nil$; $stored_i := 0$; $w_i := 0$
          fi
     end

C_i^{CM3} : { $mci_i \neq nil \wedge stored_i \geq 2 - w_i$ }
   begin report success; $lsc_i := yci_i$; $mci_i := nil$;
        $yci_i := nil$; $stored_i := 0$; $w_i := 0$
   end

E_{ij}^l, E_{ij}^d, and E_{ij}^r from section 1.2.1.2.

Thus in the protocol skeleton for the 3-way handshake the error procedure and the closing upon receipt of an error packet are changed. As non-arbitrary closes are still necessary for correct communication, we have incorporated this in the close operation. For the parameters cf, cs, and $last$ we filled in the following values: $cf = 0$ and $last = cs = 2 - w$. Thus in operation C^{CM3} the guard ensures a successful close.

Lemma 4.2.9 *Let i and j communicate using protocol skeleton CM3. Then*
   (1) lemmas 4.1.1–4.1.6 and 4.1.9–4.1.12 hold.
   (2) Let the following two conditions hold:
        (i) connections do not stay open indefinitely, and
        (ii) there are no processor breakdowns.
   Then
$$closed_i(m, y, w, s) \Rightarrow (sclosed_i(m, y, w) \wedge s + w \geq 2) \vee eclosed_i(m, y, w, s),$$
   (3) $stored_i = 0 \Rightarrow \neg\exists\, m, w : sclosed_j(m, mci_i, w) \wedge lsc_j \neq mci_i$,
   (4) $stored_i \geq 1 \Rightarrow (\exists\, w : sclosed_j(yci_i, mci_i, w) \Leftrightarrow lsc_j = mci_i)$.

Proof. (1), (2). Obvious from the protocol skeleton.
(3). Suppose that $stored_i = 0$ and $sclosed_j(m, mci_i, w)$ hold. Let this close be an (m, mci_i, w, s)-close for some s. Then there are two cases (assertion (2)).
Case 1: $s + w \geq 2$. Hence by lemma 4.1.5, $stored_i \geq 1$.
Case 2: $eclosed_j(m, mci_i, w, s)$. As $s + w = 1$ and $mci_i \neq nil$, $s = 1$ and $w = 0$. This implies $closed_i(mci_i, y', w', s')$ (lemma 4.1.10(2)).
Thus both cases lead to a contradiction. Hence we have that $stored_i = 0$ implies $\neg sclosed_j(m, mci_i, w)$. Thus also $lsc_j \neq mci_i$.
(4). The assertion holds initially. S_i^{CM3} changes mci_i if a connection is opened, but then $stored_i = 0$ and thus $\neg sclosed_j(m, mci_i, w)$ and $lsc_j \neq mci_i$ hold. If R_i^{CM3} opens a connection, j cannot know mci_i yet, thus $\neg sclosed_j(m, mci_i, w)$ and $lsc_j \neq mci_i$ hold. If R_i^{CM3} sets $stored_i$ from 0 to 1, then also $\neg sclosed_j(m, mci_i, w)$ and $lsc_j \neq mci_i$, because of (3). Other changes of $stored_i$ in R_i^{CM3} do not affect the assertion, except when i does an error close and $stored_i \geq 1$ is falsified. Operation C_i^{CM3} falsifies $stored_i \geq 1$, and R_j^{CM3} without error close and S_j^{CM3} do not change the assertion in any way. Consider the operation C_j^{CM3} or an error close in R_j^{CM3}.

Let it result in an (m', y', w', s')-close. If it is a failure close, then the assertion is not affected. Let the close be successful. Let $stored_i \geq 1$ hold (otherwise the assertion holds trivially). We have 4 cases.

Case 1: $m' = yci_i \wedge y' = mci_i$. Then $sclosed_j(yci_i, mci_i, w)$ becomes true and lsc_j is set to mci_i.

Case 2: $m' = yci_i \wedge y' \neq mci_i$. Then $sclosed_j(yci_i, mci_i, w)$ did not hold, nor $lsc_j = mci_i$. Neither holds after this close.

Case 3: $m' \neq yci_i \wedge y' = mci_i$. Hence (lemma 4.1.6) $s' = 1$ and $w' = 0$. Thus it was an error close. However, the corresponding assertion for j also held before this operation R_j^{CM3}, namely $stored_j \geq 1 \Rightarrow (\exists\, w : sclosed_i(yci_j, mci_j, w) \Leftrightarrow lsc_i = mci_j)$. Hence $sclosed_i(yci_j, mci_j, w)$ holds. Since $yci_j = y' = mci_i$, we have a contradiction as i has not closed this connection yet. Hence this case cannot occur.

Case 4: $m' \neq yci_i \wedge y' \neq mci_i$. If $lsc_j \neq mci_i$ before the close, the assertion holds afterwards too. Assume $lsc_j = mci_i$. Hence $sclosed_j(yci_i, mci_i, w)$ holds. Hence (lemma 4.1.6) $stored_j + w_j = 1$, and the close must be an error close. We also have $\neg closed_i(m'', mci_j, w'', s'')$, hence $lsc_j \neq mci_i$. Thus this close cannot be successful. Contradiction.

Summarizing, the assertion still holds after a close by j, which completes the proof. $\quad\square$

Theorem 4.2.10 *Let i and j communicate using protocol skeleton CM3. Let the following two conditions hold:*

(i) *connections do not stay open indefinitely, and*

(ii) *there are no processor breakdowns.*

Then for all closes there exist m, y, w, and w' such that the following holds:

one processor does a successful (m, y, w)-close eventually if and only if the other processor does a successful (y, m, w')-close eventually.

Proof. Let i do a successful (m, y, w)-close, and let it be an (m, y, w, s)-close. According to lemma 4.2.9 we have two cases.

Case 1: $s + w \geq 2$. Hence by lemma 4.1.5 we have that $(mci_j = y \wedge yci_j = m)$ or $closed_j(m, y, w', s')$ for some w' and s'. Using lemmas 4.2.9 and 4.1.10 we have that $closed_j(m, y, w', s')$ implies $sclosed_j(m, y, w', s')$. Let j be open still with $mci_j = y$. Then $stored_j \geq 1$ and hence (lemma 4.2.9(4)) $sclosed_i(yci_j, mci_j, w) \Leftrightarrow lsc_i = mci_j$. Thus a subsequent error close of j will be a successful (y, m, w')-close.

Case 2: $s = 1$, $w = 0$, and $eclosed_i(m, y, w, s)$. Thus j had $lsc_j = mci_i$ when it sent the error packet to i. As $stored_i = 1$, we know by lemma 4.2.9(4) that for some w', $sclosed_j(yci_i, mci_i, w')$ holds. Hence a successful close by i implies that j

does a corresponding successful close.

The reverse implication can be proved by an analogous argument.   □

Corollary 4.2.11 *For correct communication in the absence of processor break-downs, a 3-way handshake is sufficient if processors are allowed to remember one item of information about a previous connection.*

We remark that, although it is not necessary for the partial correctness of protocol skeleton $CM3$ to test whether an opening packet contains a y-field equal to nil, it is necessary now for an efficient protocol. This is because, in case the last packet of the 3-way handshake is lost, a processor needs an error packet in reply to its packet $<x, y, 0>$ in order to close. The chance of getting that reply is small if the other processor (because it already closed) reopens on receipt of $<x, y, 0>$, instead of sending an error packet.

Of course protocol skeleton $CM3$ also can be extended to handle a multiple-message exchange. It makes however no sense to do so, since to transmit n messages we still need $last \geq n + 2$.

4.2.3 Less reliable communication

If we are willing to accept a communication which is not always correct, the question still is how far one wants to go. One possibility is to accept duplication and only require that there is no loss. In that case a 2-way handshake is sufficient to achieve our goal.

Theorem 4.2.12 *Let $cf = 0$, $cs = 1$ and $last = 1$ in protocol skeleton CM, and let connections always be closed eventually. Then the problem of loss does not occur, i.e., for all closes there exist m, y, m', and w' such that the following holds:*

one processor does a successful $(m, y, 1)$-close implies that

the other processor does a successful (m', m, w')-close eventually.

Proof. Let i do a successful $(m, y, 1)$-close, hence $stored_i + w_i \geq 2$. Consequently, j was open with $mci_j = y$, $yci_j = m$ and $stored_j = 1$. Thus, when j closes this connection, it does a successful (y, m, w')-close.   □

There is however a notion of correctness which lies somewhere in between "no loss" and "correct communication". We will call this *semi-correct communication*. It is weaker than correct communication because it does not avoid all duplications. In the literature (e.g. [Tel91]), *semi-correct* is sometimes called *correct*.

Definition 4.2.3 Semi-correct communication *is the situation in which for all closes there exist m, y, w', m', and y' such that the following holds:*

> *one processor does a successful $(m, y, 1)$-close implies that*
> *the other processor does exactly one successful (m', y', w')-close with $y' = m$*
> *eventually.*

Note that semi-correct communication is strictly weaker than correct communication, because it allows that i does a failure $(m, y, 1)$-close while j does a successful $(y, m, 0)$-close, which is excluded by correct communication.

Could semi-correct communication be achieved with a 2-way handshake? The problem is of course, how to avoid duplication in the case that the sender closes successfully. The receiver now cannot wait for the sender to tell it whether it made a duplicate opening, which is the way the problem was handled in the previous cases. This is because waiting for a packet from the sender turns the 2-way handshake into a 3-way handshake. One could argue that the receiver could just wait for an error packet, to tell it how to close, but then we have the 3-way handshake discussed in section 4.2.2, where the sender just refuses to send its last packet with sequence number 1. Since the protocol skeleton does not require the sender to send this packet anyway, we even have correct communication, but we do not think it is fair to call this a 2-way handshake if we always (and not only in the case that a packet got lost) need a third (error) packet. Thus the receiver must decide on its own whether to open upon a packet and to risk a duplication, or not. Although it trivially satisfies the definition of semi-correct communication if the receiver always refuses to open upon receipt of a packet, we would hardly like to call this "communication". The receiver needs the yci value of all past successful closes in order to decide whether opening upon a received packet would introduce duplication or not, because the received packet could be a retransmission of some packet which led to a successful close long ago. We doubt that this is feasible in any practical case.

However, there is a semi-correct 2-way handshake which needs only one item of information from a previous connection, if we allow as an additional assumption on the magic function *new value* that it is strictly increasing (locally in one processor). This might seem a heavy condition to put on the function *new value*, but the two most obvious ways to implement this function both have this property. The first is to just number connections consecutively, and the other is to use the current time (on a local clock) together with the date, such that the result is non-periodic. Although both implementations in theory use unbounded numbers, in practice this is not the case since, for example, the number of milliseconds in two decades still fits into only 40 bits.

This item of information from a previous connection that will be maintained is again a *yci*-value of a past successful close. As before, it is maintained in *lsc*. The additional assumption that *new value* is strictly increasing enables us to order the values in the variables *mci*, *yci*, and *lsc*. To get a consistent ordering, we assume that the value *nil*, which is used for initializing those variables, is smaller than all values that the function *new value* can yield.

If a processor now receives a packet with an x-field less than or equal to the value it maintains in *lsc*, it knows it is an old retransmission and hence can discard it. Since successful closes are now possible with $stored = 0$ and hence $yci = nil$, we should take care not to destroy *lsc* then. However, it turns out to be sufficient to remember the *yci*-value of the last successful close with $w = 0$ (and thus $yci \neq nil$). We fill in the following values for the parameters cf, cs, and $last$: $cf = 0 - w$, and $cs = last = 1$. Thus the case that a processor does a failure close because $stored \leq cf$ cannot occur any more. Note that if i does an error $(m, y, w, 0)$-close which is successful, we know that $w = 1$ and $y = nil$, and thus we may not update lsc_i. For the other successful closes, $stored_i \geq 1$, so $yci_i \neq nil$.

We have the following (semi-correct) 2-way handshake.

Protocol skeleton $CM4$:

Initially $mci_i = nil$, $yci_i = nil$, $stored_i = 0$, $w_i = 0$, $lsc_i = nil$, $Q[i,j] = \emptyset$.

$R_i^{CM4} : \{ Q[j,i] \neq \emptyset \}$
    begin receive $<x, y, z>$ from j;
        if $x \neq$ error
        then if $mci_i = nil \wedge z = 0 \wedge x > lsc_i$
            then $mci_i := new\ value$; $yci_i := x$; $stored_i := 1$
            elif $(x = yci_i \vee stored_i = 0) \wedge y = mci_i \wedge z = stored_i$
            then $stored_i := stored_i + 1$; **if** $z = 0$ **then** $yci_i := x$ **fi**
            elif $mci_i = nil \vee y \neq mci_i \vee (x \neq yci_i \wedge stored_i = 0)$
            then if $lsc_i = x$ **then** $b := true$ **else** $b := false$ **fi**;
                send $<error, y, x, b>$
            fi
        elif $y = yci_i \wedge z = mci_i$ **co** error close **co**
        then if $stored_i \geq 1$ **then** report success; $lsc_i := yci_i$
            elif $b = true$ **then** report success
            else report failure
            fi; $mci_i := nil$; $yci_i := nil$; $stored_i := 0$; $w_i := 0$
        fi
    end

S_i^{CM4} :   **begin if** $mci_i = nil$ **then** $mci_i := new\ value$; $w_i := 1$ **fi**;
          send $< mci_i, yci_i, stored_i + w_i - 1 >$ to j
     end

C_i^{CM4} : $\{\ mci_i \neq nil \wedge stored_i \geq 1\ \}$
     begin report success; $lsc_i := yci_i$; $mci_i := nil$;
          $yci_i := nil$; $stored_i := 0$; $w_i := 0$
     end

E_{ij}^l, E_{ij}^d, and E_{ij}^r from section 1.2.1.2.

Lemma 4.2.13 *Let i and j communicate using protocol skeleton CM4, and let new value be increasing. Then*
  (1)   lemmas 4.1.1–4.1.6 and 4.1.9–4.1.12 hold.
  (2)   Let the following two conditions hold:
      (i)   connections do not stay open indefinitely, and
      (ii) there are no processor breakdowns.
     Then
     $closed_i(m, y, w, s) \Rightarrow (sclosed_i(m, y, w) \wedge s \geq 1) \vee eclosed_i(m, y, w, s),$
  (3) lsc_i is increasing.

Proof. (1), (2). Obvious from the protocol skeleton.
(3). Let $w_i = 0$. Then it is clear from the protocol skeleton that $yci_i > lsc_i$. Let $w_i = 1$ and $stored_i \geq 1$. Consider the operation R_j^{CM4} in which j opened the connection with $mci_j = yci_i$. At that moment we had $mci_i > lsc_j$, otherwise j would not have opened this connection, and $lsc_i < mci_j$, since mci_j was set to a new value which is strictly greater than all previous values. Hence $yci_i > lsc_i$ as soon as i sets $stored_i$ to 1 and sets yci_i. Since i is open still and neither yci_i nor lsc_i is changed, $yci_i > lsc_i$ still holds. Since lsc_i is not changed with a successful close if $yci_i = nil$, lsc_i is increasing.   □

Theorem 4.2.14 *Let i and j communicate using protocol skeleton CM4, and let the following conditions hold:*
  (i)   connections do not stay open indefinitely,
  (ii) there are no processor breakdowns, and
  (iii) new value is increasing.
Then for all closes there exist m, m', y, y', and w' such that the following holds:
     one processor does a successful $(m, y, 1)$-close implies that
     the other processor does exactly one successful (m', y', w')-close with $y' = m$
     eventually.

Proof. Let i do a successful $(m, y, 1)$-close. Let it be an $(m, y, 1, s)$-close. There are two cases (lemma 4.2.13).

Case 1: $s \geq 1$. Thus $s + w \geq 2$, and lemma 4.1.5 implies $closed_j(y, m, 0, s')$ with $s' \geq 1$, and hence a successful close, or $mci_j = y$, $yci_j = m$, and $stored_j \geq 1$, in which case j's close will be successful, too.

Case 2: $s = 0$. Hence it is an error close, and as it was successful, the error packet received was $< \text{error}, nil, m, true >$. Thus $sclosed_j(m', m, w')$ holds for some m' and w'.

Thus in both cases j does a successful close. Assume j does two: an (m', m, w')-close and an (m'', m, w'')-close. By lemma 4.1.6 we have that $w' = w'' = 0$. Let the close with $mci_j = m''$ be the last one. Hence just before the close $m = yci_j > lsc_j$. Since at the other close yci_j was set to m, and lsc_j is increasing, we also have $lsc_j \geq m$ just before the close with $mci_j = m''$. Contradiction. Thus j does exactly one successful close. $\qquad\square$

Theorem 4.2.15 *For semi-correct communication in the absence of processor breakdowns, a 2-way handshake is sufficient if processors are allowed to remember one item of information about a previous connection and the function new value is strictly increasing.*

Again, for an efficient working protocol we need to test whether $y = nil$ in an opening packet. Further, we can refrain from sending error packets if $x < lsc$. Since in a 2-way handshake the *seq*-field is always 0, we can just as well leave this field out too in an implementation.

Note that the protocol skeleton contains a feature that is not necessary for its semi-correctness. Namely, if a processor with $w = 1$ and $stored = 0$ receives an error packet, the way it closes depends on the bit in the error packet. This is not necessary since the processor could close as a failure always, even if the other one closed as a success. This still complies with the definition of semi-correctness. This suggests two ways to change the protocol skeleton.

First, let a processor with $w = 1$ and $stored = 0$ always close as a failure on receipt of an error packet. Then we do not need the extra bit in the error packets, nor the non-arbitrary closes, and hence we could refrain from sending error packets altogether. At the end of this section we incorporate this in operations $\text{R}^{CM4'}$ and $\text{C}^{CM4'}$ to compare it with the timer-based protocol in the next section.

Secondly, consider why a processor with $w = 1$ would want to close with $stored = 0$, apart from the case that the acknowledgement was lost (this case is handled correctly with use of the bit in the error packet). Originally, this was necessary to prevent deadlock if both processors happened to open simultaneously. If we can exclude this possibility, we have a correct 2-way handshake. The obvious way to do so is to let the processors have a fixed w, say i is always sender ($w = 1$) and j is always receiver ($w = 0$). In general, this clearly is not acceptable, but it might be inherent in some special application that the message transport is one way.

Theorem 4.2.16 *Let i and j communicate using protocol skeleton $CM4$, and let the following four conditions hold:*
  (i) connections do not stay open indefinitely,
  (ii) there are no processor breakdowns,
  (iii) new value is increasing, and
  (iv) $w_i = 1$ and $w_j = 0$ always.
Then for all closes there exist m, y, and m' such that the following holds:
     i does a successful $(m, y, 1)$-close eventually if and only if
     j does a successful $(m', m, 0)$-close eventually.

Proof. Left to the reader. □

Although the equivalence in theorem 4.2.16 is not sufficient for correct communication by definition (i might close successfully with $yci_i = nil$), we still feel this communication should be regarded as correct (one processor closes successfully if and only if the other processor closes successfully).

For reason of comparison with timer-based protocols, we now change protocol skeleton $CM4$ by deleting the error packets and doing failure closes if $stored_i = 0$, as suggested above.

Protocol skeleton $CM4'$:

Initially $mci_i = nil$, $yci_i = nil$, $stored_i = 0$, $w_i = 0$, $lsc_i = nil$, $Q[i, j] = \emptyset$.

E_{ij}^l, E_{ij}^d, and E_{ij}^r from section 1.2.1.2,

$R_i^{CM4'} : \{ Q[j, i] \neq \emptyset \}$
     begin receive $<x, y, z>$ from j;
          if $mci_i = y = nil \wedge z = 0 \wedge x > lsc_i$
          then $mci_i := new\ value$; $yci_i := x$; $stored_i := 1$
          elif $(x = yci_i \vee stored_i = 0) \wedge y = mci_i \wedge z = stored_i$
          then $stored_i := stored_i + 1$; **if** $z = 0$ **then** $yci_i := x$ **fi**
          else *error* $(<x, y, z>)$
          fi   **co** procedure *error* could be "skip". **co**
     end

$S_i^{CM4'}$:   **begin if** $mci_i = nil$ **then** $mci_i := new\ value$; $w_i := 1$ **fi**;
                    send $< mci_i, yci_i, stored_i + w_i - 1 >$ to j
            end

$C_i^{CM4'}$: $\{\ mci_i \neq nil\ \}$
        begin if $stored_i \geq 1$ **then** report success; $lsc_i := yci_i$
            else report failure
            fi; $mci_i := nil$; $yci_i := nil$; $stored_i := 0$; $w_i := 0$
    end

Theorem 4.2.17 *Let i and j communicate using protocol skeleton $CM4'$, and let the following conditions hold:*
  (i)   connections do not stay open indefinitely,
  (ii) there are no processor breakdowns, and
  (iii) new value is increasing.
Then for all closes there exist m, m', y, y', and w' such that the following holds:
    one processor does a successful $(m, y, 1)$-close implies that
    the other processor does exactly one successful (m', y', w')-close with $y' = m$
    eventually.

Proof. Use the proof from theorem 4.2.14, case 1, and note that case 2 does not occur as a processor with $stored = 0$ does not close successfully.   □

We saw above that if processors are allowed to remember one item of information about a previous connection it is possible to have correct communication with a 3-way handshake and to have semi-correct communication with a 2-way handshake. One can pose the question whether it is perhaps possible to have semi-correct communication with a 3-way handshake if we are *not* willing to use the extra memory necessary for a correct 3-way handshake. However, it turns out to be not much of a relaxation if we only have to avoid duplication when the sender closes successfully, as we can see from the proof of lemma 4.1.15. A receiver of an error packet which is in state $w = 0$ and $stored = 1$ still does not have enough information to decide how to close, and the information it needs pertains to an already closed connection. Even the knowledge that *new value* is increasing is not sufficient if the processors are not allowed to remember the highest value seen after a connection is closed.

4.2.4 The use of time

The assumptions on which timer-based protocols for connection management rely differ in two respects from our original assumptions. The first one is that packets do not have arbitrary delays: there is some finite time after which we can assume that a packet is lost, if it has not arrived yet. The second one is that processors can use time: they have local clocks, and the local clocks are in some way related. The way the first assumption is usually implemented uses time, too. Messages are timestamped when sent, and if any processor encounters a packet with a timestamp which is older than some fixed lifetime (the *packet lifetime*), it is destroyed. Thus, if the communication network allows arbitrary delays, we need that the local clocks all show more or less the same time. In other words, the processors' clocks may drift away from real time, but the drift of all clocks should remain ρ-bounded, that is, in real time δ a clock is increased by an amount δ', where $\delta/(1 + \rho) \leq \delta' \leq \delta.(1 + \rho)$ (see e.g. [Tel91]). The way duplication is avoided in timer-based protocols is basically the same as in the 2-way handshakes from section 4.2.3: do not open a connection when it is a duplication. More specifically: do not open a connection upon receipt of an old packet. Before, "old" meant: with an x-field less than or equal to lsc, now "old" means: with a timestamp $\leq$ local time $-$ packet lifetime. The way this is handled is that connections are left open until no more packets from the current connection can arrive. However, if, once a connection is opened, processors have to be able to conclude that no more "live" packets of the current connection can arrive, processors also must agree upon sending retransmissions for a fixed time only. This has one serious drawback: if packets can be sent only for a fixed time, all these packets might be lost in the communication network. In all previous protocol skeletons we had the possibility to just continue trying to get through and send retransmissions until some answer is received, whether it is the expected answer or an error packet. This is the reason why timer-based protocols only achieve semi-correct communication. As an illustration we give the protocol skeleton for a timer-based semi-correct 2-way handshake for single-message communication, leaving out all features that facilitate multiple-message flow as in e.g. the protocol given by Fletcher and Watson [FW78]. We incorporate the feature of destroying outdated packets in the protocol skeleton to comply with the assumption of unbounded delays. Apart from the atomic operations S^{CM5}, R^{CM5}, and C^{CM5} for both processors, we add an atomic action TIME which increases the local clocks of both processors by the same amount τ. This can be interpreted as: during time τ the processors did no S^{CM5}, R^{CM5}, or C^{CM5} operations. The idea of the atomic action time is due to Tel [Tel91]. Thus we assume the local clocks show exactly the same time. It is easy to adapt the protocol skeleton to clocks which have a drift which is ρ-bounded, see e.g. [Tel91]. The problem of how to keep local clocks in a distributed system synchronized is non-trivial (cf. [LL84]), but lies outside the scope of this chapter.

The protocol skeleton has the following features. In this case it is necessary for the semi-correctness of the protocol skeleton that a processor can distinguish opening packets from acknowledgements, thus we will include this in the skeleton. The variable mci_i now contains the time the current connection was opened, while yci_i will not be used any more. As it is a 2-way handshake, we fill in 1 for cs and 0 for cf. The parameter mst_w is the maximum time during which a packet may be sent. It may depend on the value of w. The parameter mpl is the maximum time during which a packet can live in the communication network. The parameter mct_w is the minimum connection time (to prevent duplication). It may depend on the value of w. It is necessary for correctness that it is strictly larger than 0, to ensure that different connections indeed have different identifiers.

Protocol skeleton $CM5$:

Initially $mci_i = nil$, $clock_i = clock_j$, $stored_i = 0$, $w_i = 0$, $Q[i,j] = \emptyset$.

TIME: **begin** choose $\tau \in \mathbb{R}^+$; $clock_i := clock_i + \tau$; $clock_j := clock_j + \tau$ **end**

S_i^{CM5} : $\{ mci_i = nil \lor clock_i - mci_i < mst_{w_i} \}$
      begin if $mci_i = nil$ **then** $mci_i := clock_i$; $w_i := 1$ **fi**;
            send $< stored_i + w_i - 1, clock_i, D >$ to j
      end

R_i^{CM5} : $\{ Q[j,i] \neq \emptyset \}$
      begin receive $< z, t, d >$ from j;
            if $clock_i - t < mpl$
            then if $mci_i = nil \land z = 0 \land d \neq ack$
                  then $mci_i := clock_i$; $D := ack$; $stored_i := 1$
                  elif $((w_i = 1 \land d = ack) \lor (w_i = 0 \land d \neq ack)) \land z = stored_i$
                  then $stored_i := stored_i + 1$
                  else *error* $(< z, t, d >)$
                  fi   **co** procedure *error* could be "skip". **co**
            fi
      end

C_i^{CM5} : $\{ mci_i \neq nil \land clock_i - mci_i \geq mct_{w_i} \}$
      begin if $stored_i \geq 1$ **then** report success **else** report failure **fi**;
            $mci_i := nil$; $stored_i := 0$; $w_i := 0$
      end

E_{ij}^l, E_{ij}^d, and E_{ij}^r from section 1.2.1.2.

   Clearly the correctness of the protocol skeleton depends on the way the constants

mst_0, mst_1, mpl, mct_0, and mct_1 are chosen. Although the assumptions on which this timer-based protocol skeleton is based are different from those of the previous protocol skeletons, we will show that it is a refinement of protocol skeleton $CM4'$ from section 4.2.3. For this purpose we define a timer-based protocol skeleton $CM5'$, where we extend protocol skeleton $CM5$ with the variables yci and lsc and the packet fields x and y. Thus we can compare situations in the protocol skeletons $CM4'$ and $CM5'$, and hence in $CM4'$ and $CM5$. We will add the name of the protocol skeleton as a superscript if we need to make the distinction. For example, we will show that $valid^{CM5'}(<x, y, z, t, d>)$ implies $valid^{CM4'}(<x, y, z>)$.

Protocol skeleton $CM5'$:

Initially $mci_i = nil$, $clock_i = clock_j$, $stored_i = 0$, $w_i = 0$, $Q[i, j] = \emptyset$,
$\qquad\qquad yci_i = nil$, $lsc_i = nil$.

E_{ij}^l, E_{ij}^d, and E_{ij}^r from section 1.2.1.2,

TIME: **begin** choose $\tau \in \mathbb{R}^+$; $clock_i := clock_i + \tau$; $clock_j := clock_j + \tau$ **end**

$\text{S}_i^{CM5'}$: $\{ mci_i = nil \vee clock_i - mci_i < mst_{w_i} \}$
     begin if $mci_i = nil$
         then $mci_i := clock_i$; $w_i := 1$; $D := \text{data} \neq ack$
         fi; send $<mci_i, yci_i, stored_i + w_i - 1, clock_i, D>$ to j
     end

$\text{R}_i^{CM5'}$: $\{ Q[j, i] \neq \emptyset \}$
     begin receive $<x, y, z, t, d>$ from j;
         if $clock_i - t < mpl$
         then if $mci_i = nil \wedge z = 0 \wedge d \neq ack$
             then $mci_i := clock_i$; $D := ack$; $stored_i := 1$; $yci_i := x$
             elif $((w_i = 1 \wedge d = ack) \vee (w_i = 0 \wedge d \neq ack)) \wedge z = stored_i$
             then $stored_i := stored_i + 1$; **if** $z = 0$ **then** $yci_i := x$ **fi**
             else *error* $(<x, y, z, t, d>)$
             fi   **co** procedure *error* could be "skip". **co**
         fi
     end

$\text{C}_i^{CM5'}$: $\{ mci_i \neq nil \wedge clock_i - mci_i \geq mct_{w_i} \}$
     begin if $stored_i \geq 1$ **then** $lsc_i := yci_i$; report success
         else report failure
         fi; $mci_i := nil$; $yci_i := nil$; $stored_i := 0$; $w_i := 0$
     end

Lemma 4.2.18 *Let i and j communicate using protocol skeleton $CM5'$. Then*

 (1) lemmas 4.1.1 and 4.1.2(1)–(2) hold,

 (2) $clock_i = clock_j$,

 (3) $clock_i$ is increasing,

 (4) $mci_i \neq nil \Rightarrow mci_i \leq clock_i$,

 (5) $yci_i \neq nil \Rightarrow \exists\, y', z, t, d : accepted_i(<yci_i, y', z, t, d>)$,

 (6) $closed_i(m, y, w, s) \wedge y \neq nil \Rightarrow \exists\, y', z, t, d : accepted_i(<y, y', z, t, d>)$,

 (7) $closed_i(m, y, w, s) \Rightarrow clock_i - m \geq mct_w \wedge (y \neq nil \Rightarrow y < clock_i) \wedge$
$$(mci_i \neq nil \Rightarrow mci_i - m \geq mct_w),$$

 (8) $lsc_i \neq nil \Rightarrow \exists\, m, w, s : closed_i(m, lsc_i, w, s)$,

 (9) $<x, y, z, t, ack> \in Q[i, j] \Rightarrow x \leq t \leq clock_i \wedge t < x + mst_0 \wedge$
$$((mci_i = x \wedge w_i = 0) \vee \exists\, s : closed_i(x, y, 0, s)),$$

 (10) $<x, y, z, t, d> \in Q[i, j] \wedge d \neq ack \Rightarrow x \leq t \leq clock_i \wedge t < x + mst_1 \wedge$
$$((mci_i = x \wedge w_i = 1) \vee \exists\, y', s : closed_i(x, y', 1, s)),$$

 (11) $mci_i \neq nil \wedge <x', y', z, t, d> \in Q[i, j] \wedge mci_i \neq x' \Rightarrow$
$$t < mci_i \vee t \geq mci_i + mct_{w_i},$$

 (12) $closed_i(x, y, w, s) \wedge <x', y', z, t, d> \in Q[i, j] \wedge x \neq x' \Rightarrow$
$$t < x \vee t \geq x + mct_w.$$

Proof. Directly from the protocol skeleton. □

Lemma 4.2.19 *Let i and j communicate using protocol skeleton $CM5'$. Let $mct_1 > 2mpl + mst_0 + mst_1$ and $mct_0 > mpl + mst_1$. Then*

 (1) $w_i = 0 \wedge mci_i \neq nil \Rightarrow 0 \leq mci_i - yci_i < mpl + mst_1$,

 (2) $w_i = 1 \wedge stored_i \geq 1 \Rightarrow 0 \leq yci_i - mci_i < mpl + mst_1$,

 (3) $mci_i = nil \wedge lsc_i \neq nil \wedge <x, nil, 0, t, d> \in Q[j, i] \wedge clock_i - t < mpl \Rightarrow$
$$x < lsc_i,$$

 (4) $mci_i \neq nil \wedge <x, y, z, t, d> \in Q[j, i] \wedge valid_i^{CM5'}(<x, y, z, t, d>) \Rightarrow$
$$y = mci_i,$$

 (5) $closed_i(m, y, w, s) \wedge s \geq 1 \wedge stored_i \geq 1 \Rightarrow yci_i > y$,

 (6) $<x, y, z, t, d> \in Q[j, i] \wedge valid_i^{CM5'}(<x, y, z, t, d>) \Rightarrow$
$$valid_i^{CM4'}(<x, y, z>).$$

Proof. (1). Use lemma 4.2.18(5) and (10) and the fact that the packet upon which i opened the connection contained a t-field which was tested for $clock_i - t < mpl$.
(2). Use lemma 4.2.18(7) and assertion (1).
(3). $lsc_i \neq nil$ implies $closed_i(m, y, w, s)$ with $y = lsc_i$ for some m, w, and s, and hence $clock_i - m > mct_w$. We have two cases.
Case 1: $w = 1$. By assertion (2) we have $y - m < mpl + mst_1$ and hence $clock_i - lsc_i > mct_1 - mpl - mst_1 > mpl + mst_0$. Using lemma 4.2.18(12) for j we have

that $t \geq x > lsc_i + mct_0$, which implies $x > lsc_i$, or that $t < lsc_i + mst_0$. Using lemma 4.2.18(3) and (9), the latter leads to a contradiction.

Case 2: $w = 0$. By assertion (1) we have $m - y \geq 0$, and hence $clock_i - lsc_i > mct_0 > mpl + mst_1$. Using lemma 4.2.18(12) for j we have that $t \geq x > lsc_i + mct_1$, which implies $x > lsc_i$, or that $t < lsc_i + mst_1$. The latter leads to a contradiction.

(4). We have the following cases.

Case 1: $w_i = 0$. Hence $d \neq ack$ and since $stored_i \geq 1$, $z \geq 1$ and $y \neq nil$. By lemma 4.2.18(1), (5), and (9) we have $t \geq y$ and thus $0 \leq clock_i - y < mpl + mst_1$. Since $clock_i - mci_i \geq 0$, we have $mci_i - y < mpl + mst_1 < mct_0$. Hence $mci_i - y \geq 0$ implies $mci_i = y$. Assume $mci_i < y$. Since i has not closed the connection between mci_i and $clock_i$ and $clock_i \geq y$, mci_i at time y equals $mci_i = y$.

Case 2: $w_i = 1$. Hence $d = ack$ and by lemma 4.2.18(9) and assertion (1) we have $mci_i - y \leq clock_i - y < 2mpl + mst_0 + mst_1 < mct_1$. Thus for the same reasons as in the first case, $mci_i = y$.

(5). $s \geq 1$ and $stored_i \geq 1$ ensure that $y \neq nil$, $yci_i \neq nil$, and $sclosed_i(m, y, w, s)$. By the fact that lemma 4.2.18(7) already held before the current connection was opened, we have $y < mci_i$. Thus the case that $w_i = 1$ implies by assertion (2) that $y < yci_i$. Let $w_i = 0$. Then by assertion (3) we have $lsc_i < yci_i$. If $y = lsc_i$, then $y < yci_i$. If not, then there was another (m', y', w', s')-close in between for some m', y', w', and s', and $mci_i - m' > mct_{w'}$ and $m' - m > mct_w$ so $mci_i - m > 2mpl + 2mst_1$. As yci_i and y differ by at most $mpl + mst_1$ from mci_i and m, respectively, $y < yci_i$.

(6). Note that assertion (3) ensures that $<x, nil, 0, t, d> \in Q[j, i]$ together with $valid_i^{CM5'}(<x, nil, 0, t, d>)$ implies $valid_i^{CM4'}(<x, nil, 0>)$. All other packets are only $valid_i^{CM5'}$ if $mci_i \neq nil$. Hence we can use assertion (4). Since yci_i-values unequal to nil uniquely identify connections (assertion (5)), a valid y-value implies a valid x-value. The test of whether a z-value is valid is the same in both protocol skeletons, thus we have proved the conclusion. $\qquad\square$

Theorem 4.2.20 *Protocol skeleton $CM5$ is a refinement of protocol skeleton $CM4'$.*

Proof. The only difference between the protocol skeletons $CM5$ and $CM5'$ is that in $CM5$ all those packet fields and variables which are not used in $CM5'$ are discarded. Since acceptance of a packet in $R^{CM5'}$ implies acceptance of that packet in operation $R^{CM4'}$, $R^{CM5'}$ is a refinement of $R^{CM4'}$. The operation $S^{CM5'}$ contains an extra restriction upon sending compared to $S^{CM4'}$, hence operation $S^{CM5'}$ is a refinement of $S^{CM4'}$. Operation $C^{CM5'}$ is a refinement of $C^{CM4'}$, as the former only contains an extra guard. Since operation TIME is a restriction of the function *new value*, protocol skeleton $CM5$ is a refinement of protocol skeleton $CM4'$.   □

Corollary 4.2.21 *For semi-correct communication in the absence of processor breakdowns, a 2-way handshake is sufficient if processors have access to synchronized local clocks.*

We remark that although the straightforward extension of protocol skeleton $CM5$ for multiple-message communication as shown in section 4.2.1 works, it will greatly improve if there is not just a constant time available to send the sequence of messages, but some time dependent on the length of the sequence. In section 2.2 the block acknowledgement protocol is discussed and implementations with one timer and a sequence of timers, respectively, are compared. Also in the timer-based protocol of Fletcher and Watson [FW78] each message in the sequence has its own timer. For a partial correctness proof of this protocol which also uses system-wide invariants, we refer to [Tel91].

5

Commit Protocols

Commit protocols are used for concurrency control in distributed data bases. Thus they belong to the application layer. For an introduction to this area we recommend the book by Bernstein *et al.* [BHG87, Chapter 7].

If a data base is distributed over several sites, it is very possible that a data base operation which is logically a single action in fact involves more than one site of the data base. For example, consider the transfer of a sum of money *sm* from one bank account to another. The balance of the first bank account has to be decreased by *sm*, while the balance of the second has to be increased by *sm*. These two subactions might have to take place at different sites. It is imperative that *both* subactions are executed, and not one. If it is not possible to execute one of them, e.g. because its site is temporarily down, they should both be not executed.

In data base management such a logically single action is called a *transaction*, and it should behave as if it is an atomic action. At some point in the execution of the transaction it has to be decided whether the transaction is (going to be) executed as a whole and will never be revoked (*commit*), or that the transaction cannot be completed, and parts already done will be undone (*abort*). In general, an algorithm to ensure that the transaction can be viewed as an atomic action is called an *atomic commitment protocol*. Thus all processes participating in an atomic commitment protocol have to reach agreement upon whether to commit or to abort the transaction under consideration.

This suggests that the problem of atomic commitment is related to the problem of distributed consensus, or the Byzantine generals problem. However, due to differences in the model of computation and the exact requirements for the solutions of both problems, the similarity is but superficial (see e.g. [Had90, Gra90]).

Atomic commitment protocols are usually presented as if one fixed set of processes has to reach agreement about one transaction. In reality, however, there are a lot of transactions, each of which has its own set of processes that try to reach agreement simultaneously. Moreover, it is possible that subactions from different transactions, e.g. located at the same site, conflict (think of writing the same data base item), so that only one of them can be executed, and the other consequently has to be aborted. Hence it is assumed that each process individually might want to abort the transaction, thus forcing the whole transaction to abort.

In contrast with the situation in the previous chapter, the identification of different transactions is no issue in data base management. In connection management, the problem is caused by the requirement that no information is stored between connections and that all information is lost when a site goes down. In data base management, to guard against loss of information when sites go down, crucial information is stored on so-called *stable storage*. As stable storage is available anyway in data base management, it is also used to record information about transactions, and in the atomic commitment protocol several stages in the progress towards commitment are recorded on (local) stable storage. This is called the *distributed transaction log*, or in short *log*. Usually it is incorporated in the data base log.

It is most important that atomic commitment protocols tolerate site failures. Some protocols also tolerate communication failures such as the loss of messages. It is assumed that the lower layers of the communication network handle garbled messages, retransmission and rerouting of messages. Sometimes it is even assumed that the delay of messages has a fixed bound, and together with the assumption that no messages are lost, this means that if a process does not receive an answer from another process within some fixed time, we can draw the conclusion that this other process is down. Hence the use of timeouts in these protocols.

The general setup of the commit protocols we discuss in this chapter is the same. They differ in the number of stages used towards commitment: the 2-phase commit protocol is comparable to a 3-way handshake, and the 3-phase commit protocols are comparable to a 5-way handshake. Further differences lie in the amount of coordination required between processes after recovering from failures. The part of the protocol that deals with this recovery for the processes that did not fail is called the *termination protocol*. The recovery of the processes that did fail and were repaired is described by the *recovery protocol*. Sometimes, the termination protocol can be used for that also.

The 2-phase commit protocol is the one used in practice. However, it is subject to *blocking*, that is, it is possible that a process has to wait for other processes to come up after a failure, before it can proceed with its own part of the commit protocol. The 3-phase commit protocols have been designed to overcome this problem. In section 5.1 we discuss the 2-phase commit protocol, and prove its safety and liveness. In section 5.2 we discuss 3-phase commit protocols.

5.1 The 2-phase Commit Protocol

We first describe some properties of all atomic commitment protocols in section 5.1.1. In section 5.1.2 we discuss the 2-phase commit protocol without all features to cope with possible failures, and prove its safety in absence of failures. In section 5.1.3 we then give the 2-phase commit protocol due to Gray [Gra78] and Lampson and Sturgis [LS76], and prove the safety and liveness of the version presented in Bernstein *et al.* [BHG87].

5.1.1 Atomic commitment protocols

We give the general setup of atomic commitment protocols and their correctness criteria as formulated by Bernstein *et al.* [BHG87].

5.1.1.1 General setup. Usually, atomic commitment protocols are asymmetric, that is, not all participating processes run the same program. Instead, one designated process is the "leader". In this case, the designated process is called the *coordinator*, while the other processes are called the *participants*.

Atomic commitment protocols proceed in *phases* (see section 1.1.2.2). A phase consists of the sending of messages from the coordinator to all participants left (participants can leave the protocol early), and (except for the last phase) awaiting the answers. Thus it is similar to simulated synchronous computation (section 1.1.2.4). However, while the basis of the message exchange in simulated synchronous computation is a sliding window protocol with a window of size 2, here the window size is 1, as is also the case in connection management (see section 4.1.1.1). In fact, atomic commitment protocols can be seen as connection management protocols with one sender (the coordinator) and several receivers (the participants).

In the first phase, all processes cast a *vote*: *yes* or *no*, which states their intention to either commit or abort. In a later phase processes reach a *decision*, which is either *commit* or *abort*. (If the decision is to abort it may occur in an earlier phase than the decision to commit.) A prerequisite for the decision to commit is that all processes voted *yes*.

Atomic commitment protocols are designed to tolerate site failures, hence it is always possible that a process cannot send a message because its site is down. To avoid indefinite waiting for the next message in the exchange, timeouts are used. (Timeouts are not necessary for the safety of atomic commitment protocols, only for their progress.) What action has to be taken upon a timeout depends on the current phase of the process. Likewise, it depends on the phase reached how a process has to proceed after recovering from a site failure. Thus information about the phase reached is written in stable storage (on the log).

Two situations arise: either a process can independently decide what to do next (i.e., *independent recovery*), or it has to communicate with other processes. In the latter case we say that the process is *uncertain*. An uncertain process may be subject to blocking if the other processes that it has to communicate with are down. It has been proven that atomic commitment protocols that tolerate both site and communication failures and never block do not exist. If we assume that there are no communication failures, atomic commitment protocols that tolerate only site failures are still subject to blocking, if the site failure is total (i.e., all sites go down), see e.g. [SS83, Ske86].

5.1.1.2 *Correctness criteria.*

Bernstein *et al.* [BHG87] formulated correctness criteria for atomic commitment protocols. For the commit protocols that we will discuss in detail, we will prove their safety and liveness by our usual methods of system-wide invariants and decreasing functions in a well-founded domain. We will then show that the criteria of Bernstein *et al.* are indeed fulfilled.

Definition 5.1.1 *An atomic commitment protocol is an algorithm for processes to reach decisions such that:*

(1) *All processes that reach a decision reach the same one.*

(2) *A process cannot reverse its decision after it has reached one.*

(3) *The commit decision can only be reached if all processes voted* yes.

(4) *If there are no failures and all processes voted* yes, *then the decision will be to commit.*

(5) *Consider any execution containing only failures that the algorithm is designed to tolerate. At any point in this execution, if all existing failures are repaired and no new failures occur for sufficiently long, then all processes will eventually reach a decision.*

It is interesting to compare these criteria with the achievements in connection management, which was discussed in the previous chapter. In that case, "commit" corresponds to "successful close", and "abort" to "unsuccessful close". The vote *yes* of a participant corresponds to the opening of a connection with parameter $w = 0$, while the vote *no* corresponds to the sending of an error packet.

A non-essential difference between atomic commitment and connection management is that in the latter, the connection is between 2 processes, while in atomic commitment, usually more processes take part in a transaction. In connection management, the goal could be formulated (section 4.1.2.1) as agreement on "successful closes", which corresponds to agreement on the decision to commit in commit protocols. However, in connection management no agreement is required for "unsuccessful closes", while in atomic commitment agreement on the decision to abort is required also. In fact, only requirement (5) is not met by the connection management protocols.

However, there are differences in the assumptions about the network. In connection management, processes do not know beforehand if and with whom they are supposed to set up a connection. In atomic commitment, processes know that they are supposed to take part in an atomic commitment protocol with what coordinator and about which transaction. Thus identification of different connections is an issue, while transactions can be easily kept apart (by their a priori known identification). Connection management protocols tolerate communication failures and not site failures, while atomic commitment protocols tolerate site failures and only sometimes communication failures. This last distinction is mainly due to the fact that in atomic commitment it is allowed to use stable storage, while in connection management it is not. In fact, the condition "no site failures" can be dropped if in the connection management protocols variables are in stable storage. As the identification issue can be circumvented if processes are allowed to store information about previous connections (in which case a 3-way handshake gives correct connection management), we are not surprised that the 2-phase commit protocol is in fact a (multiple) 3-way handshake.

5.1.2 The basic protocol

We first discuss the 2-phase commit protocol without the additions necessary to cope with several possible errors and show how it operates in a failure-free environment. We will denote it by $2P0$.

The coordinator begins by sending a message to the participants, requesting their votes. The participants send a message with their vote *yes* or *no* back to the coordinator. The participants that vote *no* immediately decide to abort. Upon receipt of the votes of all participants, the coordinator decides: commit if all participants voted *yes* and its own vote is *yes*, too; and abort in all other cases. The coordinator then sends its decision to the processes that voted *yes*. Upon receipt of the decision of the coordinator, a participant decides accordingly. During the execution of the protocol the following records are written on the log in stable storage: *start*, by the coordinator to indicate that it initiated the algorithm, *yes*, by participants, to record their vote, and *commit* or *abort*, by all processes, to record their decision. (As a participant that votes *no* immediately decides to abort, it is not necessary to record the vote *no* separately.) We will see in section 5.1.3 how these are used for recovery.

5.1.2.1 The basic protocol skeleton. We use the following notation in the protocol skeleton. The coordinator is named c, while the identifier i is used for arbitrary participants. Participants can execute operations A_i^{2P0} (awaken) and R_i^{2P0} (receive). The coordinator can also execute operation P_c^{2P0} (new phase) besides A_c^{2P0} and R_c^{2P0}.

All processes have variables $awake$, to indicate whether they are currently engaged in the commit protocol, st, to indicate their current inclination (yes (1) or no (0)) towards commit (2) or abort (0), and log, to model the stable storage (as a set). In addition, participants have a variable $stored_i$, which counts the number of messages received from the coordinator (see also section 2.1.1). The coordinator has for each participant i a variable $stored_c[i]$, to count the number of messages received from i, and a variable $mes_c[i]$, to record the contents (i.e., yes (1) or no (0)) in the message from i. Furthermore, the coordinator records the current phase in $phase_c$, whether to go to the next phase or not in the boolean variable $nphs_c$, while the set of participants can be found in $partn_c$.

We denote messages as $<z, b>$, where z is the sequence number (see section 2.1.1), and b the contents: 1 for yes, 2 for commit and 0 for no or abort. (It is clear from the sequence number which one is meant.) Casting of a vote is simply denoted as $st_i := vote$. We get the following protocol skeleton.

Protocol skeleton $2P0$:

Initially $partn_c = \{$ processes that are participants for this transaction $\}$,
$\qquad\qquad$ $awake_c = nphs_c = false,\ log_c = \emptyset,\ phase_c = 0,\ st_c = 0,$
$\qquad\qquad$ $\forall i \in partn_c$:$\quad$ $awake_i = false,\ log_i = \emptyset,\ Q[i, c] = Q[c, i] = \emptyset,$
$\qquad\qquad\qquad\qquad$ $stored_i = 0,\ st_i = 0,\ stored_c[i] = 0.$

A_c^{2P0} : $\{\neg awake_c \land log_c = \emptyset\}$
$\qquad$ **begin** $log_c := \{strt\};\ awake_c := true;$
$\qquad\qquad$ **forall** $i \in partn_c$ **do** $mes_c[i] := 0;$ send $<0, 0>$ to i **od**
$\qquad$ **end**

R_c^{2P0} : $\{\exists i : Q[i, c] \neq \emptyset\}$
$\qquad$ **begin** receive $<z, b>$ from i;
$\qquad\qquad$ **if** $awake_c \land \neg nphs_c \land z = stored_c[i]$
$\qquad\qquad$ **then** $stored_c[i] := stored_c[i] + 1;\ mes_c[i] := b;$
$\qquad\qquad\qquad$ **if** $\forall j \in partn_c :\ stored_c[j] = 1$
$\qquad\qquad\qquad$ **then** $st_c := vote;\ nphs_c := true$
$\qquad\qquad\qquad$ **fi**
$\qquad\qquad$ **fi**
$\qquad$ **end**

P_c^{2P0} : $\{\ awake_c \wedge nphs_c\}$

    begin $st_c := \min\{st_c, \min_{i \in partn_c} mes_c[i]\}$; $phase_c := phase_c + 1$;

        if $st_c = 0$ **then** $log_c := log_c \cup \{abt\}$

        else $st_c := 2$; $log_c := log_c \cup \{com\}$

        fi; **forall** $i \in partn_c$ **do if** $mes_c[i] = 1$ **then** send $<1, st_c>$ to i **fi od**;

        $awake_c := false$; $nphs_c := false$

    end

A_i^{2P0} : $\{\neg awake_i \wedge log_i = \emptyset\}$ **begin** $awake_i := true$ **end**

R_i^{2P0} : $\{Q[c, i] \neq \emptyset\}$

    begin receive $<z, b>$ from c;

        if $\neg awake_i \wedge log_i = \emptyset$ **then do** A_i^{2P0} **fi**;

        if $awake_i \wedge z = stored_i$

    then $stored_i := stored_i + 1$;

        if $stored_i = 1$ **then** $st_i := vote$ **else** $st_i := b$ **fi**;

        if $st_i = 0$ **then** $awake_i := false$; $log_i := log_i \cup \{abt\}$

        elif $st_i = 1$ **then** $log_i := log_i \cup \{yes\}$

        else $awake_i := false$; $log_i := log_i \cup \{com\}$

        fi; **if** $stored_i = 1$ **then** send $<0, st_i>$ to c **fi**

    fi

    end

5.1.2.2 Partial correctness. The assertions we use for the proof of the partial correctness of this protocol skeleton are formulated in a slightly more complex way than necessary. This is done to show the similarity to the 3-phase commit protocol. For protocol skeleton 2P0 we can prove the following invariants.

Lemma 5.1.1 *Using protocol skeleton 2P0, the following assertions hold invariantly for all $i \in partn_c$, $j \in partn_c \cup \{c\}$, $j \neq i$:*

(1) $\neg awake_c \wedge log_c = \emptyset \wedge phase_c = st_c = stored_c[i] = 0 \vee$
    $awake_c \wedge log_c = \{strt\} \wedge phase_c = 0 \wedge (st_c = 0 \vee st_c = 1 \wedge nphs_c) \vee$
    $\neg awake_c \wedge log_c = \{strt, abt\} \wedge phase_c = 1 \wedge st_c = 0 \vee$
    $\neg awake_c \wedge log_c = \{strt, com\} \wedge phase_c = 1 \wedge st_c = 2,$

(2) $log_i = \emptyset \wedge stored_i = st_i = 0 \vee$
    $awake_i \wedge log_i = \{yes\} \wedge stored_i = 1 \wedge st_i = 1 \vee$
    $\neg awake_i \wedge log_i = \{abt\} \wedge stored_i = 1 \wedge st_i = 0 \vee$
    $\neg awake_i \wedge log_i = \{yes, abt\} \wedge stored_i = 2 \wedge st_i = 0 \vee$
    $\neg awake_i \wedge log_i = \{yes, com\} \wedge stored_i = 2 \wedge st_i = 2,$

(3) $stored_i = stored_c[i] = phase_c \lor$
      $stored_i - 1 = stored_c[i] = phase_c \lor$
      $stored_i = stored_c[i] = phase_c + 1,$

(4) $<z, b> \in Q\,[c, i] \;\Rightarrow\; z = phase_c \land b = st_c \land stored_i = stored_c[i] = phase_c,$

(5) $<z, b> \in Q\,[i, c] \;\Rightarrow$
      $z = 0 = stored_i - 1 \land b = st_i \land stored_i - 1 = stored_c[i] = phase_c,$

(6) $strt \in log_c \land stored_i = stored_c[i] = phase_c \;\Rightarrow$
      $<phase_c, st_c> \;\in!\;Q\,[c, i] \lor stored_c[i] = 1 \land mes_c[i] = st_i = 0,$

(7) $stored_i - 1 = stored_c[i] = phase_c \;\Rightarrow$
      $<stored_i - 1, st_i> \;\in!\;Q\,[i, c] \lor stored_i > 1,$

(8) $stored_i = stored_c[i] = phase_c + 1 \;\Rightarrow\; mes_c[i] = st_i,$

(9) $\forall k \in partn_c : stored_c[k] = phase_c + 1 \;\Leftrightarrow\; nphs_c,$

(10) $|st_i - st_j| \leq 1.$

Proof.   Initially, the premises of all implications are false. Also, the integer variables are 0, *log*'s are empty, and *awake*'s are *false*. Hence the first clauses of the disjuctions and thus all assertions hold.

(1). Initially, the first clause holds. Operation A_c^{2P0} sets $awake_c$ to *true* and writes $strt$ on log_c, hence the second clause holds afterwards. If the second clause holds, operation R_c^{2P0} can set st_c to 1, but only when it sets $nphs_c$ to *true*. Operation P_c^{2P0} validates either the third or the fourth clause, while the second must have held beforehand.

(2). Initially the first clause holds, while operation A_i^{2P0} does not change that. Operation R_i^{2P0}, on receipt of a first message $<0, 0>$ from c, sets $stored_i$ to 1, sets st_i to a vote of either 1 or 0, and accordingly writes *yes* or *abt* on log_i, validating either the second or third clause, respectively. On receipt of a second message from c, which is either $<1, 0>$ or $<1, 2>$ by (4) and (1), operation R_i^{2P0} validates either the fourth or the fifth clause, as the second must have held beforehand.

(3). Initially the first clause holds. Operation A_c^{2P0} does not change this. Operation R_c^{2P0} receives a message from i, hence we know by (5) that the second clause held, and by (9) that $nphs_c$ does not. Thus $z = stored_c[i]$ and as $stored_c[i]$ is increased by 1, the third clause holds now. Also $nphs_c$ might be set to *true*, if this was the last message c was waiting for. Operation P_c^{2P0} can only be executed if the third clause held (by (9)), and as $phase_c$ is increased by 1, the first clause holds now. Operation A_i^{2P0} does not influence this assertion, while operation R_i^{2P0} increases $stored_i$ by 1. As a message is received from c, we know from (4) that the first clause held beforehand, thus the second holds afterwards.

(4). The premise is validated in operations A_c^{2P0} and P_c^{2P0}. In both cases the values sent are $phase_c$ and st_c. In the proof of (3) it was already argued that the first clause of (3) held after operations A_c^{2P0} and P_c^{2P0}. By (5) we know that operation R_c^{2P0} is not enabled while the premise of (4) holds, thus $stored_c[i]$ cannot be changed. Operation R_i^{2P0} would increase $stored_i$, but also deletes the message from the queue and hence invalidates the premise. (By (6) we know that there is only one such message.)

(5). The premise is only validated in operation R_i^{2P0}. If a message is sent, the values sent are $stored_i - 1 = 0$ and st_i. By (4) we know that before R_i^{2P0} the first clause of (3) held, thus afterwards the second clause holds. Operation R_c^{2P0} invalidates the premise and the conclusion because there is only one message (by (7)), and operation P_c^{2P0} is not enabled by (9).

(6). The premise is validated in operations A_c^{2P0} and P_c^{2P0}. In both operations messages with the denoted values are sent to all participants i, one to each, except in P_c^{2P0} if $mes_c[i] = 0$ (and $stored_c[i] = 1$ by (9) and the guard of P_c^{2P0}). Afterwards these operations are disabled so it is not possible that a second identical message is sent. Operation R_i^{2P0} invalidates the conclusion, but as the sequence number of the message equals $stored_i$ and i is $awake$ or does awaken (by (2)), $stored_i$ is increased and the premise invalidated.

(7). The premise is validated in operation R_i^{2P0}, upon receipt of a message from c. By (4) we know that the fields in the message contain the "right" values, and that i sends one message back to c if $stored_i$ is 1, otherwise i has finished its part of the protocol (and thus $stored_i$ is larger than 1). Operation R_c^{2P0} invalidates the conclusion by receiving the message, but also invalidates the premise by increasing $stored_c[i]$. By (9) we know that P_c^{2P0} is not enabled as long as the premise is true.

(8). The premise is validated in operation R_c^{2P0}, upon receipt of a message from i. By (5) we know that the first field of this message is equal to $phase_c$, and thus the second field is stored in $mes_c[i]$, thus now $mes_c[i] = st_i$. The conclusion might be invalidated in operation R_i^{2P0}, but by (4) we know that it is not enabled as long as the premise holds. Operation P_c^{2P0} invalidates the premise (but not the conclusion).

(9). Only in operation R_c^{2P0} is $nphs_c$ set to $true$, if indeed $stored_c[k]$ is 1 and thus equal to $phase_c + 1$ as $phase_c$ is 0 (by (1) and the test "**if** $awake_c$" in R_c^{2P0}) for all participants k. In operation P_c^{2P0} $phase_c$ is increased but also $nphs_c$ is set to $false$. In operation R_c^{2P0} $stored_c[k]$ could be increased, but not as long as $stored_c[k] = phase_c + 1$ by (4), as there is no message to receive.

(10). Initially all st's are 0. As long as $phase_c = 0$ and $stored_i$ is 0 or 1, the values of the st's are 0 or 1 (by (1) and (2)), hence the relation holds. By (3) and (9) we know that when $phase_c$ is set to 1 in operation P_c^{2P0}, $stored_i$ is 1 for all i, and in case st_c is set to 0 if some st_i's are 0 (and maybe some 1) the relation still holds, while if st_c is set to 2, we know that for all i, $mes_c[i] = st_i = 1$ (by (9), (3), and

(8)), thus the relation also holds. Finally, the case that $stored_i$ is set to 2 remains, but according to (4) and the text of operation R_i^{2P0}, st_i is set to the value of st_c. Hence the relation continues to hold.   □

Lemma 5.1.1(3) shows that the 2-phase commit protocol operates with respect to each participant i as a sliding window protocol with a window size of 1 (section 2.1.1).

   We are now ready to prove the safety of protocol skeleton $2P0$, namely, that upon termination (TERM) all processes have decided and have decided the same. As protocol skeleton $2P0$ is not formulated in a strictly message-driven manner, TERM means: all queues are empty and all operations are disabled.

Theorem 5.1.2 *Using protocol skeleton $2P0$, TERM implies that all processes have reached the same decision.*

Proof. Initially, all queues are empty, but operations A_c^{2P0} and A_i^{2P0} are enabled. A message under way from i to c or from c to i can always be received, in either R_c^{2P0} or R_i^{2P0}. Using that operation A_c^{2P0} is not enabled (if TERM holds), we know that $awake_c$ or $log_c \neq \emptyset$. Hence in both cases $strt \in log_c$ (by lemma 5.1.1(1)). Consider the value of $phase_c$, which is either 0 or 1. Assume it is 0. Then by TERM and lemma 5.1.1(3), (6), and (7) we conclude that for all i: $stored_i = stored_c[i] = phase_c + 1$. Hence $nphs_c$ holds, and by lemma 5.1.1(1) $awake_c$ also. Thus P_c^{2P0} is enabled, which is in contradiction with TERM. Thus the value of $phase_c$ is 1, and by lemma 5.1.1(1) c has decided. Using lemma 5.1.1(3) and $phase_c = 1$, we conclude that in the first case of lemma 5.1.1(3), i has decided to abort (by (6) and TERM $st_i = 0$, and because $stored_i = 1$ we can use (2) to conclude i has aborted), in the second and third case that $stored_i$ is 2, and thus also that i has decided. Lemma 5.1.1(1) and (2) show that a decision implies a value of st of either 0 or 2. By lemma 5.1.1(10) they must either be all 0 (abort) or all 2 (commit). Thus all processes have decided the same.   □

5.1.2.3 *Total correctness.* In order to prove the liveness of protocol skeleton $2P0$ we first prove that it does not deadlock and then that a finite number of operations leads to termination.

Lemma 5.1.3 *Protocol skeleton $2P0$ does not deadlock.*

Proof. Deadlock implies that all operations are disabled. As operations R_c^{2P0} and R_i^{2P0} are enabled if there exists a message to receive, this implies that message queues $Q[i,c]$ and $Q[c,i]$ are empty. Hence there is termination (TERM), and no deadlock.   □

To prove the liveness of protocol skeleton $2P0$ we define a function F^{2P0} from the system state to the set W_3 of 3-tuples of non-negative integers. For the total ordering $<_{W_3}$ on W_3 we refer to section 1.2.2.3. This order relation on W_3 is well founded. Using protocol skeleton $2P0$, we define F^{2P0} for a given system state as follows:

$$
\begin{aligned}
F^{2P0} &= (l, a, m), \text{where} \\
l &= 3.|\{i \mid log_i = \emptyset\}| + 2.|\{i \mid strt \in! \ log_i \lor yes \in! \ log_i\}| + \\
&\quad 1.|\{i \mid abt \in log_i \lor com \in log_i\}|, \\
a &= |\{i \mid awake_i \neq true\}|, \\
m &= \sum_{i,j} |\{<z, b> \ \in Q\,[i, j]\}|.
\end{aligned}
$$

Theorem 5.1.4 *Protocol skeleton $2P0$ terminates in finite time.*

Proof. Let the number of processes taking part in the protocol be n. Then the initial value of F^{2P0} is $(3n, n, 0)$. Operation A_c^{2P0} decreases the l and a-coordinate by 1, and increases the m-coordinate by $n - 1$. Operation R_c^{2P0} decreases the m-coordinate by 1. Operation P_c^{2P0} decreases the l-coordinate by 1, and possibly increases the m-coordinate. Operation A_i^{2P0} decreases the a-coordinate by 1. Operation R_i^{2P0} decreases the l-coordinate by at least 1, and does not increase the m-coordinate. The a-coordinate might or might not be changed. Thus function F^{2P0} is strictly decreased by all operations of protocol skeleton $2P0$, and the protocol skeleton terminates in finite time. $\qquad\square$

Let us now compare the achievements of protocol skeleton $2P0$ with the requirements of definition 5.1.1(1)–(5). That all decisions reached are the same ((1)) follows from theorem 5.1.2 in case of termination, and from lemma 5.1.1(1), (2), and (10) in case there is no termination yet. That a process cannot reverse its decision ((2)) follows from lemma 5.1.1(1) and (2). That the commit decision can only be reached if all processes voted *yes* ((3)) follows from lemma 5.1.1(10) and (2). That the decision will be to commit if all processes voted *yes* ((4)) follows from lemma 5.1.1(2), (8), (9), and operation P_c^{2P0}. That all processes will eventually reach a decision ((5)) follows from theorem 5.1.4. Thus protocol skeleton $2P0$ is an atomic commitment protocol which is designed to tolerate no failures at all.

5.1.3 Complete 2-phase commit protocol

In order to make protocol skeleton $2P0$ fault tolerant, we consider what problems arise when failures occur. Assume there is a communication failure. Then a message is lost or delayed for a long time. The would-be receiver of this message is expecting it and can detect the failure by means of a timer. However, if this timer goes off, the receiver process does not know whether the message is lost or whether the sender is not able to send the message because its site is down. Assume that process i's site fails. Then the contents of all variables except log_i are lost, and process i cannot participate in the commit protocol any more for the moment. This poses two problems: for i, namely, what to do upon recovery, and possibly for other processes, how to know whether i had already decided and if so, what i had decided.

Thus we have to augment protocol skeleton $2P0$ with timeout actions and a termination protocol. If the coordinator times out, the message that c was expecting is a message with a vote, say from i. As c itself has not voted yet, it can as well vote *no* and abort, as this decision does not depend on whether i voted *yes* or *no* or not at all. Likewise, if a participant i times out for the request message of c, it can safely abort. However, if a participant i times out for the decision message from c, i.e., it had voted *yes*, process i cannot unilaterally decide. It then initiates the termination protocol. We say that the process is in its *uncertainty period*, and it asks other processes what the decision was, hoping that there is a process that has decided and is up. Unfortunately, this might not be the case, and then process i is *blocked*. During the execution of the termination protocol, process i might of course time out again, if there is no process that can answer its question. Process i then has no other possibility than to keep on asking.

Recovery from a site failure is as follows. The process first examines its stable storage for log's for transactions. (There might very well be log's for several transactions, but we describe only what has to be done for one.) If there is a decision (commit or abort) on the log, the transaction had terminated and nothing has to be done. If there is only a *strt* record on the log, the process was the coordinator and it can safely decide to abort. If the log is empty, the process is a participant and can safely abort. However, if there is *yes* on the log and no decision, then the process is a participant in its uncertainty period. Thus it cannot recover independently and has to ask other processes what decision was taken. Hence it initiates the termination protocol.

The simplest termination protocol possible is for process i to ask only the coordinator, because that always knows (or at that moment can take) the decision. However, this has the disadvantage that i has to wait until the coordinator is up again. Thus we use here a cooperative termination protocol, where i just asks all other processes. Hence a process has to know the identity of the other participants, especially after a site failure, and this information also has to be written on log_i. As it is only necessary after a vote of *yes*, we assume that the coordinator sends this information in its initial request message. A process that receives a request in the termination protocol about the decision taken simply sends the answer if it knows it. This termination protocol can still lead to blocking if there is no process up that has already decided; however, the chance that this is the case in practice is much smaller.

5.1.3.1 The protocol skeleton.

We assume that the transmission errors possible are deletion errors, modeled by the operations E_{ij}^l and E_{ji}^l, defined in section 1.2.1.2. It is not necessary to take duplication and reordering of messages into account, as the messages are uniquely identified by the transaction and their sequence number (they are simply ignored in the protocol skeleton). It is assumed that messages have only a fixed transmission delay, and if they are delayed long, this causes a so-called *timeout failure*. We just model this by the loss operations E_{ij}^l and E_{ji}^l.

To model site failures, we add operations D_i^{2PC}, and for recovery U_i^{2PC}. In operation D_i^{2PC} all variables except log_i are set to *nil*, while in operation U_i^{2PC} the *log* is examined to decide whether independent recovery is possible, or whether the termination protocol has to be initiated, which is then acted upon accordingly. Note that a *log* might exist for several transactions, and for each transaction it has to be decided whether the transaction has terminated already, or whether independent recovery or initiation of the termination protocol is necessary. In the protocol skeleton, however, we only consider the case of one transaction.

As participants may have to communicate with each other in the termination protocol instead of only with the coordinator, we add a receive operation RT_i^{2PC} for this. We also need operation TIME, for running the timers that trigger the timeout operations T_i^{2PC}. There is no separate recovery protocol; a process that comes up again after a failure just uses the termination protocol if it is uncertain.

Additional variables used in protocol skeleton $2PC$ compared to $2P0$ are the following. All processes have a boolean system variable up_i, which is used to model the status of a process when its site is "up" or "down". Each process has a timer tim_i, which is a non-negative integer that can be set to a certain constant tp (timeout period) by the process, and which is decreased by the system operation TIME (see section 1.2.1.5). In addition, a participant i has a boolean variable $itrm_i$, which records whether it has initiated the termination protocol. As participants need to know each other in the termination protocol, the coordinator includes this information in its first message, and as participants may need this information upon recovery from a site failure, it is written on log_i. The message that requests information in the termination protocol about the decision taken is denoted as $<t, ?>$. We get the following protocol skeleton. Lines belonging to the termination protocol are marked by a "t" in the margin.

Protocol skeleton $2PC$:

Initially $partn_c = \{$ processes that are participants for this transaction $\}$,
$\qquad awake_c = nphs_c = false,\ log_c = \emptyset,\ up_c = true,\ phase_c = 0,\ st_c = 0,$
$\qquad \forall i \in partn_c: \quad awake_i = false,\ log_i = \emptyset,\ up_i = true,\ stored_c[i] = 0,$
$\qquad\qquad\qquad\qquad Q[i,c] = Q[c,i] = \emptyset,\ st_i = stored_i = 0,\ itrm_i = false,$
$\qquad\qquad\qquad\qquad \forall j \in partn_c:\ j \neq i:\ Q[i,j] = Q[j,i] = \emptyset.$

TIME : $\{\ \exists j:\ tim_j > 0\ \}$
$\qquad$ **begin** choose $\delta \in \mathbb{N}^+$;
$\qquad\qquad$ **forall** processes $i:\ up_i$ **do** $tim_i := \max\{tim_i - \delta, 0\}$ **od**
$\qquad$ **end**

A_c^{2PC} : $\{up_c \wedge \neg awake_c \wedge log_c = \emptyset\}$
$\qquad$ **begin** $log_c := \{strt\}$; $awake_c := true$; $tim_c := tp$;
$\qquad\qquad$ **forall** $i \in partn_c$ **do** $mes_c[i] := 0$; send $<0, partn_c>$ to i **od**
$\qquad$ **end**

R_c^{2PC} : $\{up_c \wedge \exists i: Q[i,c] \neq \emptyset\}$
$\qquad$ **begin** receive $<z, b>$ from i;
$\qquad\qquad$ **if** $awake_c \wedge \neg nphs_c \wedge z = stored_c[i]$
$\qquad\qquad$ **then** $stored_c[i] := stored_c[i] + 1$; $mes_c[i] := b$;
$\qquad\qquad\qquad$ **if** $\forall j \in partn_c:\ stored_c[j] = 1$ **then** $st_c := vote$; $nphs_c := true$ **fi**
t$\qquad\qquad$ **elif** $b = ?$
t$\qquad\qquad$ **then** $stored_c[i] := 1$; $mes_c[i] := 1$;
t$\qquad\qquad\qquad$ **if** $abt \in log_c$ **then** send $<1, 0>$ to i
t$\qquad\qquad\qquad$ **elif** $com \in log_c$ **then** send $<1, 2>$ to i
t$\qquad\qquad\qquad$ **fi**
$\qquad\qquad\quad$ **fi**
$\qquad$ **end**

T_c^{2PC} : $\{up_c \wedge awake_c \wedge \neg nphs_c \wedge tim_c = 0\}$ **begin** $st_c := 0$; $nphs_c := true$ **end**

P_c^{2PC} : $\{up_c \wedge awake_c \wedge nphs_c\}$
$\qquad$ **begin** $st_c := \min\{st_c, \min_{i \in partn_c} mes_c[i]\}$; $phase_c := phase_c + 1$;
$\qquad\qquad$ **if** $st_c = 0$ **then** $log_c := log_c \cup \{abt\}$
$\qquad\qquad$ **else** $st_c := 2$; $log_c := log_c \cup \{com\}$
$\qquad\qquad$ **fi**; **forall** $i \in partn_c$ **do if** $mes_c[i] = 1$ **then** send $<1, st_c>$ to i **fi od**;
$\qquad\qquad$ $awake_c := false$; $nphs_c := false$
$\qquad$ **end**

A_i^{2PC} : $\{up_i \wedge \neg awake_i \wedge log_i = \emptyset\}$ **begin** $awake_i := true$; $tim_i := tpo$ **end**

R_i^{2PC} : $\{up_i \wedge Q[c,i] \neq \emptyset\}$
       begin receive $<z,b>$ from c;
           if $\neg awake_i \wedge log_i = \emptyset$ **then do** A_i^{2PC} **fi**;
           if $awake_i \wedge \neg itrm_i \wedge z = stored_i$
           then $stored_i := stored_i + 1$;
               if $stored_i = 1$ **then** $st_i := vote$ **else** $st_i := b$ **fi**;
               if $st_i = 0$ **then** $awake_i := false$; $log_i := log_i \cup \{abt\}$
               elif $st_i = 1$ **then** $log_i := \{b \cup \{c\}, yes\}$
               else $awake_i := false$; $log_i := log_i \cup \{com\}$
               fi;
               if $stored_i = 1$
               then send $<0, st_i>$ to c; **if** $st_i = 1$ **then** $tim_i := tp$ **fi**
               fi

t   **elif** $awake_i \wedge itrm_i \wedge z = 1$
t   **then if** $b = 0$ **then** $log_i := log_i \cup \{abt\}$ **else** $log_i := log_i \cup \{com\}$ **fi**;
t $itrm_i := false$; $awake_i := false$
           fi
       end

RT_i^{2PC} : $\{up_i \wedge \exists j \neq c : Q[j,i] \neq \emptyset\}$
t   **begin** receive $<z,b>$ from j;
t   **if** $b = ?$
t   **then if** $stored_i = 0$
t   **then** $st_i := 0$; $awake_i := false$; $log_i := log_i \cup \{abt\}$
t   **fi**;
t   **if** $abt \in log_i$ **then** send $<1,0>$ to j
t   **elif** $com \in log_i$ **then** send $<1,2>$ to j
t   **fi**
t   **elif** $awake_i \wedge itrm_i \wedge z = 1$
t   **then if** $b = 0$ **then** $log_i := log_i \cup \{abt\}$ **else** $log_i := log_i \cup \{com\}$ **fi**;
t $itrm_i := false$; $awake_i := false$
t   **fi**
t   **end**

T_i^{2PC} : $\{up_i \wedge awake_i \wedge tim_i = 0\}$
       begin if $stored_i = 0$ **then** $st_i := 0$; $awake_i := false$; $log_i := log_i \cup \{abt\}$
t   **else** $itrm_i := true$; $tim_i := tp$; $X := \{participants\}$ from log_i;
t   **forall** $j \neq i : j \in X$ **do** send $<t,?>$ to j **od**
           fi
       end

D_c^{2PC} : $\{up_c\}$
  begin $up_c := false$; $awake_c := nil$; $partn_c := nil$; $st_c := nil$; $tim_c := nil$;
     $nphs_c := nil$; $phase_c := nil$; $stored_c := nil$; $mes_c := nil$
  end

D_i^{2PC} : $\{up_i\}$
  begin $up_i := false$; $awake_i := nil$; $itrm_i := nil$; $st_i := nil$;
    $tim_i := nil$; $stored_i := nil$
  end

U_i^{2PC} : $\{\neg up_i\}$
  begin $up_i := true$;
    if there exists a log_i for a transaction
    then if $abt \notin log_i \wedge com \notin log_i \wedge\ yes \notin log_i$
      then $log_i := log_i \cup \{abt\}$; $awake_i := false$; $st_i := 0$;
        if $strt \notin log_i$ **then** $itrm_i := false$ **fi**
      elif $yes \in log_i \wedge abt \notin log_i \wedge com \notin log_i$
t   **then** $awake_i := true$; $stored_i := 1$; $st_i := 1$;
t $itrm_i := true$; $tim_i := tp$;
t   **forall** $j \neq i : j \in X \in log_i$ **do** send $<t,?>$ to j **od**
      else $awake_i := false$; **if** $strt \notin log_i$ **then** $itrm_i := false$ **fi**
      fi
    fi
  end

E_{ij}^l and E_{ji}^l : defined as in section 1.2.1.2.

5.1.3.2 *Partial correctness.*

A usual assumption in our proofs that certain assertions are invariant for a protocol skeleton is that the defined operations are executed atomically. This abstraction makes no difference if the operations that are executed at the same time are independent of each other, but in case of the operation D "going down" this is an over-simplification. In practice, it is possible that a site goes down while a process is executing some operation. This can leave the system in a different state from what is possible if operations are always executed atomically. Hence, to achieve a better correspondence with reality, we relax this assumption somewhat. All operations are executed one at a time, and only the operation D_i^{2PC} can interrupt the execution of another operation of the same process i, leaving this other operation unfinished.

This has the following effect on the assertions that we can prove. Consider for example operation A_c^{2PC}. It contains among others the statements $log_c := \{strt\}$

and send $<0, partn_c>$ to i, in this order. Consider the skeleton consisting of A_c^{2PC} and D_c^{2PC} only. If operations are always executed atomically, the following equivalence holds: $strt \in log_c \Leftrightarrow <0, partn_c> \in Q[c, i]$. However, if D_c^{2PC} can interrupt the execution of A_c^{2PC}, we only have: $<0, partn_c> \in Q[c, i] \Rightarrow strt \in log_c$. If the order of the statements in A_c^{2PC} is reversed, the reverse implication holds. We have to keep this in mind when proving protocol skeleton $2PC$ correct. As timers are not necessary for the partial correctness of protocol skeleton $2PC$, the values of the timers are not mentioned in the proof. Because loss of messages is always possible using protocol skeleton $2PC$, it is not possible to infer the existence of a message. Furthermore, the existence of a message does not imply a unique state of its sender, because the intended receiver process can have timed out and sent a message back while the unreceived message remains in the message queue. Likewise, as processes can go down, often the caveat "$\vee \neg up_i$" or "$\wedge up_i$" has to be added in assertions.

In protocol skeleton $2P0$ the values of st do not differ by more than 1 and ensure that upon termination, the decisions are consistent. We would like to use the same invariant here; however, the value of an st can be undefined if the process is down. It is possible to define ghost variables which reflect the value that st would have had, but using this for correctness results in a much longer proof; hence we give a shorter proof using the contents of the log's. It is still true, though, that the values of the (ghost) st do not differ by more than 1. The crucial observation on the contents of the log's that leads to a proof that the decision is consistent is the following. In case of an abort decision, there is at least one process that voted no (represented on the log by an abt without a yes entry), while in case of a decision to commit, all processes voted yes. For protocol skeleton $2PC$ we can now prove the following invariants.

Lemma 5.1.5 *Let X denote $partn_c \cup \{c\}$. Using protocol skeleton $2PC$, the following assertions hold invariantly for all $i \in partn_c$, $j \in partn_c \cup \{c\}$, $j \neq i$:*

(1) $up_c \Rightarrow \neg awake_c \wedge log_c = \emptyset \wedge st_c = phase_c = 0 \vee$
$\qquad awake_c \wedge log_c = \{strt\} \wedge phase_c = 0 \wedge (st_c = 0 \vee st_c = 1 \wedge nphs_c) \vee$
$\qquad \neg awake_c \wedge log_c = \{strt, abt\} \vee \neg awake_c \wedge log_c = \{strt, com\},$

(2) $up_i \Rightarrow log_i = \emptyset \wedge st_i = stored_i = 0 \wedge \neg itrm_i \vee$
$\qquad awake_i \wedge log_i = \{X, yes\} \wedge stored_i = 1 \wedge st_i = 1 \vee$
$\qquad \neg awake_i \wedge \neg itrm_i \wedge (log_i = \{abt\} \vee$
$\qquad\qquad log_i = \{X, yes, abt\} \vee log_i = \{X, yes, com\}),$

(3) $<0, b> \in Q[c, i] \Rightarrow strt \in log_c \wedge yes \notin log_i \wedge b = \{participants\},$

(4) $<0, 0> \in Q[i, c] \vee (up_c \wedge awake_c \wedge mes_c[i] = 0 \wedge stored_c[i] = 1) \Rightarrow$
$\qquad yes \notin log_i \wedge abt \in log_i,$

(5) $<0, 1> \in Q[i, c] \vee (up_c \wedge awake_c \wedge mes_c[i] = 1) \Rightarrow yes \in log_i,$

(6) $up_c \wedge awake_c \wedge nphs_c \ \Rightarrow\ st_c = 0 \vee \forall k \in partn_c : stored_c[k] = 1,$

(7) $<1,0> \in Q\,[c,i] \ \Rightarrow\ yes \in log_i \wedge abt \in log_c,$

(8) $<1,2> \in Q\,[c,i] \vee com \in log_i \ \Rightarrow\ yes \in log_i \wedge com \in log_c,$

(9) $abt \in log_i \wedge yes \in log_i \ \Rightarrow\ abt \in log_c \vee \exists k \in partn_c : (yes \notin log_k \wedge abt \in log_k),$

(10) $com \in log_c \ \Rightarrow\ \forall k \in partn_c : (yes \in log_k \wedge abt \notin log_k),$

(11) $<t,?> \in Q\,[i,j] \ \Rightarrow\ yes \in log_i,$

(12) $<1,0> \in Q\,[j,i] \ \Rightarrow\ abt \in log_j \wedge yes \in log_i,$

(13) $<1,2> \in Q\,[j,i] \ \Rightarrow\ com \in log_j \wedge yes \in log_i.$

Proof. Initially, the premises of the implications are false, except for (1) and (2), where the first clause of the conclusion also holds, hence all assertions hold.

(1). Operation A_c^{2PC} sets $awake_c$ to *true* and writes $strt$ on log_c, so log_c now only contains $strt$, hence the second clause now holds. Operation D_c^{2PC} does not affect log_c and sets up_c to *false*. Operation P_c^{2PC} sets $phase_c$ to 1, and writes abt to log_c if st_c is 0, and com if st_c is 2, and sets $awake_c$ to *false*. Hence the third or fourth clause of the conclusion now holds. Operation U_c^{2PC} writes abt on log_c if it only contains $strt$ and sets $awake_c$ to *false*.

(2). Operation A_i^{2PC} sets $awake_i$ to *true*, and log_i is $\emptyset$, so the first clause still holds. In operation R_i^{2PC} either $awake_i$ is set to *false* and abt written on log_i, or yes and the set $partn_c \cup \{c\}$ are written on log_i, validating the third or second clause of the conclusion. That the second field of the message received is indeed the required set follows from (3) and the tests in R_i^{2PC}. If yes is written, $stored_i$ and st_i were set to 1. Operation U_i^{2PC} only sets $awake_i$ to *true* if yes (and thus the set of participants) is on log_i, and abt or com not. In that case $stored_i$ and st_i are set to 1 and $itrm_i$ is set to *true*. Otherwise, if the log contains something else, $awake_i$ and $itrm_i$ are set to *false*. Finally, if the log was still empty, abt is also written. Thus any but the first clause can be validated. Operations RT_i^{2PC} and T_i^{2PC} only change the contents of log_i if st_i is changed and they set $awake_i$ (and $itrm_i$, if necessary) to *false*, too.

(3). Operation A_c^{2PC} validates the premise together with the conclusion, as initially log_i is $\emptyset$. Process c only sends messages with a 0 as first field in operation A_c^{2PC}. Moreover, operation A_c^{2PC} is only executed once because of its guard $log_c = \emptyset$. Hence there is only one such message sent to i, and when it is received (which might result in $yes \in log_i$), no such message remains in queue $Q\,[c,i]$ or can be sent again.

(4). A message $<0,0>$ is only sent in operation R_i^{2PC}, upon receipt of a message $<0,b>$. By (3) we know $yes \notin log_i$ beforehand, and as st_i was 0, abt is written on log_i. Hence the conclusion holds. The clause $up_c \wedge awake_c \wedge mes_c = 0 \wedge stored_c[i] = 1$ can only be validated by operation R_c^{2PC} upon receipt of $<0,0>$

from i. Hence we know $abt \in log_i$ and $yes \notin log_i$ held beforehand, and now still holds. Once abt is on log_i nothing more is written on log_i.

(5). A message $<0,1>$ is only sent in operation R_i^{2PC}, upon receipt of a message $<0,b>$. By (3) we know $yes \notin log_i$ beforehand, and as st_i was 1, yes is written on log_i. Hence the conclusion holds. The clause $up_c \wedge awake_c \wedge mes_c[i] = 1$ can be validated by operation R_c^{2PC} upon receipt of $<0,1>$ from i, but also upon receipt of $<t,?>$ from i. Hence we know $yes \in log_i$ (in the latter case by (11)) held beforehand, and now still holds.

(6). The premise is validated in operations R_c^{2PC} and T_c^{2PC}. In operation R_c^{2PC} it is validated if $\forall k \in partn_c : stored_c[k] = 1$, and in operation T_c^{2PC} it is validated together with $st_c = 0$. Only operation D_c^{2PC} falsifies the conclusion, but also sets up_c to $false$.

(7). A message $<1,0>$ can be sent in operations P_c^{2PC} and R_c^{2PC}. If it is sent in P_c^{2PC}, abt is written on log_c and as $mes_c[i]$ is 1 (because only in that case is a message sent), we know by (5) that $yes \in log_i$. If it is sent in operation R_c^{2PC}, this is done upon receipt of a message $<t,?>$ from i, only if $abt \in log_c$. With (11) we know $yes \in log_i$.

(8). A message $<1,2>$ can be sent in operations P_c^{2PC} and R_c^{2PC}. If it is sent in P_c^{2PC}, com is written on log_c and as $mes_c[i]$ is 1, we know by (5) that $yes \in log_i$. If it is sent in operation R_c^{2PC}, this is done upon receipt of a message $<t,?>$ from i, only if $com \in log_c$. With (11) we know $yes \in log_i$. The clause $com \in log_i$ is only validated in operation R_i^{2PC} upon receipt of a message $<1,2>$, either from c or from some other process j. Hence we know that the conclusion held beforehand (in the latter case by (13) and using (8) for j instead of i).

(9). The premise can only be validated by operations R_i^{2PC} and RT_i^{2PC} upon receipt of a message $<1,0>$ from either c or some $j \neq c$. (Operations T_i^{2PC} and U_i^{2PC} can write abt on log_i, but not if $yes \in log_i$, because then $stored_i$ is 1 by (2)). If $<1,0>$ is received from c we know by (7) that $abt \in log_c$. If $<1,0>$ is received from some $j \neq c$, we know by (12) that $abt \in log_j$. Thus either $yes \notin log_j$ and the conclusion of (9) holds for $k = j$, or $yes \in log_j$ and the premise of (9), and hence the conclusion of (9), held beforehand for j. Hence the conclusion still holds.

(10). Only operation P_c^{2PC} can validate the premise. If com is written on log_c then st_c was 2 and hence $mes_c[i]$ was 1 for all participants i. With (5) we have $yes \in log_i$. Assume there is a participant j with $abt \in log_j$. Then we can use (9) for j. Hence either $abt \in log_c$ which is not the case by (1), or there is some participant k with $yes \notin log_k$, but we know all participants have yes on their log. Hence the conclusion holds.

(11). The premise is validated in operation T_i^{2PC} or U_i^{2PC}, only when at that moment up_i and $itrm_i$. Hence with (2) $yes \in log_i$.

(12). A message $<1,0>$ from j to i is only sent in operation RT_j^{2PC} upon receipt of a message $<t,?>$ from i. Hence with (11) $yes \in log_i$. The message $<1,0>$ is sent because $abt \in log_j$.

(13). A message $<1,2>$ from j to i is only sent in operation RT_j^{2PC} upon receipt of a message $<t,?>$ from i. Hence with (11) $yes \in log_i$. The message $<1,2>$ is sent because $com \in log_j$.   □

We are now ready to prove that if decisions are taken, then they are taken consistently.

Theorem 5.1.6 *Using protocol skeleton* $2PC$, *the following assertion holds:*
$$\exists i \in partn_c \cup \{c\} : com \in log_i \;\Rightarrow\; \forall j \in partn_c \cup \{c\} : abt \notin log_j$$

Proof. If $i = c$, we can use lemma 5.1.5(1) and (10) to reach the conclusion. If $i \neq c$, we first use lemma 5.1.5(8).   □

Corollary 5.1.7 *Using protocol skeleton* $2PC$, *the following assertion holds:*
$$\exists i \in partn_c \cup \{c\} : abt \in log_i \;\Rightarrow\; \forall j \in partn_c \cup \{c\} : com \notin log_j$$

This concludes the proof of the safety of the 2-phase Commit Protocol. We will now investigate its liveness.

5.1.3.3   Total correctness. For total correctness, we have to prove that eventually, all processes will decide (if all failures have been repaired).

Lemma 5.1.8 *Protocol skeleton* $2PC$ *does not deadlock.*

Proof. We show that for every process engaged in the $2PC$ protocol that has not terminated yet, there is a non-failure (i.e., not D_i^{2PC} or D_c^{2PC}) operation enabled, or TIME is enabled. First consider the coordinator c. If up_c does not hold, U_c^{2PC} is enabled. Otherwise, up_c holds. If $awake_c$ does not hold, either log_c is $\emptyset$ and A_c^{2PC} is enabled, or $strt \in log_c$ and by lemma 5.1.5(1) c has terminated. Thus assume $awake_c$ holds. If $nphs_c$ holds, P_c^{2PC} is enabled. If there is a message to receive by c, R_c^{2PC} is enabled. Finally, consider tim_c. If it is 0, T_c^{2PC} is enabled, and otherwise TIME is enabled. Thus one of these operations is always enabled.

Consider a participant i. If up_i does not hold, U_i^{2PC} is enabled. Otherwise, up_i holds. If $awake_i$ does not hold, either log_i is $\emptyset$ and A_i^{2PC} is enabled, or $log_i \neq \emptyset$ and by lemma 5.1.5(2) i has terminated. Thus assume $awake_i$ holds. If there is a message to be received by i, R_i^{2PC} or RT_i^{2PC} is enabled. Finally, consider tim_i. If it is 0, T_i^{2PC} is enabled, and otherwise TIME is enabled. Thus one of these operations is always enabled.   □

To investigate if all operations lead to progress towards termination, we define a function F^{2PC} from the set of system states to the set W_4 of 4-tuples of non-negative integers, with the total ordering $<_{W_4}$ on W_4 as in section 1.2.2.3. This order relation on W_4 is well founded. Using protocol skeleton $2PC$, we define F^{2PC} for a given system state as follows:

$$
\begin{aligned}
F^{2PC} &= (l, a, m, t), \text{ where} \\
l &= 3.|\{i \mid log_i = \emptyset\}| + 2.|\{i \mid log_i = \{strt\} \vee log_i = \{X, yes\}\}| + \\
&\quad 1.|\{i \mid abt \in log_i \vee com \in log_i\}|, \\
a &= |\{i \mid awake_i \neq true\}| + |\{c \mid nphs_c \neq true\}| + |\{i \neq c \mid itrm_i \neq true\}|, \\
m &= \sum_{i,j} 2.|\{<z, b> \in Q[i, j] \mid z = 0 \vee z = t\}| + |\{<z, b> \in Q[i, j] \mid z = 1\}|, \\
t &= \sum_{i \text{ with } tim_i \neq nil} tim_i.
\end{aligned}
$$

Lemma 5.1.9 *Function F^{2PC} is strictly decreased by all operations of protocol skeleton $2PC$ except possibly U_i^{2PC}, D^{2PC} and T_i^{2PC}.*

Proof. Let $n = |partn_c \cup \{c\}|$, the number of processes involved in the protocol. Then initially, $F^{2PC} = (3n, 2n, 0, 0)$. In figure 5.1 we summarize the effect of all operations on the 4-tuples of F^{2PC}. If the effect on F^{2PC} depends on the outcome of a test inside an operation, the effects are given for each condition. In nearly all operations, it is the case that the leftmost coordinate of the tuple that shows an effect, shows a negative effect. This means by the definition of $<_{W_4}$ that F^{2PC} strictly decreases. The only operations that do not decrease F^{2PC} are D_i^{2PC}, T_i^{2PC} in case $itrm_i$ held before, and U_i^{2PC} in case i had terminated already. $\square$

Theorem 5.1.10 *If all failures are repaired, and no new failures occur, protocol skeleton $2PC$ can terminate in finite time.*

Proof. That all site failures are repaired means that operations U_i^{2PC} are executed for all processes i that were down, hence up_i holds for all processes afterwards. That all communication failures are repaired means that there is no more loss of messages but also that there are no more timeout failures, i.e., all messages reach their destination within a fixed time. In our model, we translate this into the condition that after the repair the system operation TIME is only executed if no other operations are enabled. To trigger the compensation for messages which were lost before the repairs, we assume that part of the repair is a system operation TIME with some $\delta \geq tp$. Now a process i might have an enabled operation T_i^{2PC}, which

Op.	condition	l	a	m	t
A_c^{2PC}		-1	-1	$+2(n-1)$	$+tp$
R_c^{2PC}	$<0,b>$rec. $\wedge \neg$exp.	0	0	-2	0
	$<0,b>$rec. $\wedge$ exp.	0	0	-2	0
	idem $\wedge$ "last" message	0	-1	-2	0
	$<t,?>$rec. $\wedge$ term.	0	0	$-2+1$	0
	$<t,?>$rec. $\wedge \neg$term.	0	0	-2	0
T_c^{2PC}		0	-1	0	0
P_c^{2PC}		-1	$+2$	$+\leq n-1$	0
U_c^{2PC}	$log_c = \{strt\}$	-1	0	0	0
	term.	0	0	0	0
D_c^{2PC}		0	$+\leq 2$	0	$-tim_c$
A_i^{2PC}		0	-1	0	$+tpo$
R_i^{2PC}	extra contribution of A_i^{2PC}		-1		
	$<0,b>$rec. $\wedge$ exp. $\wedge\ vote = 0$	-2	$+1$	$-2+2$	0
	$<0,b>$rec. $\wedge$ exp. $\wedge\ vote = 1$	-1	0	$-2+2$	$+tp$
	$<1,b>$rec. $\wedge$ exp. $\wedge \neg itrm_i$	-1	$+1$	-1	0
	$<1,b>$rec. $\wedge$ exp. $\wedge\ itrm_i$	-1	$+2$	-1	0
	message rec. $\wedge \neg$exp.	0	0	$-2 \vee -1$	0
RT_i^{2PC}	$<t,?>$rec. $\wedge\ log_i = \emptyset$	-2	$+1$	$-2+1$	0
	$<t,?>$rec. $\wedge$ term.	0	0	$-2+1$	0
	$<1,b>$rec. $\wedge\ itrm_i \wedge awake_i$	-1	$+2$	-1	0
T_i^{2PC}	$stored_i = 0$	-2	$+1$	0	0
	$stored_i = 1 \wedge \neg itrm_i$	0	-1	$+2(n-1)$	$+tp$
	$stored_i = 1 \wedge itrm_i$	0	0	$+2(n-1)$	$+tp$
U_i^{2PC}	$log_i = \emptyset$	-2	0	0	0
	$log_i = \{X, yes\}$	0	-2	$+2(n-1)$	$+tp$
	term.	0	0	0	0
D_i^{2PC}		0	$+\leq 2$	0	$-tim_i$
TIME		0	0	0	$-\geq 1$
E_{ij}^l		0	0	$-1 \vee -2$	0

term. terminated, i.e. *abt* or *com* on *log*   rec. received
exp. expected,   i.e. *awake* $\wedge$ right sequence number $\wedge$ ($\neg itrm_i$ resp. $\neg nphs_c$)

Figure 5.1 THE EFFECT OF ALL $2PC$ OPERATIONS ON THE FUNCTION F^{2PC}.

might increase F^{2PC}. However, each process can do at most one timeout operation: the coordinator because it will decide then, and for a participant, because if it does not decide and sends out $<t, ?>$ messages, at least the coordinator will answer with a decision message (operation R_c^{2PC}; or R_c^{2PC} followed by P_c^{2PC}). All other operations strictly decrease F^{2PC}. Thus we know that protocol skeleton $2PC$ terminates within a finite number of operations. That this termination is a real termination, by decision and not by deadlock, follows from lemma 5.1.8.   □

This completes the correctness proof for protocol skeleton $2PC$. Let us now check whether the requirements for commit protocols given in definition 5.1.1(1)–(5) due to Bernstein *et al.* [BHG87] are met. That all decisions reached are the same ((1)) follows from theorem 5.1.6 and corollary 5.1.7. That decisions are never reversed ((2)) is also implied by theorem 5.1.6 and corollary 5.1.7. That the decision to commit can only be reached if all processes voted *yes* ((3)) follows from lemma 5.1.5(10) and (13). That if there are no failures and all processes voted *yes*, the decision will be to commit ((4)) follows from lemma 5.1.5(1), (2), and (9). That after the repair of all failures and if no new failures occur for sufficiently long then all processes will reach a decision ((5)) follows from theorem 5.1.10.

5.2 The 3-phase Commit Protocol

The several variants of the 3-phase commit protocol are all designed to minimize the problem of blocking. In the 2-phase commit protocol, it is the case that all participants are in an uncertain state when the coordinator decides to commit. In the 3-phase commit protocols, the decision to commit is delayed until the participants have left their uncertain state (unless they happened to fail). This is done by requiring another message exchange, thus leading to the "third phase". The state of a process that is no longer uncertain but knows that it will eventually decide to commit, is called *committable*. Thus it is no longer possible that the states "committed" and "uncertain" coexist in different processes: "committable" can coexist with either, but only with one at a time.

Unfortunately, there are no non-blocking atomic commitment protocols if it is possible that *all* processes fail (a *total failure*); see [SS83, Ske86].

First we discuss the basic 3-phase commit protocol without timeout actions and termination protocol (section 5.2.1). In section 5.2.2 we present a version which is resilient to site failures only, provided there is no total failure. Finally we discuss an adaptation of this protocol for the case of total failures.

5.2.1 The basic protocol

The text of the basic 3-phase protocol is similar to the 2-phase protocol; we only need some extra tests to distinguish the larger number of cases in the former. We do not need any new variables, unless one counts $phase_c$ as such, as that was not really used in protocol skeleton 2P0. The variable st is used more extensively: it not only records the vote *yes* or *no*, but also records the progress towards commit. For a particiant i, a value of 0 for st_i represents the vote *no* and for the coordinator the decision to abort. A value of 1 represents the vote *yes*, while the values of 2 and 3 represent the states of committable and committed, respectively.

The message $<1,2>$, which was called the commit message in protocol skeleton 2P0, is now called *precommit*. The message $<1,2>$ that a participant sends in reply is called the *ack* message, while the commit message now is $<2,3>$. The precommit and ack messages are distinguished only by the direction in which they are transmitted. We get the following protocol skeleton.

Protocol skeleton 3P0:

Initially $partn_c = \{$ processes that are participants for this transaction $\}$,
$\qquad awake_c = nphs_c = false,\ phase_c = 0,\ log_c = \emptyset,\ st_c = 0,$
$\qquad \forall i \in partn_c: \quad awake_i = false,\ log_i = \emptyset,\ Q\,[i,c] = Q\,[c,i] = \emptyset,$
$\qquad\qquad stored_i = 0,\ stored_c[i] = 0,\ st_i = 0.$

A_c^{3P0} : $\{\neg awake_c \wedge log_c = \emptyset\}$
$\qquad$ **begin** $log_c := \{strt\};\ awake_c := true;$
$\qquad\qquad$ **forall** $i \in partn_c$ **do** $mes_c[i] := 0;$ send $<0,0>$ to i **od**
$\qquad$ **end**

P_c^{3P0} : $\{awake_c \wedge nphs_c\}$
$\qquad$ **begin** $phase_c := phase_c + 1;$
$\qquad\qquad$ **if** $phase_c = 2$ **then** $st_c := 3$
$\qquad\qquad$ **else** $st_c := \min\{st_c, \min_{i \in partn_c} mes_c[i]\};$ **if** $st_c = 1$ **then** $st_c := 2$ **fi**
$\qquad\qquad$ **fi**;
$\qquad\qquad$ **if** $st_c = 0$ **then** $awake_c := false;\ log_c := log_c \cup \{abt\}$
$\qquad\qquad$ **elif** $st_c = 2$ **then** $log_c := log_c \cup \{pcom\}$
$\qquad\qquad$ **else** $awake_c := false;\ log_c := log_c \cup \{com\}$
$\qquad\qquad$ **fi**; $nphs_c := false;$
$\qquad\qquad$ **forall** $i \in partn_c$
$\qquad\qquad$ **do if** $mes_c[i] \geq 1$ **then** send $<phase_c, st_c>$ to i **fi od**
$\qquad$ **end**

A_i^{3P0} : $\{\neg awake_i \wedge log_i = \emptyset\}$ **begin** $awake_i := true$ **end**

R_c^{3P0} : $\{\exists i : Q\,[i,c] \neq \emptyset\}$
>   **begin** receive $<z,b>$ from i;
>>   **if** $awake_c \wedge \neg nphs_c \wedge z = stored_c[i]$
>>   **then** $stored_c[i] := stored_c[i] + 1;\ mes_c[i] := b;$
>>>   **if** $\forall j \in partn_c:\ stored_c[j] = phase_c + 1$
>>>   **then** $nphs_c := true;$ **if** $phase_c = 0$ **then** $st_c := vote$ **fi**
>>>   **fi**
>>   **fi**
>   **end**

R_i^{3P0} : $\{Q\,[c,i] \neq \emptyset\}$
>   **begin** receive $<z,b>$ from c; **if** $\neg awake_i \wedge log_i = \emptyset$ **then** do A_i^{3P0} **fi**;
>>   **if** $awake_i \wedge z = stored_i$
>>   **then** $stored_i := stored_i + 1;$
>>>   **if** $stored_i = 1$ **then** $st_i := vote$ **else** $sti := b$ **fi**;
>>>   **if** $st_i = 0$ **then** $awake_i := false;\ log_i := log_i \cup \{abt\}$
>>>   **elif** $st_i = 1$ **then** $log_i := log_i \cup \{yes\}$
>>>   **elif** $st_i = 3$ **then** $awake_i := false;\ log_i := log_i \cup \{com\}$
>>>   **fi**; **if** $stored_i = 1 \vee st_i = 2$ **then** send $<stored_i - 1, st_i>$ to c **fi**
>>   **fi**
>   **end**

5.2.1.1 *Partial correctness.* For protocol skeleton $3P0$ we can prove the following invariants.

Lemma 5.2.1 *Using protocol skeleton $3P0$, the following assertions hold invariantly for all $i \in partn_c$:*

(1) $\neg awake_c \wedge log_c = \emptyset \wedge phase_c = st_c = stored_c[i] = 0 \vee$
$awake_c \wedge log_c = \{strt\} \wedge phase_c = 0 \wedge (st_c = 0 \vee st_c = 1 \wedge nphs_c) \vee$
$awake_c \wedge log_c = \{strt, pcom\} \wedge phase_c = 1 \wedge st_c = 2 \vee$
$\neg awake_c \wedge log_c = \{strt, abt\} \wedge phase_c = 1 \wedge st_c = 0 \vee$
$\neg awake_c \wedge log_c = \{strt, com\} \wedge phase_c = 2 \wedge st_c = 3,$

(2) $log_i = \emptyset \wedge stored_i = st_i = 0 \vee$
$awake_i \wedge log_i = \{yes\} \wedge (stored_i = st_i = 1 \vee stored_i = st_i = 2) \vee$
$\neg awake_i \wedge log_i = \{abt\} \wedge stored_i = 1 \wedge st_i = 0 \vee$
$\neg awake_i \wedge log_i = \{yes, abt\} \wedge stored_i = 2 \wedge st_i = 0 \vee$
$\neg awake_i \wedge log_i = \{yes, com\} \wedge stored_i = st_i = 3,$

(3) $stored_i = stored_c[i] = phase_c \vee$
$stored_i - 1 = stored_c[i] = phase_c \vee$
$stored_i = stored_c[i] = phase_c + 1,$

(4) $<z,b> \in Q\,[c,i] \Rightarrow z = phase_c \wedge b = st_c \wedge stored_i = stored_c[i] = phase_c,$

(5) $<z,b> \in Q\,[i,c] \Rightarrow$
$$z = stored_i - 1 \wedge b = st_i \wedge stored_i - 1 = stored_c[i] = phase_c,$$

(6) $strt \in log_c \wedge stored_i = stored_c[i] = phase_c \Rightarrow$
$$<phase_c, st_c> \in!\, Q\,[c,i] \vee stored_c[i] = 1 \wedge mes_c[i] = st_i = 0,$$

(7) $stored_i - 1 = stored_c[i] = phase_c \Rightarrow$
$$<stored_i - 1, st_i> \in!\, Q\,[i,c] \vee (stored_i = 2 \wedge st_i = 0 \vee stored_i = 3),$$

(8) $stored_i = stored_c[i] = phase_c + 1 \Rightarrow mes_c[i] = st_i,$

(9) $\forall k \in partn_c : stored_c[k] = phase_c + 1 \Leftrightarrow nphs_c,$

(10) $|st_i - st_j| \le 1.$

Proof. As the proof is more or less analogous to the proof of lemma 5.1.1, we will only give those parts of the proof that are different.

(1). In case the second clause holds, operation P_c^{3P0} either sets st_c to 1, $phase_c$ to 1, and writes $pcom$ on log_c, validating the third clause, or it decides to abort, validating the fourth clause. When the third clause holds, operation P_c^{3P0} validates the fifth clause by deciding to commit.

(2). Operation R_i^{3P0}, on receiving a message for the first time and voting, has the same effect as in protocol skeleton $2P0$, validating either the second or the third clause. However, if it receives a second message, we know by (4) and (1) that it either remains at the second clause, now with $stored_i = st_i = 2$, or that it validates the fourth clause. At the receipt of a third message, it validates the fifth clause.

(3)–(5). Analogous to the proof of lemma 5.1.1(3)–(5).

(6). The premise is validated in operations A_c^{3P0} and P_c^{3P0}. In both operations exactly one message is sent to every participant i, with fields as specified, unless i voted *no*, i.e., $stored_c[i] = 1$ and $st_i = mes_c[i] = 0$. The test in operation P_c^{3P0} only considers $mes_c[i]$, but by (8) $st_i = mes_c[i]$ before operation P_c^{3P0}, and by (10) st_c is 0 or 1. Thus by the premise and (1), $stored_c[i]$ is 1.

(7). The premise is validated in operation R_i^{3P0}, and exactly 1 message with these contents is sent to c, if $stored_i$ is 1 or st_i is 2. By (2) the negation of this condition is $stored_i = 2 \wedge st_i = 0$ or $stored_i = st_i = 3$.

(8). Analogous to the proof of lemma 5.1.1(8).

(9). Both sides of the equivalence are validated in R_c^{3P0} simultaneously, and operation P_c^{3P0} invalidates both.

(10). Analogous to the proof of lemma 5.1.1(10). $\square$

5.2.1.2 *Total correctness.*

In order to prove the liveness of protocol skeleton $3P0$ we first prove that it does not deadlock and then that a finite number of operations lead to termination.

Lemma 5.2.2 *Protocol skeleton 3P0 does not deadlock.*

Proof. Deadlock implies that all operations are disabled. As operations R_c^{3P0} and R_i^{3P0} are enabled if there exists a message to receive, this implies that message queues $Q[i,c]$ and $Q[c,i]$ are empty. Hence there is termination (TERM), and no deadlock. □

To prove the liveness of protocol skeleton 3P0 we define a function F^{3P0} from the system state to the set W_3 of 3-tuples of non-negative integers. It resembles function F^{2P0}, but it has to take the extra phase into account, so it is slightly more complex. Using protocol skeleton 3P0, we define F^{3P0} for a given system state as follows:

$$
\begin{aligned}
F^{3P0} &= (l, a, m), \quad \text{where} \\
l &= 2.|\{i \mid log_i = \{strt\} \vee log_i = \{strt, pcom\} \vee log_i = \{yes\}\}| + \\
&\quad 3.|\{i \mid log_i = \emptyset\}| + 1.|\{i \mid abt \in log_i \vee com \in log_i\}|, \\
a &= |\{i \mid awake_i \neq true\}| + \sum_i (3 - st_i), \\
m &= \sum_{i,j} |\{<z, b> \, \in Q[i,j]\}|.
\end{aligned}
$$

Theorem 5.2.3 *Protocol skeleton 3P0 terminates in finite time.*

Proof. Let the number of processes taking part in the protocol be n. Then the initial value of F^{3P0} is $(3n, 4n, 0)$. Operation A_c^{3P0} decreases the l and a-coordinate by 1, and increases the m-coordinate by $n - 1$. Operation R_c^{3P0} decreases the m-coordinate by 1 and possibly the a-coordinate by 1 (by a vote of 1). Operation P_c^{3P0} either decreases the l-coordinate by 1 (by a decision), or decreases the a-coordinate by 1 (by increasing st_c), and possibly increases the m-coordinate. Operation A_i^{3P0} decreases the a-coordinate by 1. Operation R_i^{3P0} either decreases the l-coordinate by at least 1, or decreases the a-coordinate by increasing st_i. It does not increase the m-coordinate. Thus function F^{3P0} is strictly decreased by all operations of protocol skeleton 3P0, and the protocol skeleton terminates in finite time. □

Let us now compare the achievements of protocol skeleton 3P0 with the requirements of definition 5.1.1(1)–(5). That all decisions reached are the same ((1)) follows from lemma 5.2.1(1), (2), and (10). That a process cannot reverse its decision ((2)) follows from lemma 5.2.1(1) and (2). That the commit decision can only be reached if all processes voted *yes* ((3)) follows from lemma 5.2.1(2) and (10). That the decision will be to commit if all processes voted *yes* ((4)) follows from lemma 5.2.1(2), (8), (9), and the text of operation P_c^{3P0}. That all processes will eventually reach a decision ((5)) follows from theorem 5.2.3. Thus protocol skeleton $3P0$ is an atomic commitment protocol which is designed to tolerate no failures at all.

5.2.2 3-phase commit assuming no communication failures

For this protocol we assume that there are no communication failures. This does not only mean that messages do not get lost, but also that messages are not subject to timing failures. Hence, if a process i sent a message to j and expects an answer (i.e., i set its timer upon sending the message), and the timer goes off, then we know that process j must have failed. As conclusions are now going to be drawn from the value of timers, one needs timer values in the assertions for the safety proof of this protocol. Also a timer field in messages will be needed, as in section 2.2, to ensure their timely disappearance from the message queues in case a message is undeliverable because the would-be receiver has failed. Finally we need a system operation TIME to simulate the progress of time (see section 1.2.1.5).

We need several protocols to augment the basic protocol to overcome the effect of process failures. First, we need a termination protocol to enable the remaining processes to decide when the coordinator fails. Second, we need an election protocol to choose a new coordinator to coordinate the termination protocol. Third, we need a recovery protocol for the processes that failed to decide upon their repair. Of course, (new) coordinators can also fail during the execution of the election and termination protocols, so several instances of these can run simultaneously. The reason that we need a new coordinator if the old one fails is that we want to do something about the problem of blocking. In the 2-phase commit protocol, no coordinator was necessary for termination, as each process just asked around until it found another processs that had decided. As we do not want processes to be blocked, the remaining processes now decide together. As we need the analog of the basic commit protocol, it is centralized, and we need a new coordinator. It is also possible to use a decentralized termination protocol if one makes use of majority voting. This is discussed by Skeen [Ske81].

We first assume that there is no *total failure*, i.e., not all processes fail. By no total failure we do not mean that there always is a process that is up, but that there is a process that never fails. We will discuss later what adaptations are necessary to cope with total failures. Unfortunately, total failures introduce the possibility of blocking again.

5.2.2.1 *No total failures.* Only processes that have never failed during the execution of the $3PC$ protocol are allowed to take part in the termination protocol. The termination protocol proceeds as follows. Once a new coordinator has been decided on (in the election protocol, see below) the new coordinator requests the current state of all processes (processes that do not answer have failed by our assumptions). If there are processes that have decided, the decision is sent to the other processes by the new coordinator. If there is a process that is committable, the new coordinator first sends a precommit message to the processes that are uncertain, and awaits their acknowledgement messages. Only when all processes that have not failed so far are committable does the new coordinator decide to commit and send the commit message to all processes. Otherwise (in case all processes are uncertain or have not voted yet), the new coordinator decides to abort and informs the other processes. If during the execution of the termination protocol the new coordinator fails, the election protocol is invoked again and a new instantiation of the termination protocol is invoked with another new coordinator. As there is no total failure, there is always some process left which can decide. Of course it is helpful if a process which receives messages from two different instantiations of the termination protocol can decide which one to disregard because it is no longer current.

For the election protocol we take a very simple one, based on the process identities. We suppose the identities are totally ordered and we choose the process with the smallest identity as the leader. Each process maintains a set of processes that have not failed so far, and also this set is occasionally written on the *log*. If a process infers that some other process has failed, then it deletes the failed process from the set of non-failed processes, and if necessary it decides the new coordinator by taking the minimum of the process identities. If it turns out that it itself is the new coordinator, it starts (a new instantiation of) the termination protocol, and otherwise it sends a message "you are the new coordinator" to the chosen one. There are two ways in which a process can infer that an old coordinator has failed. The first is that it times out on a message to the old coordinator, and the second is that it receives a "you are the new coordinator" message – in that case all processes with an identity smaller than its own must have failed. If a process receives messages from two coordinators, we know that the one with the highest identity is the most recent one, because otherwise the coordinator with the smallest identity would have remained coordinator. Hence the one with the smallest identity must have failed.

The recovery protocol is as follows. A process that failed first checks its *log* upon repair. If it had decided, we are finished. If it had not voted yet, the process can safely abort. If it is uncertain or committable, it has to ask the other processes how they decided. As we assumed that there is no total failure and hence that there is at least one process that has never failed, we know that that process will eventually decide, either in the original commit protocol if the original coordinator never failed, or in (one instantiation of) the termination protocol. Note that even if the state of the failed process was committable, we cannot be sure that the eventual decision by the remaining processes will be to commit. This could happen in the following way. Assume the old coordinator failed while it was busy sending precommit messages, so precommit messages were sent to some, but not all participants. Assume further that all participants that received precommit messages, and thus entered the committable state, failed. Thus all participants that never failed will be in the uncertain state and will decide to abort in the termination protocol. Hence a participant which was committable when it failed is so to speak uncertain when it recovers. This is the reason that participants do not record on their *log* when they become committable.

In the recovery protocol for the (old) coordinator, we made a change that will improve performance. In the original version of the 3-phase commit protocol, the coordinator only logs *start* and *com/abt*. This means that if the coordinator fails after *start* and before the decision, it has to request from the remaining participants what the outcome of the decision was. However, in the 2-phase commit protocol, the coordinator could decide to abort independently in that case. In 3-phase commit, the coordinator can independently decide to abort on recovery if it has sent no precommit messages yet, and only has to request the decision of the others if such messages are sent. This is the case because in the termination protocol, abort is decided if no participant is committable yet. Thus the coordinator writes *pcom* on its log before sending the precommit messages, to enable it to recover independently in more cases than in the original protocol.

The protocol skeleton of the 3-phase commit protocol that tolerates site failures has to take care of many more details than either protocol skeleton $3P0$ or $2PC$. Thus we omit the actual text and the correctness proof, as we consider those too lengthy for this book. Note, however, that an essential difference from all preceding commit protocols is that it is no longer the case that its correctness is based on a maximum difference in the values of the st's of only 1. This property now only holds amongst those processes that never have been down. Processes that have been down might have a difference in st value of at most 2 from other processes. As abt corresponds to a value of 0 and com to a value of 3, this is sufficient to ensure consistency in decisions taken.

The proof of the partial correctness of protocol skeleton $2PC$ is based on the following discriminating feature: either there is a process that voted *no*, in which case the decision will be to abort, or all processes voted *yes*, in which case the decision will be to commit. However, in protocol skeleton $3PC$ it is no longer true that if all processes voted *yes*, the decision will be to commit. The decision might also be to abort, namely in the case that all committable processes (i.e., those that "knew" that all processes voted *yes*) failed, leaving the decision to the uncertain processes. In protocol skeleton $2PC$ the uncertain processes were blocked until a knowledgeable process comes up; in protocol skeleton $3PC$ the processes are not blocked, but this possibility of abort when all processes voted *yes* is the price we pay. Note, however, that this is not in contradiction with requirement (4) of definition 5.1.1 of a commit protocol, as this can only happen when failures occur.

The proof of the partial correctness of protocol skeleton $3PC$ relies on the following observations. As there is at least one process that never fails and communication is reliable, there is at least one process that participates in all instantiations of the termination protocol. Thus it is not possible to have two different instantiations of the termination protocol that decide differently. As precommit messages are only sent from a (new) coordinator to a participant, they are always sent from a process with a small identity to one with a higher identity. As a new coordinator only sends precommit messages if one of its participants was committable before, that participant must have received its precommit message from a (new) coordinator with a still smaller identity. This enables us to conclude that the original coordinator has once sent precommit messages and thus that all processes voted *yes*.

5.2.2.2 *Total failures.*

If it is possible that there is a total failure, there is an extra problem to take care of in the recovery protocol. If, as assumed in the previous section, there is some process that never failed, we know that if there is a decision taken, this process knows that decision (eventually). Thus any process recovering will know what the decision was if it asks that particular process (and it will answer because it has not failed). In the case of a total failure, however, if a recovering process requests what the decision was, the processes that took this decision may have all failed in the meantime. On the other hand, there never may have been any decision, and the processes participating in the recovery protocol now may have to decide. This is in contrast with the situation in the protocol sketched in the previous section, where in the recovery protocol only decisions made in the termination or original commit protocol are copied.

The problem here is for the recovering processes to decide which of two situations is the case. One: a decision was taken, but all processes knowing what the decision is have failed. In that case the recovering processes are blocked until one of them is repaired. Two: no decision was taken yet, so waiting until other processes are repaired makes no sense. In that case the recovering processes have to use some termination protocol to decide. It is suggested in the literature (e.g. [BHG87,

Ske85]) that the key to this problem is the notion of the *last process to fail*. The idea is that this process has come furthest towards a decision and will know (upon repair) whether any decision has been taken or not. Thus recovering processes should remain blocked until the last process to fail is repaired, upon which they can safely proceed.

Thus the extension of the recovery protocol in case total failures are possible should be the following. If a process upon recovery finds that it has voted *yes* and has not decided yet, it not only requests from the other processes their current state, but also the set of processes that were still up before their failure. From these sets it is possible to determine whether the last process to fail has already recovered (see [BHG87]). If this is not the case the processes are blocked, otherwise they execute the termination protocol.

However, in the case of centralized protocols, the last process to fail is not necessarily the process that has come furthest towards a decision. This is because (new or old) coordinators decide before their participants. The following example shows how this can lead to inconsistency. Consider the following scenario: all processes except two fail, and the remaining processes execute the termination protocol. The new coordinator of these decides to commit, and fails before it can send its final message. If the remaining process times out it will decide to commit. However, if it fails before timeout, the last entry in its *log* will be *yes*, and it will thus have an uncertain state upon recovery. If this process now acts upon the (correct) assumption that it was the last process to fail and recovers independently, it will take the decision to abort, resulting in an inconsistent decision. In the same way it is possible to construct a scenario in which the original coordinator fails first, just after deciding to commit, and that all subsequent coordinators fail before committing, thus eventually leading to an abort of the last process to fail when that recovers before the original coordinator. In general, any process that has been coordinator might have committed while no other process realizes this when they all have failed. (As long as a process has not failed, it would be committable, but that state is lost upon failure.)

Thus we make the following change to the recovery protocol. A recovering process not only requests current states and the set of processes that were still up before their failure, but also the set of all previous coordinators. If the last process to fail *and* all its previous coordinators have recovered, it is safe to execute the termination protocol.

Bibliography

[AAG87] Y. Afek, B. Awerbuch, and E. Gafni. Applying static network protocols to dynamic networks. In *Proc. 28th FoCS*, pages 358–370, Los Angeles, CA, 1987.

[AB93] Y. Afek and G.M. Brown. Self-stabilization over unreliable communication media. *Distributed Computing*, 7:27–34, 1993.

[AWYU82] A.V. Aho, A.D. Wyner, M. Yannakakis, and J.D. Ullman. Bounds on the size and transmission rate of communications protocols. *Comp. & Maths. with Appls.*, 8:205–214, 1982.

[Bar64] P. Baran. On distributed communications networks. *IEEE Trans. on Commun. Syst.*, CS-12:1–9, 1964.

[Bel76] D. Belsnes. Single-message communication. *IEEE Trans. on Commun.*, COM-24:190–194, 1976.

[BGM91] G.M. Brown, M.G. Gouda, and R.E. Miller. Block acknowledgment: redesigning the window protocol. *IEEE Trans. on Commun.*, 39:524–532, 1991.

[BHG87] P.A. Bernstein, V. Hadzilacos, and N. Goodman. *Concurrency Control and Recovery in Database Systems*. Addison-Wesley Publ. Comp., Reading, MA, 1987.

[BK86] J.A. Bergstra and J.W. Klop. Verification of an alternating bit protocol. In W. Bibel and K.P. Jantke, editors, *Math. methods of spec. and synthesis of software systems '85*, pages 9–23, Berlin, 1986. Math. Research 31, Akademie Verlag.

[BK88] J.A. Bergstra and J.W. Klop. Process theory based on bisimulation semantics. In J.W. de Bakker, W.-P. de Roever, and G. Rozenberg, editors, *Linear time, branching time and partial order in logics and models for concurrency*, pages 50–122, Berlin, 1988. LNCS vol. 354, Springer-Verlag.

[Boc75] G.V. Bochmann. Logical verification and implementation of protocols. In *Proc. 4th Data Communications Symp.*, pages 8-5–8-20, Quebec, Canada, 1975.

[BS89] R.J.R. Back and K. Sere. Stepwise refinement of action systems. In J.L.A. van de Snepscheut, editor, *Mathematics of program construction*, pages 115–138, Berlin, 1989. LNCS vol. 375, Springer-Verlag.

191

[BSW69] K.A. Bartlett, R.A. Scantlebury, and P.T. Wilkinson. A note on reliable full-duplex transmission over half-duplex links. *Commun. ACM*, 12:260–261, 1969.

[Car82] D.E. Carlson. Bit-oriented data link control. In P.E. Green Jr., editor, *Computer network architectures and protocols*, pages 111–143, New York, NY, 1982. Plenum Press.

[Chu78] K. Chu. A distributed protocol for updating network topology. Technical Report RC7235, IBM T.J. Watson Research Center, Yorktown Heights, NY, 1978.

[CK74]   V.E. Cerf and R.E. Kahn. A protocol for packet network intercommunication. *IEEE Trans. on Commun.*, COM-22:637–648, 1974.

[CM88]   K.M. Chandy and J. Misra. *Parallel Program Design, A Foundation*. Addison-Wesley Publ. Comp., Reading, MA, 1988.

[Dij74] E.W. Dijkstra. Self-stabilization in spite of distributed control. *Commun. ACM*, 11:643–644, 1974.

[dR85]   W.-P. de Roever. The quest for compositionality. In E.J. Neuhold, editor, *The role of abstract models in computer science, Proc. of the IFIP working conference 1985*, Amsterdam, 1985. North Holland.

[DS88]   N.J. Drost and A.A. Schoone. Assertional verification of a reset algorithm. Technical Report RUU-CS-88-5, Dept. of Computer Science, Utrecht Univ., Utrecht, 1988.

[Fel68] W. Feller. *An introduction to probability theory and its applications*. John Wiley & Sons, Inc., New York, NY, 1968.

[Fin79] S.G. Finn. Resynch procedures and a failsafe network protocol. *IEEE Trans. on Commun.*, COM-27:840–845, 1979.

[Fri78] D.U. Friedman. *Communication complexity of distributed shortest path algorithms*. PhD thesis, MIT, Cambridge, MA, 1978.

[FW78]   J.G. Fletcher and R.W. Watson. Mechanisms for a reliable timer-based protocol. *Computer Networks*, 2:271–290, 1978.

[Gaf87] E. Gafni. Generalized scheme for topology-update in dynamic networks. In *Distributed algorithms*, pages 187–196, Berlin, 1987. LNCS vol. 312, Springer-Verlag.

[Ger89] R.T. Gerth. *Syntax-directed verification of distributed systems*. PhD thesis, Utrecht Univ., Utrecht, 1989.

[Gra78] J.N. Gray. Notes on database operating systems. In *Operating systems: an advanced course*, pages 393–481, Berlin, 1978. LNCS vol. 60, Springer-Verlag.

[Gra90] J. Gray. A comparison of the Byzantine agreement problem and the transaction commit problem. In B. Simons and A. Spector, editors, *Workshop on fault tolerant distributed computing, 1986, Pacific Grove, CA*, pages 10–17, Berlin, 1990. LNCS vol. 448, Springer-Verlag.

[Had90] V. Hadzilacos. On the relationship between the atomic commitment and consensus problems. In B. Simons and A. Spector, editors, *Workshop on fault tolerant distributed computing, 1986, Pacific Grove, CA*, pages 201–208, Berlin, 1990. LNCS vol. 448, Springer-Verlag.

[Hal85] F. Halsall. *Introduction to data communications and computer networks.* Addison-Wesley Publ. Comp., Wokingham, UK, 1985.

[HdR86] J. Hooman and W.-P. de Roever. The quest goes on: a survey of proof systems for partial correctness of csp. In J.W. de Bakker, W.-P. de Roever, and G. Rozenberg, editors, *Current trends in concurrency*, pages 343–395, Berlin, 1986. LNCS vol. 224, Springer-Verlag.

[HF85] J.Y. Halpern and R. Fagin. A formal model of knowledge, action, and communication in distributed systems: preliminary report. In *Proc. 4th PoDC*, pages 224–236, Minaki, Canada, 1985.

[HM84] J.Y. Halpern and Y. Moses. Knowledge and common knowledge in a distributed environment. In *Proc. 3rd PoDC*, pages 50–61, Vancouver, Canada, 1984.

[Hoa78] C.A.R. Hoare. Communicating sequential processes. *Commun. ACM*, 21:666–677, 1978.

[HZ87] J.Y. Halpern and L.D. Zuck. A little knowledge goes a long way: simple knowledge-based derivations and correctness proofs for a family of protocols. In *Proc. 6th PoDC*, pages 269–280, Vancouver, Canada, 1987. Extended version available as: Report RJ5857, IBM Almaden Research Center, San Jose, CA, 1987 (revised 1989).

[JM80] J.M. Jaffe and F.H. Moss. A responsive distributed routing algorithm for computer networks. Technical Report RC8479, IBM T.J. Watson Research Center, Yorktown Heights, NY, 1980.

[JRT86] T.A. Joseph, Th. Räuchle, and S. Toueg. State machines and assertions: an integrated approach to modeling and verification of distributed systems. *Science of Computer Programming*, 7:1–22, 1986.

[Kel76] R.M. Keller. Formal verification of parallel programs. *Commun. ACM*, 19:371–384, 1976.

[Knu81] D.E. Knuth. Verification of link-level protocols. *BIT*, 21:31–36, 1981.

[Kro78] S. Krogdahl. Verification of a class of link-level protocols. *BIT*, 18:436–448, 1978.

[Lam78] L. Lamport. Time, clocks, and the ordering of events in a distributed system. *Commun. ACM*, 21:558–565, 1978.

[Lam80] L. Lamport. The 'Hoare logic' of concurrent programs. *Acta Inform.*, 14:21–37, 1980.

[Lam82] L. Lamport. An assertional correctness proof of a distributed algorithm. *Science of Computer Programming*, 2:175–206, 1982.

[Lam90]   L. Lamport. A theorem on atomicity in distributed algorithms. *Distributed Computing*, 4:59–68, 1990.

[LL84]   J. Lundelius and N. Lynch. An upper and lower bound for clock synchronization. *Information and Control*, 62:190–204, 1984.

[LS76]   B. Lampson and H. Sturgis. Crash recovery in a distributed data storage system. Computer science laboratory, Xerox, Palo Alto Research Center, Palo Alto, CA, 1976.

[Lyn68]   W.C. Lynch. Reliable full-duplex file transmission over half-duplex telephone lines. *Commun. ACM*, 11:407–410, 1968.

[Mis90]   J. Misra. Soundness of the substitution axiom. Notes on UNITY: 14-90, Univ. of Texas at Austin, Austin, TX, 1990.

[MP88]   Z. Manna and A. Pnueli. The anchored version of the temporal framework. In J.W. de Bakker, W.-P. de Roever, and G. Rozenberg, editors, *Linear time, branching time and partial order in logics and models for concurrency*, pages 201–284, Berlin, 1988. LNCS vol. 354, Springer-Verlag.

[MS79]   P.M. Merlin and A. Segall. A failsafe distributed routing protocol. *IEEE Trans. on Commun.*, COM-27:1280–1287, 1979.

[OG76]   S.S. Owicki and D. Gries. An axiomatic proof technique for parallel programs I. *Acta Inform.*, 6:319–340, 1976.

[RSB90]   P. Ramanathan, K.G. Shin, and R.W. Butler. Fault-tolerant clock synchronization in distributed systems. *IEEE Computer*, 23:10-33–10-42, 1990.

[San90]   B. Sanders. Eliminating the substitution axiom from UNITY logic. Technical Report 128, Dept. Informatik, ETH Zürich, Zürich, 1990.

[SBvL87] A.A. Schoone, H.L. Bodlaender, and J. van Leeuwen. Diameter increase caused by edge deletion. *J. of Graph Theory*, 11:409–427, 1987.

[Sch80]   M. Schwartz. Routing and flow control in data networks. Technical Report RC8353, IBM T.J. Watson Research Center, Yorktown Heights, NY, 1980.

[SdR87]   F.A. Stomp and W.-P. de Roever. A correctness proof of a distributed minimum-weight spanning tree algorithm. Technical Report 87-4, Dept. of Informatics, Univ. of Nijmegen, Nijmegen, 1987.

[Seg81]   A. Segall. Advances in verifiable fail-safe routing procedures. *IEEE Trans. on Commun.*, COM-29:491–497, 1981.

[SH86]   F.R. Soloway and P.A. Humblett. On distributed network protocols for changing topologies. Technical Report LIDS-P-1564, MIT, Cambridge, MA, 1986.

[SK87]   M. Sloman and J. Kramer. *Distributed systems and computer networks*. Prentice-Hall, Inc., Englewood Cliffs, NJ, 1987.

[Ske81]   D. Skeen. A decentralized termination protocol. In *Proceedings Symposium on reliability in distributed software and database systems.* IEEE, 1981.

[Ske85] D. Skeen. Determining the last process to fail. *ACM Trans. on Computer Systems*, 3:15–30, 1985.

[Ske86] D. Skeen. Non-blocking commit protocols. In M. Stonebraker, editor, *The Ingres papers: anatomy of a relational database system*, Reading, MA, 1986. Addison-Wesley Publishing Co.

[SS83] D. Skeen and M. Stonebraker. A formal model of crash recovery in a distributed system. *IEEE Trans. on Software Engin.*, SE-9:219–227, 1983.

[Ste76] N.V. Stenning. A data transfer protocol. *Computer Networks*, 1:99–110, 1976.

[Taj77] W.D. Tajibnapis. A correctness proof of a topology information maintenance protocol for a distributed computer network. *Commun. ACM*, 20:477–485, 1977.

[Tan88] A.S. Tanenbaum. *Computer Networks*. Prentice-Hall, Inc., Englewood Cliffs, NJ, second edition, 1988.

[Tel91] G. Tel. *Topics in distributed algorithms*. Cambridge Univ. Press, Cambridge, UK, 1991.

[Tel94] G. Tel. *Introduction to distributed algorithms*. Cambridge Univ. Press, Cambridge, UK, 1994.

[Tom75] R.S. Tomlinson. Selecting sequence numbers. In *Proc. ACM SIGCOMM/SIGOPS Interprocess Commun. Workshop*, pages 11–23. ACM, 1975.

[Tou80] S. Toueg. A minimum-hop path failsafe and loop-free distributed algorithm. Technical Report RC8530, IBM T.J. Watson Research Center, Yorktown Heights, NY, 1980.

[Vaa86] F.W. Vaandrager. Verification of two communication protocols by means of process algebra. Technical Report CS-R8608, Centrum voor Wiskunde en Informatica, Amsterdam, 1986.

[vGT90] A.J.M. van Gasteren and G. Tel. Comments on "On the proof of a distributed algorithm": always-true is not invariant. *Inf. Proc. Lett.*, 35:277–279, 1990.

[vH90] P.J.M. van Haaften. *Verification of routing algorithms, INF/SCR-90-16*. Master's thesis, Dept. of Computer Science, Utrecht Univ., Utrecht, 1990.

[Wei89] W.P. Weijland. *Synchrony and asynchrony in process algebra*. PhD thesis, Univ. of Amsterdam, Amsterdam, 1989.

[YK82] Y. Yemini and J.F. Kurose. Can current protocol verification techniques guarantee correctness? *Computer Networks*, 6:377–381, 1982.

[Zwi88] J. Zwiers. *Compositionality, concurrency and partial correctness*. PhD thesis, Techn. Univ. of Eindhoven, Eindhoven, 1988. Also appeared as: LNCS vol. 321, Springer-Verlag, Berlin, 1989.

Index